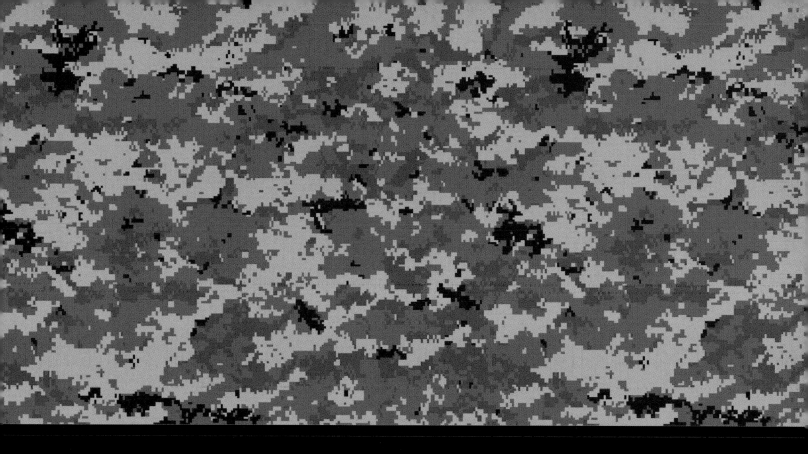

FBI HOSTAGE RESCUE & SWAT TEAMS

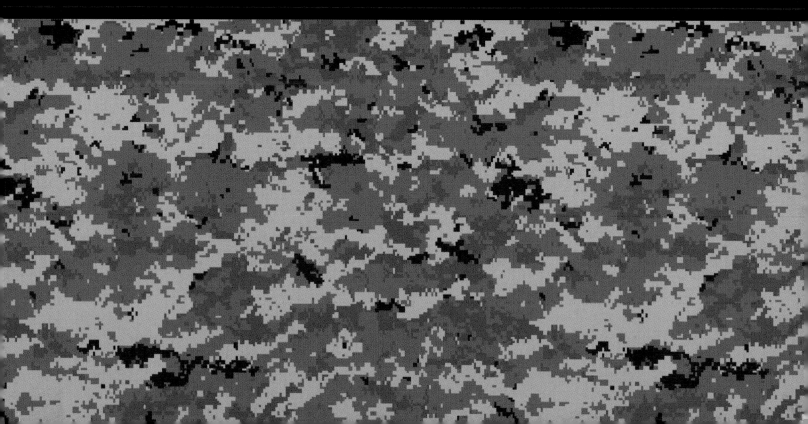

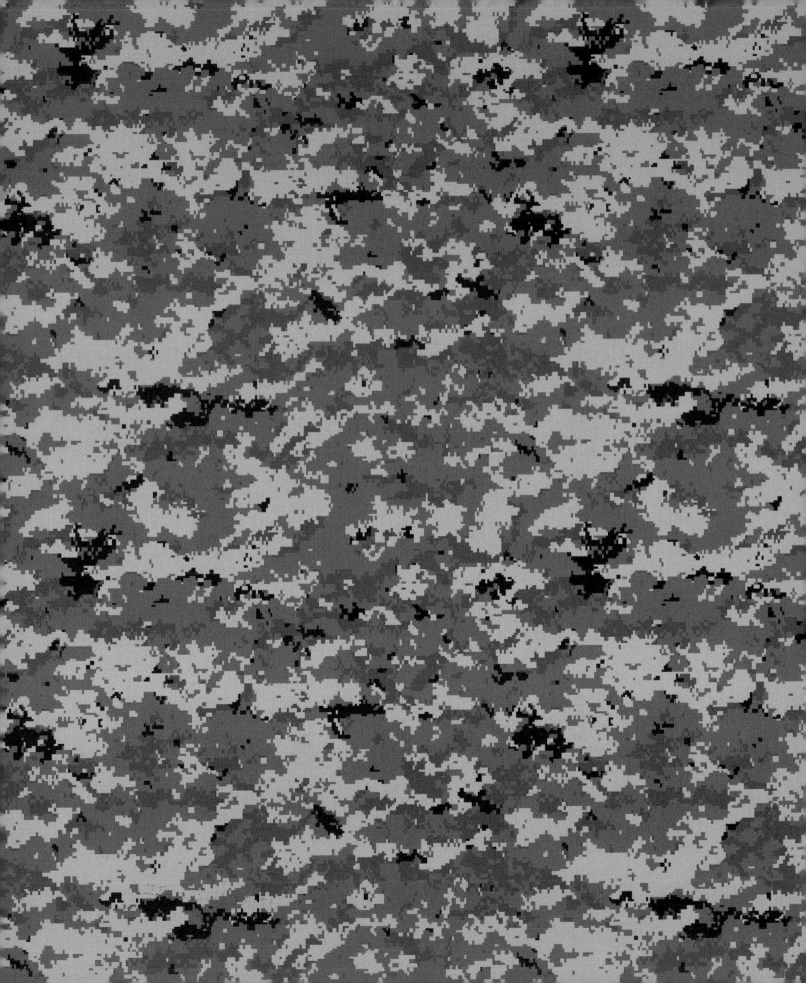

U.S. SPECIAL FORCES

FBI HOSTAGE RESCUE & SWAT TEAMS

JIM WHITING

CREATIVE ✿ EDUCATION

PUBLISHED BY Creative Education

P.O. Box 227, Mankato, Minnesota 56002

Creative Education is an imprint of The Creative Company

www.thecreativecompany.us

DESIGN AND PRODUCTION BY Christine Vanderbeek

ART DIRECTION BY Rita Marshall

PRINTED IN the United States of America

PHOTOGRAPHS BY

Alamy (Alliance Images, Chuck Eckert, Images of Africa Photobank,
SCPhotos, Marmaduke St. John), Corbis (David Brabyn, Anna Clopet,
Rauchwetter/dpa, PHILIP SEARS/Reuters, Greg Smith, Gary Stewart/
AP, Nick Ut/AP), Getty Images (Patrick AVENTURIER/Gamma-
Rapho), iStockphoto (icholakov, qingwa, spxChrome), Shutterstock
(ALMAGAMI, gst, trekandshoot), SuperStock (Marka)

LIBRARY OF CONGRESS CATALOGING-IN-PUBLICATION DATA

Whiting, Jim.

FBI hostage rescue & SWAT teams / Jim Whiting.

p. cm. — (U.S. Special Forces)

Includes bibliographical references and index.

*Summary: A chronological account of the American special forces
unit known as FBI S.W.A.T, including key details about important
figures, landmark missions, and controversies.*

ISBN 978-1-60818-462-0

1. United States. Federal Bureau of Investigation. Hostage Rescue
Team—Juvenile literature. 2. Hostages—Juvenile literature. 3.
Rescues—Juvenile literature. I. Title.

HV8144.F43W458 2014

363.2'3—dc23   2013036171

CCSS: RI.5.1, 2, 3, 8; RH.6-8.4, 5, 6, 8

FIRST EDITION

9 8 7 6 5 4 3 2 1

U.S. SPECIAL FORCES

TABLE OF CONTENTS

★ ★ ★

Minimum physical standards for HRT training are 12 pull-ups, 60 sit-ups, 50 pushups, swimming 200 meters in 7 minutes, and running 2 miles (3.2 km) in less than 15 minutes.

Students train at the FBI Academy campus located south of Washington, D.C.

INTRODUCTION

IN 1980, CUBAN PRESIDENT FIDEL CASTRO ALLOWED MORE than 100,000 of his people to come to the United States in a mass emigration event known as the Mariel Boatlift. Several thousand were dangerous criminals whom Castro wanted to get rid of. Many committed crimes in the U.S. and were imprisoned. Threatened with deportation to Cuba in 1991, dozens of those *Marielitos* housed in the Federal Correctional Facility in Talladega, Alabama, seized control of part of the prison and took 10 hostages.

The Hostage Rescue Team (HRT) of the Federal Bureau of Investigation (FBI) quickly responded, as did other federal forces. During an uneasy truce that lasted for more than a week, little progress was made in resolving the situation. At that point, authorities became convinced the hostages were in danger of being killed. HRT was ordered to retake the facility.

The operation began in the early morning darkness when HRT members blew open several doors. Rushing inside, they flung stun grenades to momentarily blind their targets. The grenades also generated a shock wave that knocked down anyone in the area. Moments later, the assault team threw "stingers," which unleashed dozens of painful rubber pellets, and fog-causing devices that also emitted a skin-irritating chemical.

"It was loud, confused, and smoky," said one team member. "It seemed like we caught them completely by surprise. There were no attempts to fight back." From start to finish, the operation took just three minutes. The hostages were unharmed, and the only *casualty* was a slightly wounded prisoner.

★ ★ ★

Communist leader Fidel Castro strictly regulated who could enter and exit Cuba.

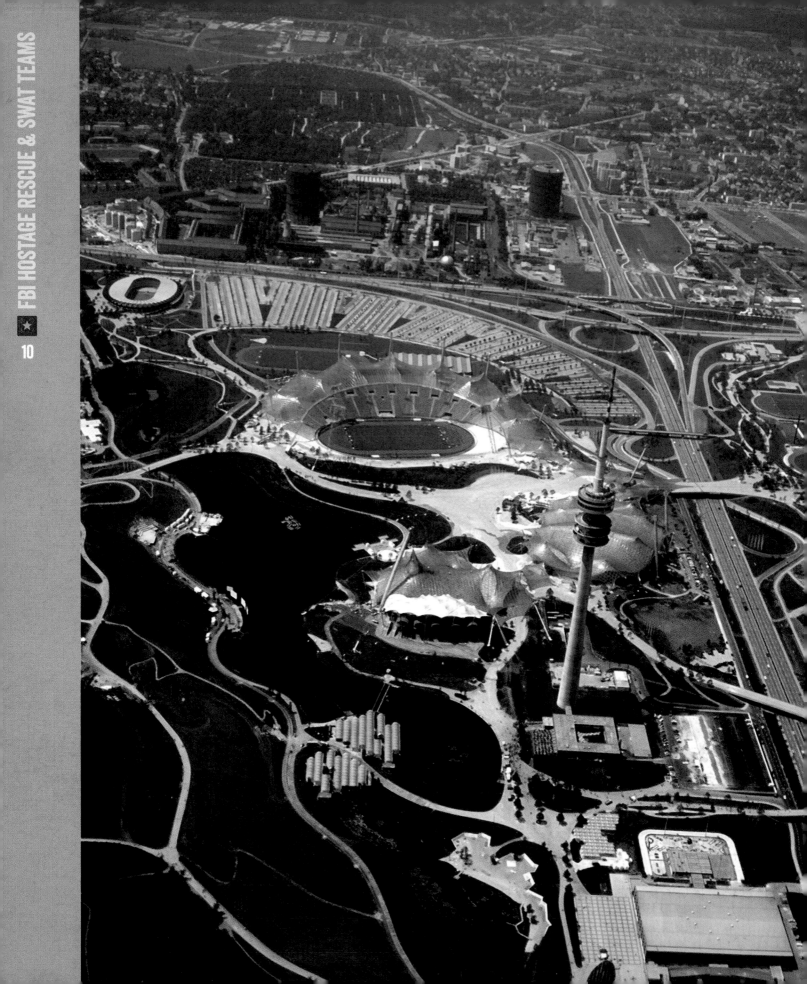

HOSTAGES AND HANDCUFFS

U.S. SPECIAL FORCES

WHEN PEOPLE THINK OF SPECIAL FORCES, THEY MIGHT ENvision U.S. Navy SEALs taking down America's most wanted man, Osama bin Laden, in 2011. Or the army's Green Berets, whose jaunty headgear visually sets them apart from other military units. Or Delta Force, the ultra-secret unit that has often been featured in movies, television, and thriller novels.

However, these highly skilled warriors can't operate on American soil. The Posse Comitatus Act, which dates back to 1878, forbids using the military for civilian law enforcement, unless the president specifically allows it. Yet long before the 9/11 terrorist attacks in 2001, the need for operators able to take on terrorists—either homegrown or from abroad—who threaten people inside the U.S. became apparent.

The first inkling of danger came at the 1972 Olympic Games in Munich, West Germany, when terrorists murdered 11 members of the Israeli team inside the Olympic Village. Terror struck much closer to home five years later. A group of gunmen took over 3 buildings in Washington, D.C., and held more than 100 hostages for 38 hours. The situation was resolved with minimal loss of life, but it illustrated the need for more advanced skills than local police possessed. "It would have been a bloodbath," said Donald Bassett, an FBI firearms instructor. "These [police] officers had never been training to do airborne assaults."

The FBI of the mid-1970s had a number of Special Weapons and Training (SWAT) teams at its disposal. These were modeled after the Los Angeles Police Department's SWAT teams, which first formed in 1967. Eventually, each of the 56 FBI field offices would have its own SWAT team, consisting of special agents

The 1972 killings inside the Olympic Park became known as the Munich Massacre.

FORCE FACTS HRT operators often "ride the skids" of their helicopters, standing on the narrow rails that serve as landing gear. They jump off when the aircraft lands.

who undertake SWAT training in addition to their other duties. But even the best SWAT teams couldn't keep up with the increasing firepower and boldness of terrorist groups.

By the early 1980s, the need for a highly skilled force capable of launching "airborne assaults" and other antiterrorist actions was becoming more apparent. Four major events were on the docket in 1984: the Republican and Democratic national conventions, the World's Fair in New Orleans, Louisiana, and especially the Summer Olympics in Los Angeles. All these events were potential terrorist magnets. "When Los Angeles won the nomination for the 1984 Olympics, the question was, 'Who would handle an event such as Munich?' And there weren't a lot of good answers. That's how the idea of a Hostage Rescue Team evolved," said FBI deputy director Sean Joyce, a former HRT member.

The HRT initiative got a big boost when then FBI Director William Webster visited the Delta Force training facility at Fort Bragg, North Carolina, late in 1981. He was impressed by the professionalism and efficiency the operators demonstrated. But when he talked with the men afterward, he noticed that they seemed to be missing one key piece of law-enforcement equipment. An operator explained the apparent omission: "We put two rounds in their forehead. The dead don't need handcuffs."

Delta's lack of handcuffs concerned Webster. He wanted a dedicated unit that trained full-time and would be capable of *deploying* anytime and anywhere in the country on short notice. He also wanted a unit that was aware of the principles of law enforcement and of constitutional requirements for making arrests. "They are FBI agents first and foremost, and they have the ability to perform special agent duties—whether it's obtaining evidence or interviewing an individual—anywhere in the world while being able to operate in all types of environments, no matter how inhospitable," Joyce added.

Final approval for Webster's plan came early in 1982, with 89

Riding the skids allows operators to save time and engage an enemy more quickly.

Supervisors of a training exercise often alter the nature of the exercise after it starts so that operators learn how to change plans in an instant and adapt to changing conditions.

men and 1 woman selected for initial training. Fifty continued on for advanced training. In planning the training regimen, the FBI drew on the expertise of American military forces and similar organizations around the world. One particularly influential special operations unit was the French National Gendarmerie Intervention Group (Groupe d'Intervention de la Gendarmerie Nationale, or GIGN). One of GIGN's leaders explained that their mission was simply "to save lives." That quickly became the new American group's motto.

Choosing a name to reflect its life-saving mission was crucial for the new unit. "Super-SWAT," the initial choice, sounded too elitist to some. "Hostage Rescue Team" struck a better note, but the name may be somewhat misleading. "Rescuing hostages is but a part of the full range of capabilities that we train and are prepared to respond to," said HRT director Steve Fiddler in 2009. Future operations would involve hijackings, manhunts, high-profile arrests, protecting dignitaries, and dealing with extremist groups in addition to actual hostage situations.

As the members of the unit neared the end of their training late in 1983, they faced one final exercise, this time a scenario involving "terrorists" who threatened to detonate a nuclear device hidden somewhere in New Mexico's Kirtland Air Force Base near Albuquerque. They had also seized a number of hostages and taken them to a remote cabin. The FBI promptly sent HRT to the scene. As negotiations with the concealed terrorists continued during the following three days, the team managed to learn the location of the hideout. They also discovered where the bomb was.

HRT focused on the hideout, and a SWAT team was tasked with recovering the bomb. Timing was critical. Both teams had to strike

Albuquerque, New Mexico, was in no real danger during the Equus Red exercise.

at exactly the same moment, neutralizing the nuclear device while preserving the lives of the hostages. HRT operators forced down the doors of the hideout, tossed in flash-bang grenades to stun the terrorists, and fanned out inside. In less than 30 seconds, every *tango* was gunned down. All the hostages were safe. And the weapon didn't detonate.

This operation served as the newly minted HRT's "final exam" and was code-named "Equus Red." Soon afterward, HRT went active. Its first deployment was to the Olympics, which went off without any problems. The following year, a group of *white supremacists* living in a compound in the Ozark Mountains of Arkansas shot two state troopers during a traffic stop. HRT conducted several nighttime operations to gather intelligence, and then—in tandem with several FBI SWAT teams—stormed part of the compound. Negotiations eventually led to the surrender of the entire group. A search revealed a *cache* of military-grade weapons and drums of *cyanide* the group's members had planned on pouring into a nearby city's water supply.

The unit's reputation took a hit after a pair of highly

SWAT teams enter locked rooms by using explosives, battering rams, or ballistics.

publicized cases in Idaho and Texas a few months apart in 1992 and 1993 resulted in the deaths of several dozen people. The outcome illustrated the need for a unified command to oversee all aspects of future situations. The Critical Incident Response Group (CIRG) was established to bring all the FBI's crisis management units together. One element of CIRG was the Tactical Support Branch, which includes HRT as well as SWAT teams.

The new approach received its first major test in 1996, when an armed confrontation with members of the Montana Freemen began. The group rejected the authority of the federal government in favor of its own system. A bank tried to foreclose on the land the group occupied, but the Freemen refused to leave. The FBI also had arrest warrants out for several men on the site. This time, the situation was resolved after an 81-day, injury-free standoff.

Since its beginnings, HRT has become involved in more than 800 actions. The majority of them were either secret or resolved peacefully, thereby remaining virtually unknown to the general public. One notable exception came early in 2013. A 65-year-old retired trucker in Midland, Alabama, shot and killed a school-bus driver, kidnapped a 5-year-old boy, and held him hostage in a heavily fortified underground bunker. After a tense, six-day standoff that drew national attention, HRT operators raided the bunker. They killed the trucker and rescued the boy unharmed. Once again, the unit proved worthy of its motto: To Save Lives.

FBI operators arrived on the scene soon after a young Alabama boy was taken hostage.

MAKING THE CUT

TRADITIONALLY, APPLYING TO HRT HAS BEEN OPEN TO ALL FBI special agents with a minimum of three years' field experience, consistently superior performance evaluations, and a willingness to serve at least three years in the unit. Even though HRT is one of the most coveted assignments in the FBI, its combination of high qualifying standards and demanding lifestyle resulted in its understaffing for many years. So in 2007, the FBI instituted the Tactical Recruitment Program (TRP) to increase the pool of potential operators. TRP now allows agents who have three years' experience in military combat or law-enforcement SWAT to apply for the HRT program with a commitment to two years in the field.

While candidates have many reasons for applying, former HRT member Christopher Whitcomb echoed the feelings of many when he wrote, "HRT represented something almost mythically grand. Every time something big happened in the United States, HRT flew in, strapped on black *Nomex* flight suits and submachine guns, and straightened it out. This is it, I thought." Jaime Atherton, a member of the original team in 1983, added, "The challenge that was involved, the chance to be a part of something new, and the ability to make a difference—that's why I joined the Bureau."

Once they decide to join, all applicants must take the two-week HRT selection course, which is held twice a year at the FBI

Dangerous assignments and training exercises make qualifying standards high for HRT agents.

FORCE FACTS During the two-week selection process, candidates are not addressed by name. They are known only by the color and number of the T-shirt they wear.

Academy in Quantico, Virginia. The first day begins before dawn and includes a series of runs, swims, multistory stair climbs, and other strenuous physical activities. Sometimes trainees are required to perform these tasks while wearing a vest weighing more than 50 pounds (22.7 kg) and carrying a 35-pound (15.9 kg) battering ram. And that's the easy day. "The process is designed to identify individuals who will perform the best in a crisis situation," said Sean Joyce. "The point is to break you down to see how you perform under stress."

To assist in the breaking-down process, trainees must ascend a rock wall and then climb a narrow ladder to a point more than 70 feet (21.3 m) high. They are required to paddle a rubber boat across a lake as a helicopter tilted on its side blows wind and waves against the craft. One of the primary objectives of such tests is to ensure that potential operators have a great deal of upper-body strength. As Danny Coulson, the original leader of HRT, explained in his book *No Heroes*, "We focused heavily on upper-body and hand strength because commanders at Delta, SEAL Team Six, and the European services had all told us that it was an operator's most important physical attribute. Often the most difficult part of a counterterrorist operation was not the fight itself but getting to the scene in the first place. That could involve climbing, jumping, swimming, running, crawling, walk-ing, or *fast-roping* out of helicopters. All these required extraor-dinary upper-body strength." As of yet, no woman has become an HRT operator in the field.

At least as important as the physical challenges are the men-tal and psychological ones that HRT operatives face. Selectees never know what is coming up next, so they have to be flexible in adjusting to each test as it arises. In addition, they never know how they are performing in the eyes of their instructors, or even to what standards they are being held. This uncertainty creates additional stress.

HRT and SWAT members must be physically fit and ready for any hostile situation.

Those who ace the selection course report to the New Operator Training School (NOTS) at the FBI Academy. The NOTS has nearly 24 buildings, including dormitories, classrooms, offices, an auditorium, gym, swimming pool, and weight room. It also has firing ranges, an outdoor track, and other facilities.

For the next eight months, the men are immersed in an increasingly demanding regimen that both enhances existing individual skills and introduces them to new ones such as scuba diving and fast-roping. Their training also integrates them as members of a team, but always, the emphasis is on speed. In hostage situations, even a few seconds can make the difference between life and death.

One of the most important facilities at the NOTS is the Tactical Firearms Training Center (TFTC). Its moveable walls can be reconfigured to mimic a variety of environments that operators are likely to face. The interior walls are rubber-lined to absorb bullet fragments, eliminating the potential for ricocheting. Most of the sides are open so that the smoke from flash-bang grenades and firing thousands of rounds of ammunition is quickly dispersed. Inside the center is a mockup of a commercial jetliner, which includes dozens of seated mannequins and pre-recorded screams and gunfire to add to the realism. Overhead are a series of catwalks equipped with microphones and cameras. Instructors can directly observe the action and examine the feeds to respond to the trainees' performance.

A four-story tower at one end of the TFTC overlooks the rest of the structure. It is outfitted with interior and exterior stairways, allowing for a variety of types of training such as fast-roping, *rappelling*, and hoisting gear. Another key facility on the campus is "Hogan's Alley," a 10-acre (4 ha) simulated

Quantico's FBI National Academy trains local and international law enforcement officers.

SWAT members practice approaching a criminal target at a California training facility.

town with homes, a bank, a post office, and other elements of contemporary urban life. Actors portray "townspeople" from innocent bystanders to cutthroat terrorists. Trainees gain real-world experience by engaging in house-to-house combat.

The training course culminates in a full-scale hostage rescue exercise—such as Equus Red—to test everything the trainees have learned. If they succeed, then they become full-fledged HRT operators. Yet their training isn't over. From this point until they leave the team, operators continue to train. For at least five days a week, they constantly hone their skills to make their responses as automatic as possible. Even a seemingly minor task such as changing the *magazines* on their weapons can always be improved upon, saving a precious second or two.

On most days, time is set aside for physical conditioning, to maintain and improve strength and stamina. Gear maintenance and team planning sessions are also important. But the foundation of all training is close quarters combat (CQC), firearms, and sniper training. "Those are our core skill sets," said Charles Pierce, commander of one of the HRT units. "The other things are built around that."

Operators fall into one of two groups: assaulters or sniper/observers. Operators selected as sniper/observers train at the Marine Corps' elite Scout/Sniper School, where they learn concealment techniques and target *reconnaissance* in addition to enhancing their shooting skills. Assaulters often specialize in such areas as *breaching*, communications, and treating serious wounds.

One of the most vital aspects of engaging in ongoing training involves coordinating the efforts of the snipers and assaulters. Snipers sneak into advanced positions, where they often lie almost motionless for hours as they keep in radio contact with the rest of the team. Then it's "go" time. Snipers provide covering fire for the assault team, which moves in and kills or disables the targets as quickly and efficiently as possible. If there are hostages, the goal is to rescue them unharmed. To pull off such a difficult task successfully, the squads need to continually practice coordinating their efforts.

The same general philosophy of "saving lives" underlies FBI SWAT teams. To be eligible, field agents must have a minimum of two years' service. Potential members must pass a pistol qualification course and physical fitness test, plus a psychological evaluation. Once accepted for their respective teams, they undergo refresher training two to four times per month. Several times a year they undergo a more extensive exercise, often utilizing vacant houses that the owners have made available for their use.

★ ★ ★

All HRT and SWAT team members must be proficient with firearms such as pistols, shotguns, and rifles.

FORCE FACTS In total, about 1,100 agents belong to SWAT teams, a little less than 10 percent of the nearly 14,000 special agents working for the FBI.

THE CALL COMES IN, AND HRT GOES OUT

AT ANY TIME OF DAY OR NIGHT, "THE CALL"—A SITUATION beyond the scope and capabilities of local law enforcement and with the possibility of becoming life-threatening—comes in to HRT headquarters at Quantico. Immediately, the scene becomes an extremely well-organized beehive of activity. The men have been through this scenario many times, both during training exercises and in real-life missions. Team leaders assemble for a briefing, while everyone else gathers their equipment.

The most important piece of equipment—and the primary weapon for HRT operators—is the HK MP5 submachine gun with a collapsible stock. Developed in the 1960s by a team of German engineers, the MP5 has become an "industry standard," used by more than 40 nations and numerous military, law enforcement, and security organizations. The MP5 has been specially modified for HRT purposes with laser-aiming devices, tactical front-facing lights, and pistol grips on the forward part of the gun.

The men may also carry Remington M870 12-gauge shotguns. These pump-action weapons have barrels in several lengths, pistol grips, and feature rails for mounting accessories such as lights and *foregrips*. In one variation, the M870p "Masterkey" system, a cut-down version of the M870 is mounted beneath the barrel of a conventional M4 or M16 assault rifle. That system provides deadly force for the operator in CQC and helps retain the MP5's value as an automatic weapon. In another variation, the weapon is loaded with special breaching rounds to blow

SWAT team members use headsets for communication and ballistic shields for added cover.

Hallways can be dangerous because of the limited maneuverability they allow. Operators often blow holes in walls so that they can move from room to room in greater safety.

away door hinges and locks.

HRT's secondary armament for many years was the Springfield Armory's M1911A1 .45 caliber pistol, based on a design dating back to 1911 but still noted for its reliability. It has begun to be phased out by Glock 22 and Glock 23 *polymer* pistols.

The men wear flame-retardant suits and gloves, heavy boots, and thick plastic kneepads. Everyone has a Kevlar helmet and goggles strong enough to withstand blast pressures and to protect the eyes from flying debris. They wear bulletproof vests that have external webbing for carrying pouches filled with extra ammunition, and any other gear depends on the profile of the mission at hand. There's also room on the vests for medical packs and—setting HRT apart from the long-ago demonstration by Delta Force—handcuffs.

Radios are an essential element of HRT gear so that the team members can stay in touch with each other during the chaos of an assault. If the situation they are responding to may involve weapons of mass destruction (WMD), they have gas masks equipped with valves to enable them to drink liquids and enhanced voice box amplifiers to maintain communication.

Since many operations involve smashing down doors, the team is equipped with battering rams and collapsible sledgehammers. Another key piece of assault gear is the Halligan bar. Named for the New York City firefighter who invented it in the late 1940s, the device is commonly described as a "crowbar on steroids." Varying in length from 18 inches to more than 4 feet (46–122 cm), the bar is forked at one end, with a heavy blade and a tapered point at the other.

Once their gear is ready, the men attend a meeting that outlines the objectives and rules of the upcoming mission. When that's over, everyone helps load gear such as tents, food, electric generators, lanterns, and an array of other equipment onto trucks. They then head to Andrews Air Force Base to board an

Constant practice prepares FBI teams to gather gear as quickly as possible before deployment.

FORCE FACTS Nine "enhanced" SWAT teams in major cities such as Atlanta and Los Angeles undergo additional training. They offer assistance to HRT and may be deployed worldwide.

awaiting transport aircraft—usually a C-130 Hercules or C-141 Starlifter.

By the time the operators arrive, larger vehicles have already been loaded into the aircraft. Because of their long practice and experience in fast deployments, the team is almost always "wheels up" within four hours of receiving The Call. As Christopher Whitcomb, who made many such flights, notes, "The four-engine jet aircraft sagged under the weight of HRT and its support staff, their gear, a four-wheel-drive van containing a remote control robot, the Chevy Suburban ambulance, a four-wheel-drive box truck, and the MD-530 helicopter."

Once aloft, the men settle in for what is often several hours of discomfort. Most operators have to wear earplugs to combat the roar of the engines. They sit rigidly on narrow canvas benches bolted to each side of the aircraft, their knees jammed against some large piece of equipment. Without windows, it's hard to gauge progress. On top of everything else, it's not uncommon for air traffic controllers to route HRT flights into areas of turbulence so that commercial flights can take advantage of the smoothest air.

Since many HRT flights take place at night, operators are likely to be sleep-deprived when they arrive on-scene. However, their training kicks in and overrides any sense of fatigue. The airplane has barely stopped moving when the team unloads it, climbs into transport vehicles, and speeds to the incident site.

While most of its operations take place inside the U.S., HRT sometimes ventures overseas. The team provided security for then FBI director Louis Freeh during a visit to Israel in 1995. Another group helped apprehend Mohamed Rashed Daoud Al-Owhali, who was wanted in connection with terrorist bombings in Kenya and Tanzania in 1998 that killed 324 and

From combat missions to special ops, the C-130 Hercules is known for its versatility.

wounded thousands more. Still others traveled to war-torn Kosovo in 1999 to provide security for FBI agents looking for evidence of war crimes committed during the conflict that had begun the previous year and was recently concluded. In 2011, HRT operators played key roles after the hijacking of the American yacht *S/V Quest* by Somali pirates. While the four hostages were killed before they could be rescued, the operators took the lead in compiling evidence to use in court against the pirates.

With the widespread publicity the unit has received, it isn't surprising that HRT appears often in popular media. One of the more notable mentions came in best-selling thriller author David Baldacci's 2001 novel *Last Man Standing*, in which an HRT unit is ambushed. A character named Web London is the only survivor, and he must overcome the suspicions of fellow agents who believe he froze up at the critical moment. Baldacci wanted to give as accurate a picture of HRT as possible. "I visited the HRT's headquarters, toured the facilities, spent time with HRT

Osama bin Laden helped finance the 1998 bombing of the U.S. embassy in Nairobi, Kenya.

operators, asked a zillion questions, read everything I could find on them," Baldacci said in an interview for Readersread.com. "I really wanted to get into their heads and hearts to bring it all to life on the pages. I think I succeeded.... I learned to ride a horse and fired machine guns, among other activities, while researching *Last Man Standing*." Reviewers and readers agreed. *Publishers Weekly* called it "Baldacci's most accomplished thriller," and the novel made it to the *New York Times* list of best-selling books.

HRT sometimes appears in the novels of best-selling author Tom Clancy. Clancy's books are noted for their extreme realism, and he sought the same effect in video games based on the exploits of HRT. Clancy helped Red Storm Entertainment develop the Rainbow Six series of tactical shooter games in the 1990s. The games feature operators who rescue hostages and take out terrorists. Clancy originally modeled the operators after HRT but changed the game's characters to an international team to broaden its appeal worldwide. In 2003, GameCube released the video-game version of Clancy's 1991 novel *The Sum of All Fears*. In it, players command HRT units with a variety of armaments in 11 different scenarios, all with the goal of preventing the release of a dangerous weapon on American soil. "For more than 15 years, Tom Clancy has presented the gritty, realistic counterpoint to most action games' abstract ideal of combat," gaming writer Joe Keiser summarized in 2012. "You could bleed out from a single bullet wound. Reflexes would rarely play a role in victory. Instead, success would come from careful operations, selection of *ordnance*, and the Planning Stage, a pre-battle strategizing session that let you lay out the positions and pathing of your computer-controlled operatives."

State law enforcement agencies often cooperate and train with FBI SWAT teams.

Units often leave Quantico and travel to other parts of the country to train in environments such as mountains, deserts, and large seaports that can't be duplicated at the Academy.

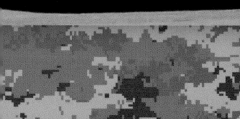

HRT AND SWAT IN ACTION

WHILE SPEAKING SPECIFICALLY ABOUT NEGOTIATORS SUCH as himself, longtime FBI agent Gary Noesner undoubtedly expressed the feelings of HRT members as well when he said, "I've gone into every situation wanting to see the person do what I think is in their best interest, which is put their weapon down ... and surrender peacefully." Despite this goal and HRT's overall success rate, two of the unit's highest-profile operations ended badly when their targets refused to "surrender peacefully." The negative outcome provoked severe criticism, which led to changes being made in the structuring of HRT's overall command and in some of the unit's operational procedures.

The first incident began in August 1992 when federal marshals tried to serve an arrest warrant on Idaho survivalist and former Army Special Forces operator Randy Weaver at his cabin deep in a forested area known as Ruby Ridge. Weaver had been charged with federal weapons violations. Deeply mistrustful of the government, Weaver didn't appear in court to answer the charges. The U.S. Marshals Service declared him a dangerous fugitive as a result. Before trying to arrest Weaver, the marshals put the cabin under surveillance. An accidental confrontation led to the shooting deaths of Weaver's 14-year-old son Samuel and a marshal. The marshals then asked HRT for help.

Under standard FBI *Rules of Engagement* (ROE), agents

After the Ruby Ridge standoff, federal agents gathered evidence from the Weaver cabin.

FORCE FACTS In the past 20 years, women have become increasingly a part of SWAT teams, a reflection of the FBI's growing emphasis on recruiting women to serve as agents.

cannot use deadly force against anyone, unless they are acting in self-defense or if they believe that the life of another person is in imminent danger. In addition, they are required to issue verbal warnings before using deadly force.

Based on the confrontation that had killed Samuel Weaver and the marshal, as well as reports that the Weavers had fired on a helicopter carrying TV journalist Geraldo Rivera, the ROE at Ruby Ridge were different. Agents were authorized to open fire if they saw an adult carrying a weapon, as long as no children were at risk. They were not obligated to issue a verbal warning before firing. Acting under that modified set of ROE, an HRT sniper shot Weaver in the back as he, his daughter, and a friend—who were all carrying rifles—crossed the yard to a shed where Samuel's body was lying. As the three people fled back to the house, the sniper fired another round. It wounded the friend and killed Weaver's wife Vicki, who was holding her 10-month-old daughter and standing behind the front door—where she was invisible to the sniper. The bloody incident aroused public outcry. While Weaver was charged with multiple crimes, his only conviction was for his failure to appear in court. A senate committee eventually decided that the shooting of Vicki Weaver was unjustified. The sniper was *indicted* for manslaughter several years later, but the charges were eventually dropped.

Rudy Ridge was still fresh in the national consciousness when HRT became involved in another controversial operation the following February in Waco, Texas. Agents of the Bureau of Alcohol, Tobacco, Firearms and Explosives (ATF) tried to use a search warrant to access the grounds of a compound belonging to a small religious group called the Branch Davidians in February 1993. The agency believed that the group had been purchasing and stockpiling illegal weapons and ammunition. There were also reports of drug manufacturing and child abuse.

Like Randy Weaver, Branch Davidian leader David Koresh

HRT agents are trained to aim precisely and hold their fire until commanded.

Field office SWAT teams vary in size according to the extent of the geographical area they cover, the density of the population, and the likelihood of violent crimes in that area.

was geared up for a fight. A TV reporter inadvertently tipped off Koresh that ATF was coming. In the 45-minute firefight that ensued, 4 ATF agents were killed, while the others were forced to retreat. Six Branch Davidians also died, and dozens on both sides were wounded.

Once again, HRT was summoned. A series of fruitless negotiations began, with each side accusing the other of acting in bad faith. At the same time, HRT employed psychological devices designed to deprive the Branch Davidians of sleep and make them more willing to surrender. These tactics included having low-flying helicopters hover over the compound, shining bright searchlights through the windows, and playing loud rock-and-roll music continuously. Nothing worked, though, and the siege dragged on for nearly two months. Finally, the team launched an assault. While it's still not clear who was responsible, a fire that engulfed the compound broke out and led to the deaths of 76 Branch Davidians. The case remains controversial today.

While most high-profile cases feature HRT, sometimes FBI SWAT teams "take point" instead. One notable example of this occurred on August 3, 2011, in Mosman, Australia, a wealthy suburb of Sydney. Eighteen-year-old Madeleine Pulver was alone in her home. Suddenly, a masked man later identified as Paul Peters broke in and threatened her with a baseball bat. Then he chained a black box around Madeleine's neck and left a ransom note that included an e-mail address by which he could be reached. Part of the note read, "Plastic explosives are located inside the small black combination case delivered to you." The note added that the case was booby-trapped and would explode if anyone tried to remove it.

When the man scuttled away, Madeleine called her father for help. He called the police,

In 2000, an official report cleared FBI agents of responsibility in the Waco fire of 1993.

who responded with a bomb squad. Madeleine endured nine frightening hours before the squad determined that the bomb didn't contain explosives. What was quickly dubbed the "Collar Bomb Case" attracted worldwide attention.

Starting with the e-mail address Peters had provided, authorities tracked him to a house near Louisville, Kentucky. An FBI SWAT team was dispatched to the address. According to one of Peters's neighbors in what was normally a very quiet neighborhood, the team "came in heavy and hard.... We had guys with machine guns in our back yard," the neighbor said.

The men's training paid off, as their overwhelming force took Peters completely by surprise and captured him without firing any shots. He was *extradited* to Australia and sentenced to 13 and a half years in prison.

Often, SWAT and HRT work together. In early 1988, a man named Charlie Leaf tracked his ex-girlfriend Cheryl Hart and their four-year-old son to her parents' house in Connecticut. They had moved there to escape Leaf's constant abuse. Though he nearly killed Hart and the boy on the spot, she talked him

In the event of a crisis, a local field office SWAT team will act as a first responder.

into driving away with them.

Hart's parents alerted the FBI. Within hours, the Richmond, Virginia, field office SWAT team had tracked Leaf and his captives to a small farmhouse near Sperryville. When the team entered the house that night, Leaf threatened to kill Hart and their son. The agents backed away, and negotiations began. According to FBI agent Kevin August, Leaf's demands included safe passage to "somewhere south where there were mountains" in the FBI helicopter that had landed nearby.

After hours of negotiation, the FBI came to the conclusion that no matter what they did, Leaf intended to kill both his hostages. They decided to take him out, and HRT sniper teams were deployed near the house. The FBI allowed Leaf to see them loading the helicopter with the supplies he had demanded. He emerged from the house using Hart as a human shield, holding a knife to her throat and a gun to her head. He had tied the terrified boy to his shoulders. Leaf's head was too close to Hart's for the snipers to risk a shot. The helicopter lifted off as Leaf approached, stirring up dust and leaves to distract him. At the same time, HRT agents set off stun grenades. Leaf dropped to his knees and whispered, "Goodbye, Kitten," fully intending to kill Hart. But his change in position allowed a sniper to gain a clear shot in the split second before Leaf could pull the trigger. The crisis over, both hostages left the scene unharmed.

It was yet another example of how HRT lives up to its motto and validation of the group's key role in the American system of criminal justice—a role that former member Jaime Atherton notes was by no means a slam dunk in its early days. "You've got to remember that in 1983 when it started, there were a lot of people who said, 'As soon as the Olympics are over, you guys are going to be reassigned,'" Atherton reported.

Obviously the "guys" were not reassigned. And today, there are countless people who are glad they were not. HRT continues to prove its worth in high-risk situations, and it is poised to continue its mission in the years to come.

The FBI, headquartered in Washington, D.C., employs more than 35,000 worldwide.

★ ★ ★

FORCE FACTS Former Navy SEAL and Medal of Honor winner Thomas Norris lost an eye in the Vietnam War and became the only HRT member to operate with just one eye.

When not in the field,
HRT and SWAT teams
keep up a rigorous
practice regimen.

FORCE FACTS HRT operators commonly fire a thousand rounds of ammunition or even more every week so they can keep their shooting skills at the highest possible level.

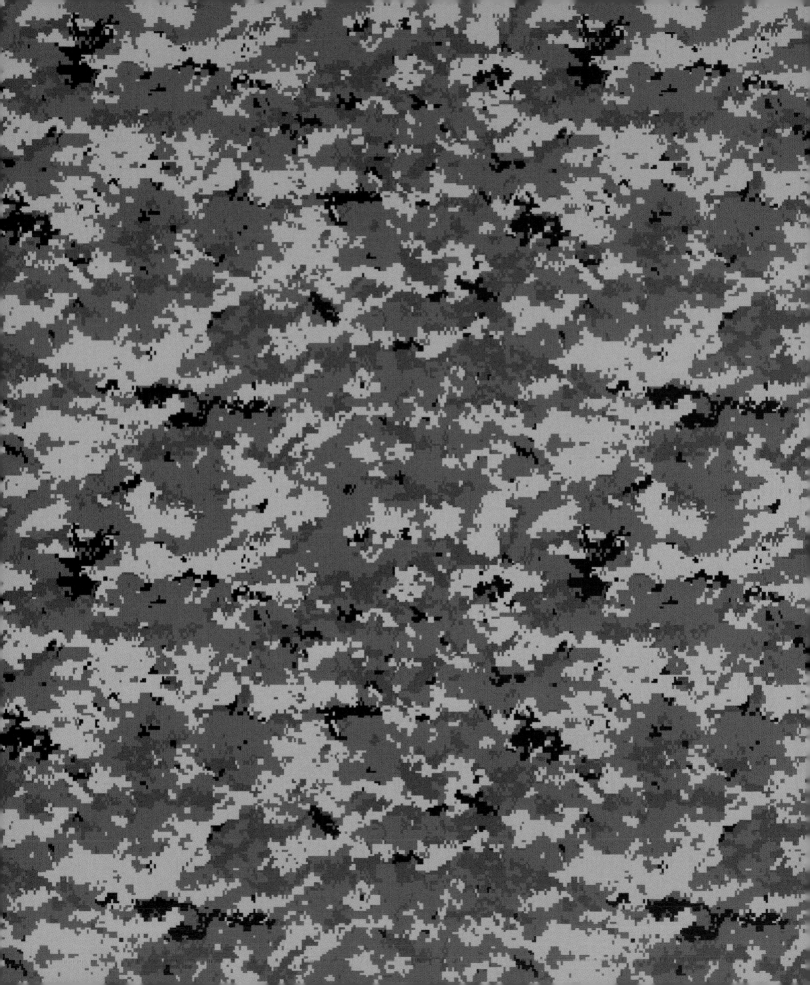

U.S. SPECIAL FORCES

GLOSSARY

breaching – breaking through a barrier

cache – a concealed storage location

casualty – a person injured or killed in an accident or a battle

cyanide – a toxic salt used as a poison

deploying – moving personnel into position for military action

extradited – took a suspect from one state or country to another to stand trial

fast-roping – sliding down a thick rope suspended from a helicopter as rapidly as possible

foregrips – handles of a weapon mounted under the front part of the barrel

indicted – charged with a crime

magazines – containers in guns that hold bullets and allow them to be fed into the firing chamber

Nomex – a lightweight, flame-resistant artificial fiber used in protective clothing for firefighters and other workers in hazardous situations

ordnance – military or law enforcement weapons, ammunition, and related equipment

polymer – a form of plastic noted for its exceptional strength

rappelling – descending a vertical surface using a rope coiled around the body and attached at a higher point

reconnaissance – a search to gain information, usually conducted in secret

Rules of Engagement – rules under which government forces can operate in conflict situations; these rules include but are not limited to the application of lethal force

tango – a code word representing the letter *T*, sometimes used as a name for "terrorist"

white supremacists – people who believe that white-skinned people are superior to people of other racial backgrounds

FORCE FACTS In the winter of 1996, HRT went directly from one operation in Puerto Rico to another in Michigan, undergoing a 125-degree temperature swing in less than 12 hours.

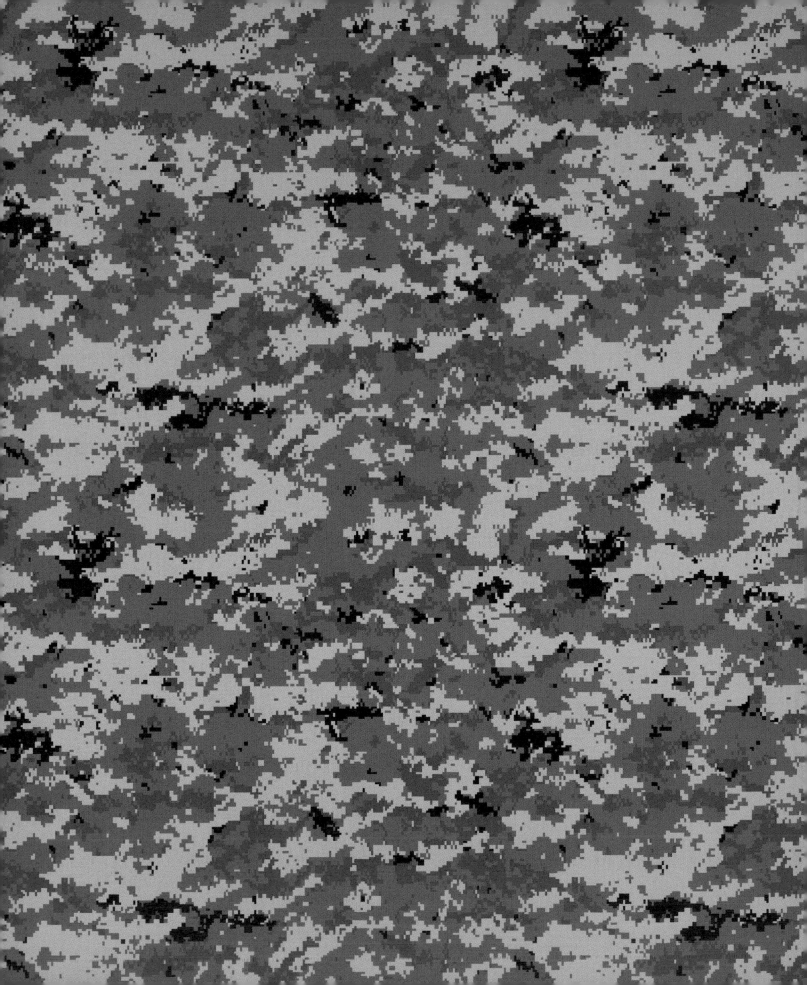

SELECTED BIBLIOGRAPHY

U.S. SPECIAL FORCES

Ackerman, Thomas H. *FBI Careers: The Ultimate Guide to Landing a Job as One of America's Finest.* Indianapolis: JIST Works, 2010.

Coulson, Danny, and Elaine Shannon. *No Heroes: Inside the FBI's Secret Counter-Terror Force.* New York: Pocket Books, 1999.

Kessler, Ronald. *Bureau: The Secret History of the FBI.* New York: St. Martin's Press, 2002.

Noesner, Gary. *Stalling for Time: My Life as an FBI Hostage Negotiator.* New York: Random House, 2010.

Pushies, Fred. *U.S. Counter-Terrorist Forces.* St. Paul, Minn.: MBI Publishing, 2002.

Theoharis, Athan G., ed. *The FBI: A Comprehensive Reference Guide.* New York: The Oryx Press, 2000.

Van Sandt, Clint, with Daniel Paisner. *Facing Down Evil: Life on the Edge as an FBI Hostage Negotiator.* New York: G. P. Putnam's Sons, 2006.

Whitcomb, Christopher. *Cold Zero: Inside the FBI Hostage Rescue Team.* New York: Warner Books, 2001.

WEBSITES

The Hostage Rescue Team

http://www.fbi.gov/news/stories/2013/february /the-hostage-rescue-team-30-years-of-service

An ongoing series beginning on the 30th anniversary of HRT covers its history, training, notable missions, and more.

"Stalling for Time" with an FBI Hostage Negotiator

http://www.npr.org/templates/story /story.php?storyId=130103016

A National Public Radio story about the Leaf hostage situation, including the link to the original radio broadcast.

READ MORE

Brush, Jim. *Special Forces.* Mankato, Minn.: Sea-to-Sea, 2012.

Cooper, Jason. *U.S. Special Operations.* Vero Beach, Fla.: Rourke, 2004.

INDEX

U.S. SPECIAL FORCES

Visit classzone.com and get connected

Online resources for students and parents

ClassZone resources provide instruction, practice, and learning support.

eEdition Plus
ONLINE

This interactive version of the text encourages students to explore science.

Content Review Online

Interactive review reinforces the big idea and key concepts of each chapter.

SciLinks

NSTA-selected links provide relevant Web resources correlated to the text.

Chapter-Based Support

Math tutorials, news, resources, test practice, and a misconceptions database help students succeed.

Now it all clicks!™

CLASSZONE.COM

McDougal Littell

McDougal Littell Science

Cells and Heredity

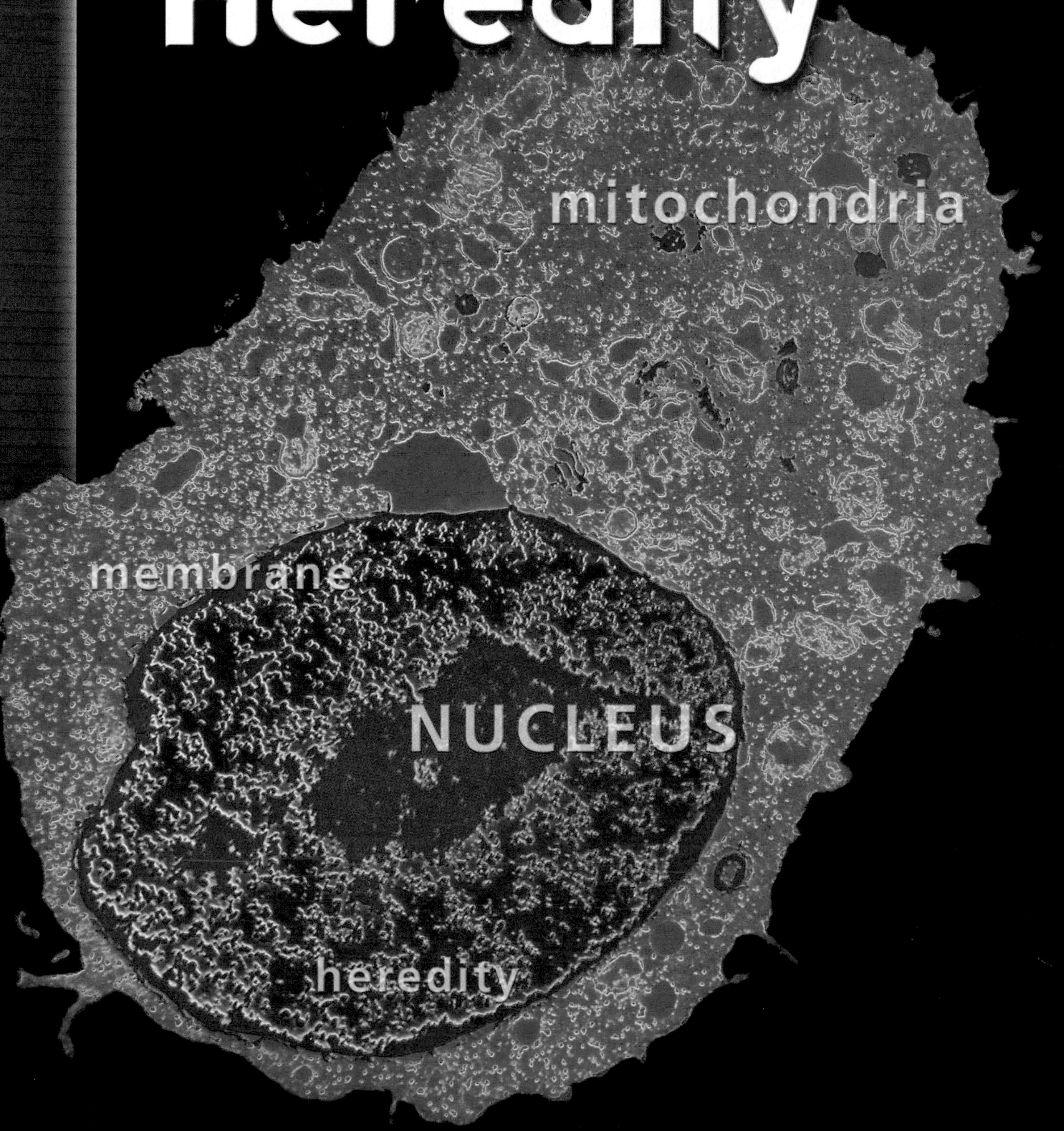

mitochondria

membrane

NUCLEUS

heredity

LIFE SCIENCE

A ▶ Cells and Heredity
B ▶ Life Over Time
C ▶ Diversity of Living Things
D ▶ Ecology
E ▶ Human Biology

EARTH SCIENCE

A ▶ Earth's Surface
B ▶ The Changing Earth
C ▶ Earth's Waters
D ▶ Earth's Atmosphere
E ▶ Space Science

PHYSICAL SCIENCE

A ▶ Matter and Energy
B ▶ Chemical Interactions
C ▶ Motion and Forces
D ▶ Waves, Sound, and Light
E ▶ Electricity and Magnetism

Acknowledgments: Excerpts and adaptations from *National Science Education Standards* by the National Academy of Sciences. Copyright © 1996 by the National Academy of Sciences. Reprinted with permission from the National Academies Press, Washington, D.C.

Excerpts and adaptations from *Benchmarks for Science Literacy: Project 2061.* Copyright © 1993 by the American Association for the Advancement of Science. Reprinted with permission.

ISBN: 0-618-33427-0   6 7 8 VJM 08 07 06 05

Internet Web Site: http://www.mcdougallittell.com

Science Consultants

Chief Science Consultant

James Trefil, Ph.D. is the Clarence J. Robinson Professor of Physics at George Mason University. He is the author or co-author of more than 25 books, including *Science Matters* and *The Nature of Science.* Dr. Trefil is a member of the American Association for the Advancement of Science's Committee on the Public Understanding of Science and Technology. He is also a fellow of the World Economic Forum and a frequent contributor to *Smithsonian* magazine.

Rita Ann Calvo, Ph.D. is Senior Lecturer in Molecular Biology and Genetics at Cornell University, where for 12 years she also directed the Cornell Institute for Biology Teachers. Dr. Calvo is the 1999 recipient of the College and University Teaching Award from the National Association of Biology Teachers.

Kenneth Cutler, M.S. is the Education Coordinator for the Julius L. Chambers Biomedical Biotechnology Research Institute at North Carolina Central University. A former middle school and high school science teacher, he received a 1999 Presidential Award for Excellence in Science Teaching.

Instructional Design Consultants

Douglas Carnine, Ph.D. is Professor of Education and Director of the National Center for Improving the Tools of Educators at the University of Oregon. He is the author of seven books and over 100 other scholarly publications, primarily in the areas of instructional design and effective instructional strategies and tools for diverse learners. Dr. Carnine also serves as a member of the National Institute for Literacy Advisory Board.

Linda Carnine, Ph.D. consults with school districts on curriculum development and effective instruction for students struggling academically. A former teacher and school administrator, Dr. Carnine also co-authored a popular remedial reading program.

Donald Steely, Ph.D. serves as principal investigator at the Oregon Center for Applied Science (ORCAS) on federal grants for science and language arts programs. His background also includes teaching and authoring of print and multimedia programs in science, mathematics, history, and spelling.

Sam Miller, Ph.D. is a middle school science teacher and the Teacher Development Liaison for the Eugene, Oregon, Public Schools. He is the author of curricula for teaching science, mathematics, computer skills, and language arts.

Vicky Vachon, Ph.D. consults with school districts throughout the United States and Canada on improving overall academic achievement with a focus on literacy. She is also co-author of a widely used program for remedial readers.

Content Reviewers

John Beaver, Ph.D.
Ecology
Professor, Director of Science Education Center
College of Education and Human Services
Western Illinois University
Macomb, IL

Donald J. DeCoste, Ph.D.
Matter and Energy, Chemical Interactions
Chemistry Instructor
University of Illinois
Urbana-Champaign, IL

Dorothy Ann Fallows, Ph.D., MSc
Diversity of Living Things, Microbiology
Partners in Health
Boston, MA

Michael Foote, Ph.D.
The Changing Earth, Life Over Time
Associate Professor
Department of the Geophysical Sciences
The University of Chicago
Chicago, IL

Lucy Fortson, Ph.D.
Space Science
Director of Astronomy
Adler Planetarium and Astronomy Museum
Chicago, IL

Elizabeth Godrick, Ph.D.
Human Biology
Professor, CAS Biology
Boston University
Boston, MA

Isabelle Sacramento Grilo, M.S.
The Changing Earth
Lecturer, Department of the Geological Sciences
San Diego State University
San Diego, CA

David Harbster, MSc
Diversity of Living Things
Professor of Biology
Paradise Valley Community College
Phoenix, AZ

Richard D. Norris, Ph.D.
Earth's Waters
Professor of Paleobiology
Scripps Institution of Oceanography
University of California, San Diego
La Jolla, CA

Donald B. Peck, M.S.
*Motion and Forces; Waves, Sound, and Light;
Electricity and Magnetism*
Director of the Center for Science Education (retired)
Fairleigh Dickinson University
Madison, NJ

Javier Penalosa, Ph.D.
Diversity of Living Things, Plants
Associate Professor, Biology Department
Buffalo State College
Buffalo, NY

Raymond T. Pierrehumbert, Ph.D.
Earth's Atmosphere
Professor in Geophysical Sciences (Atmospheric Science)
The University of Chicago
Chicago, IL

Brian J. Skinner, Ph.D.
Earth's Surface
Eugene Higgins Professor of Geology and Geophysics
Yale University
New Haven, CT

Nancy E. Spaulding, M.S.
Earth's Surface, The Changing Earth, Earth's Waters
Earth Science Teacher (retired)
Elmira Free Academy
Elmira, NY

Steven S. Zumdahl, Ph.D.
Matter and Energy, Chemical Interactions
Professor Emeritus of Chemistry
University of Illinois
Urbana-Champaign, IL

Susan L. Zumdahl, M.S.
Matter and Energy, Chemical Interactions
Chemistry Education Specialist
University of Illinois
Urbana-Champaign, IL

Safety Consultant

Juliana Texley, Ph.D.
Former K–12 Science Teacher and School Superintendent
Boca Raton, FL

English Language Advisor

Judy Lewis, M.A.
Director, State and Federal Programs for reading proficiency
and high risk populations
Rancho Cordova, CA

Teacher Panel Members

Carol Arbour
Tallmadge Middle School,
Tallmadge, OH

Patty Belcher
Goodrich Middle School,
Akron, OH

Gwen Broestl
Luis Munoz Marin Middle School,
Cleveland, OH

Al Brofman
Tehipite Middle School,
Fresno, CA

John Cockrell
Clinton Middle School,
Columbus, OH

Jenifer Cox
Sylvan Middle School,
Citrus Heights, CA

Linda Culpepper
Martin Middle School,
Charlotte, NC

Kathleen Ann DeMatteo
Margate Middle School,
Margate, FL

Melvin Figueroa
New River Middle School,
Ft. Lauderdale, FL

Doretha Grier
Kannapolis Middle School,
Kannapolis, NC

Robert Hood
Alexander Hamilton Middle School,
Cleveland, OH

Scott Hudson
Covedale Elementary School,
Cincinnati, OH

Loretta Langdon
Princeton Middle School,
Princeton, NC

Carlyn Little
Glades Middle School,
Miami, FL

Ann Marie Lynn
Amelia Earhart Middle School,
Riverside, CA

James Minogue
Lowe's Grove Middle School,
Durham, NC

Joann Myers
Buchanan Middle School,
Tampa, FL

Barbara Newell
Charles Evans Hughes Middle School,
Long Beach, CA

Anita Parker
Kannapolis Middle School,
Kannapolis, NC

Greg Pirolo
Golden Valley Middle School,
San Bernardino, CA

Laura Pottmyer
Apex Middle School,
Apex, NC

Lynn Prichard
Booker T. Washington Middle Magnet
School, Tampa, FL

Jacque Quick
Walter Williams High School,
Burlington, NC

Robert Glenn Reynolds
Hillman Middle School,
Youngstown, OH

Stacy Rinehart
Lufkin Road Middle School,
Apex, NC

Theresa Short
Abbott Middle School,
Fayetteville, NC

Rita Slivka
Alexander Hamilton Middle School,
Cleveland, OH

Marie Sofsak
B F Stanton Middle School,
Alliance, OH

Nancy Stubbs
Sweetwater Union Unified School District,
Chula Vista, CA

Sharon Stull
Quail Hollow Middle School,
Charlotte, NC

Donna Taylor
Okeeheelee Middle School,
West Palm Beach, FL

Sandi Thompson
Harding Middle School,
Lakewood, OH

Lori Walker
Audubon Middle School & Magnet Center,
Los Angeles, CA

Teacher Lab Evaluators

Andrew Boy
W.E.B. DuBois Academy,
Cincinnati, OH

Jill Brimm-Byrne
Albany Park Academy,
Chicago, IL

Gwen Broestl
Luis Munoz Marin Middle School,
Cleveland, OH

Al Brofman
Tehipite Middle School,
Fresno, CA

Michael A. Burstein
The Rashi School,
Newton, MA

Trudi Coutts
Madison Middle School,
Naperville, IL

Jenifer Cox
Sylvan Middle School,
Citrus Heights, CA

Larry Cwik
Madison Middle School,
Naperville, IL

Jennifer Donatelli
Kennedy Junior High School,
Lisle, IL

Melissa Dupree
Lakeside Middle School,
Evans, GA

Carl Fechko
Luis Munoz Marin Middle School,
Cleveland, OH

Paige Fullhart
Highland Middle School,
Libertyville, IL

Sue Hood
Glen Crest Middle School,
Glen Ellyn, IL

William Luzader
Plymouth Community Intermediate School,
Plymouth, MA

Ann Min
Beardsley Middle School,
Crystal Lake, IL

Aileen Mueller
Kennedy Junior High School,
Lisle, IL

Nancy Nega
Churchville Middle School,
Elmhurst, IL

Oscar Newman
Sumner Math and Science Academy,
Chicago, IL

Lynn Prichard
Booker T. Washington Middle Magnet
School, Tampa, FL

Jacque Quick
Walter Williams High School,
Burlington, NC

Stacy Rinehart
Lufkin Road Middle School,
Apex, NC

Seth Robey
Gwendolyn Brooks Middle School,
Oak Park, IL

Kevin Steele
Grissom Middle School,
Tinley Park, IL

Cells and Heredity

Unit Features

SCIENTIFIC AMERICAN

1 The Cell   6

the **BIG** idea

All living things are made up of cells.

2 How Cells Function   38

the **BIG** idea

All cells need energy and materials for life processes.

How do plants like these sunflowers change energy from the Sun?
page 38

Features

Visual Highlights

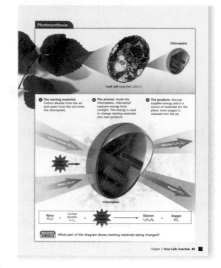

Internet Resources @ ClassZone.com

INVESTIGATIONS AND ACTIVITIES

Standards and Benchmarks

Each chapter in **Cells and Heredity** covers some of the learning goals that are described in the *National Science Education Standards* (NSES) and the Project 2061 *Benchmarks for Science Literacy.* Selected content and skill standards are shown below in shortened form. The following *National Science Education Standards* are covered in Frontiers in Science, and in Timelines in Science, as well as in chapter features and laboratory investigations: Understandings About Scientific Inquiry (A.9), Understandings About Science and Technology (E.6), Science and Technology in Society (F.5), Nature of Science (G.2), and History of Science (G.3).

Content Standards

1 The Cell

National Science Education Standards

C.1.a	Levels of organization for living systems include cells, tissues, organs, organ systems, whole organisms, and ecosystems.
C.1.b	All organisms are composed of cells—the basic unit of life. Most are single cells; others, including humans, are multicellular.
C.1.c	Cells perform the functions of life. They grow, divide, and take in nutrients.
C.1.d	Specialized cells perform specialized functions in multicellular organisms.

Project 2061 Benchmarks

5.C.1	All living things are made of cells. A microscope is needed to see cell details. Different tissues and organs are made of different kinds of cells.
5.C.3	Cells carry out the functions of organisms.
10.I.1	Many diseases are caused by microorganisms. This is the germ theory, introduced by Louis Pasteur and others in the 19th century.
10.I.2	Pasteur showed that food spoils as microorganisms enter from air, and that heat can destroy the germs.

2 How Cells Function

National Science Education Standards

B.1.b	Substances react with other substances to form new substances with different characteristic properties.
B.1.c	There are more than 100 known elements that combine in many ways to produce living and nonliving substances.
B.3.a	Energy is a property of many substances. Energy is transferred many ways.
C.1.c	Cells perform the functions of life. They take in nutrients for energy and materials.

Project 2061 Benchmarks

5.C.3	Cells carry out the functions of all organisms similarly.
5.C.4	About 2/3 of the weight of cells is water. This gives cells certain properties.
5.E.1	Food provides fuel and building material for all organisms. Plants use light to make sugars. Other organisms eat plants to get materials and energy.
5.E.3	Energy can change from one form to another in living things. Animals get energy from food. Almost all food energy comes originally from sunlight.

3 Cell Division

National Science Education Standards

C.1.c	Cells perform the functions of life. They grow and divide. This requires that they take in nutrients for energy.
C.2.a	Reproduction is a characteristic of all living systems. Some organisms reproduce asexually. Others reproduce sexually.

Project 2061 Benchmarks

5.B.1	In some organisms, all the genes come from a single parent. In organisms that have sexes, usually half of the genes come from each parent.
5.C.2	Cells repeatedly divide to make more cells for growth and repair.

4 Patterns of Heredity

National Science Education Standards

C.2.a Reproduction happens in all living systems. Some organisms reproduce asexually. Others reproduce sexually.

C.2.b In many species, females produce eggs, and males sperm, which unite to begin a new individual. The offspring gets genes from both parents. Sexually produced offspring are never identical to their parents.

C.2.c Every organism requires a set of instructions for specifying its traits. Heredity is this set of instructions passing from one generation to another.

C.2.d Heredity information is in genes in the chromosomes of each cell. Each gene carries one unit of information that influences one or more traits. A trait is determined by one or more genes. A human cell has many thousands of genes.

Project 2061 Benchmarks

5.B.1 In some organisms, all the genes come from a single parent. In organisms that have sexes, typically half of the genes come from each parent.

5.B.2 In sexual reproduction, a single specialized cell from a female joins with a specialized cell from a male.

5 DNA and Modern Genetics

National Science Education Standards

C.2.d Heredity information is in genes in the chromosomes of each cell. Each gene carries one unit of information that influences one or more traits. A trait is determined by one or more genes. A human cell has many thousand genes.

C.2.e Some traits are inherited and others result from Interactions with the environment.

F.5.c Technology influences society and can cause social, political, and economic change. Needs, attitudes, and values influence decisions about technology.

Project 2061 Benchmarks

3.C.5 New technologies increase some risks and decrease others.

3.C.6 Rarely are technology issues simple and one-sided.

5.B.3 New varieties of plants and animals have resulted from selective breeding.

5.F.1 Small differences between parents and offspring can become big differences between ancestors and distant descendants.

8.A.2 People control characteristics of plants and animals by selective breeding.

Process and Skill Standards

National Science Education Standards

A.1 Identify questions that can be answered through scientific methods.

A.2 Design and conduct a scientific investigation.

A.3 Use appropriate tools and techniques to gather and analyze data.

A.4 Use evidence to describe, predict, explain, and model.

A.5 Think critically to find relationships between results and interpretations.

A.6 Give alternative explanations and predictions.

A.7 Communicate procedures, results, and conclusions.

A.8 Use mathematics in all aspects of scientific inquiry.

A.9.a Different kinds of questions suggest different kinds of scientific investigations.

A.9.b Current scientific knowledge guides scientific investigations.

A.9.c Mathematics is important in all aspects of scientific inquiry.

A.9.d Scientific explanations emphasize evidence, have logically consistent arguments, and use scientific principles, models, and theories.

E.6.b Many different people in different cultures have made and continue to make contributions to science and technology.

G.1.a Women and men of various social and ethnic backgrounds engage in the activities of science.

G.1.b Science requires different abilities. The work of science relies on basic human qualities, such as reasoning, insight, energy, skill, and creativity.

Project 2061 Benchmarks

1.C.1 Contributions to science have been made by different people, in different cultures, at different times.

12.A.1 Know why it is important in science to keep honest, clear, and accurate records.

12.A.2 Hypotheses are valuable, even if they turn out not to be true.

12.A.3 Different explanations can often be given for the same evidence.

12.C.3 Using appropriate units, use and read instruments that measure length, volume, weight, time, rate, and temperature.

12.D.1 Use tables and graphs to organize information and identify relationships.

12.D.2 Read, interpret, and describe tables and graphs.

12.D.3 Locate information in reference books and other resources.

12.D.4 Understand information that includes different types of charts and graphs, including circle charts, bar graphs, line graphs, data tables, diagrams, and symbols.

Introducing Life Science

Scientists are curious. Since ancient times, they have been asking and answering questions about the world around them. Scientists are also very suspicious of the answers they get. They carefully collect evidence and test their answers many times before accepting an idea as correct.

In this book you will see how scientific knowledge keeps growing and changing as scientists ask new questions and rethink what was known before. The following sections will help get you started.

What Is Life Science?

Life science is the study of living things. As you study life science, you will observe and read about a variety of organisms, from huge redwood trees to the tiny bacteria that cause sore throats. Because Earth is home to such a great variety of living things, the study of life science is rich and exciting.

But life science doesn't simply include learning the names of millions of organisms. It includes big ideas that help us to understand how all these living things interact with their environment. Life science is the study of characteristics and needs that all living things have in common. It's also a study of changes—both daily changes as well as changes that take place over millions of years. Probably most important, in studying life science, you will explore the many ways that all living things—including you—depend upon Earth and its resources.

The text and visuals in this book will invite you into the world of living things and provide you with the key concepts you'll need in your study. Activities offer a chance for you to investigate some aspects of life science on your own. The four unifying principles listed below provide a way for you to connect the information and ideas in this program.

- **All living things share common characteristics.**

- **All living things share common needs.**

- **Living things meet their needs through interactions with the environment.**

- **The types and numbers of living things change over time.**

the **BIG** idea

Each chapter begins with a big idea. Keep in mind that each big idea relates to one or more of the unifying principles.

All living things share common characteristics.

Birds nest among the plants of a reed marsh as sunlight shines and a breeze blows. Which of these is alive? Warblers and plants are living things, but sunlight and breezes are not. All living things share common characteristics that distinguish them from nonliving things.

What It Means

This unifying principle helps you explore one of the biggest questions in science, "What is life?" Let's take a look at four characteristics that distinguish living things from nonliving things: organization, growth, reproduction, and response.

Organization

If you stand a short distance from a reed warbler's nest, you can observe the largest level of organization in a living thing—the **organism** itself. Each bird is an organism. If you look at a leaf under a microscope, you can observe the smallest level of organization capable of performing all the activities of life, a **cell.** All living things are made of cells.

Growth

Most living things grow and develop. Growth often involves not only an increase in size, but also an increase in complexity, such as a tadpole growing into a frog. If all goes well, the small warblers in the picture will grow to the size of their parent.

Reproduction

Most living things produce offspring like themselves. Those offspring are also able to reproduce. That means that reed warblers produce reed warblers, which in turn produce more reed warblers.

Response

You've probably noticed that your body adjusts to changes in your surroundings. If you are exploring outside on a hot day, you may notice that you sweat. On a cold day, you may shiver. Sweating and shivering are examples of response.

Why It's Important

People of all ages experience the urge to explore and understand the living world. Understanding the characteristics of living things is a good way to start this exploration of life. In addition, knowing about the characteristics of living things helps you identify

- similarities and differences among various organisms
- key questions to ask about any organism you study

All living things share common needs.

What do you need to stay alive?
What does an animal like a fish or a
coral need to stay alive? All living
things have common needs.

What It Means

Inside every living thing, chemical reactions constantly change materials into new materials. For these reactions to occur, an organism needs energy, water and other materials, and living space.

Energy

You use energy all the time. Movement, growth, and sleep all require energy, which you get from food. Plants use the energy of sunlight to make sugar for energy. Almost all animals get their energy by eating either plants or other animals that eat plants.

Water and Other Materials

Water is an important material in the cells of all living things. The chemical reactions inside cells take place in water, and water plays a part in moving materials around within organisms.

Other materials are also essential for life. For example, plants must have carbon dioxide from the air to make sugar. Plants and animals both use oxygen to release the energy stored in sugar. You and other animals that live on land get oxygen when you breathe in air. The fish swimming around the coral reef in the picture have gills, which allow them to get oxygen that is dissolved in the water.

Living Space

You can think of living space as a home—a space that protects you from external conditions and a place where you can get materials such as water and air. The ocean provides living space for the coral that makes up this coral reef. The coral itself provides living space for many other organisms.

Why It's Important

Understanding the needs of living things helps people make wise decisions about resources. This knowledge can also help you think carefully about
• the different ways in which various organisms meet their needs for energy and materials
• the effects of adding chemicals to the water and air around us
• the reasons why some types of plants or animals may disappear from an area

Living things meet their needs through interactions with the environment.

A moose chomps on the leaves of a plant. This ordinary event involves many interactions among living and nonliving things within the forest.

What It Means

To understand this unifying principle, take a closer look at the words *environment* and *interactions*.

Environment

The **environment** is everything that surrounds a living thing. An environment is made up of both living and nonliving factors. For example, the environment in this forest includes rainfall, rocks, and soil as well as the moose, the evergreen trees, and the birch trees. In fact, the soil in these forests is called "moose and spruce" soil because it contains materials provided by the animals and evergreens in the area.

Interaction

All living things in an environment meet their needs through interactions. An **interaction** occurs when two or more things act in ways that affect one another. For example, trees and other forest plants can meet their need for energy and materials through interactions with materials in soil and with air and light from the Sun. New plants get living space as birds, wind, and other factors carry seeds from one location to another.

Animals like this moose meet their need for food through interactions with other living things. The moose gets food by eating leaves off trees and other plants. In turn, the moose becomes food for wolves.

Why It's Important

Learning about living things and their environment helps scientists and decision makers address issues such as

- predicting how a change in the moose population would affect the soil in the forest
- determining the ways in which animals harm or benefit the trees in a forest
- developing land for human use without damaging the environment

The types and numbers of living things change over time.

The story of life on Earth is a story of changes. Some changes take place over millions of years. At one time, animals similar to modern fish swam in the area where this lizard now runs.

What It Means

To understand how living things change over time, let's look closely at the terms *diversity* and *adaptation*.

Diversity

You are surrounded by an astonishing variety of living things. This variety is called **biodiversity.** Today, scientists have described and named 1.4 million species. There are even more species that haven't been named. Scientists use the term *species* to describe a group of closely related living things. Members of a **species** are so similar that they can produce offspring that are able to reproduce. Lizards, such as the one you see in the photograph, are so diverse that they make up many different species.

Over the millions of years that life has existed on Earth, new species have originated and others have disappeared. The disappearance of a species is called **extinction.** Fossils, like the one in the photograph, provide evidence of some of the organisms that lived millions of years ago.

Adaptation

Scientists use the term **adaptation** to mean a characteristic of a species that allows members of that species to survive in a particular environment. Adaptations are related to needs. A lizard's legs are an adaptation that allows it to move on land.

Over time, species either develop adaptations to changing environments or they become extinct. The history of living things on Earth is related to the history of the changing Earth. The presence of a fishlike fossil indicates that the area shown in this photograph was once covered by water.

Why It's Important

By learning how living things change over time, you will gain a better understanding of the life that surrounds you and how it survives. Discovering more about the history of life helps scientists to

- identify patterns of relationships among various species
- predict how changes in the environment may affect species in the future

The Nature of Science

You may think of science as a body of knowledge or a collection of facts. More important, however, science is an active process that involves certain ways of looking at the world.

Scientific Habits of Mind

Scientists are curious. They are always asking questions. A scientist who observes that the number of plants in a forest preserve has decreased might ask questions such as, "Are more animals eating the plants?" or "Has the way the land is used affected the numbers of plants?" Scientists around the world investigate these and other important questions.

Scientists are observant. They are always looking closely at the world around them. A scientist who studies plants often sees details such as the height of a plant, its flowers, and how many plants live in a particular area.

Scientists are creative. They draw on what they know to form a possible explanation for a pattern, an event, or a behavior that they have observed. Then scientists create a plan for testing their ideas.

Scientists are skeptical. Scientists don't accept an explanation or answer unless it is based on evidence and logical reasoning. They continually question their own conclusions as well as conclusions suggested by other scientists. Scientists trust only evidence that is confirmed by other people or methods.

A white-tailed deer feeds on many plants, including the trillium shown here.

By measuring the growth of this tree, a scientist can study interactions in the ecosystem.

Science Processes at Work

You can think of science as a continuous cycle of asking and seeking answers to questions about the world. Although there are many processes that scientists use, scientists typically do each of the following:

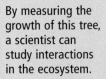

- Observe and ask a question
- Determine what is known
- Investigate
- Interpret results
- Share results

Observe and Ask a Question

It may surprise you that asking questions is an important skill. A scientific investigation may start when a scientist asks a question. Perhaps scientists observe an event or a process that they don't understand, or perhaps answering one question leads to another.

Determine What Is Known

When beginning an inquiry, scientists find out what is already known about a question. They study results from other scientific investigations, read journals, and talk with other scientists. A biologist who is trying to understand how the change in the number of deer in an area affects plants will study reports of censuses taken for both plants and animals.

Investigate

Investigating is the process of collecting evidence. Two important ways of collecting evidence are observing and experimenting.

Observing is the act of noting and recording an event, a characteristic, a behavior, or anything else detected with an instrument or with the senses. For example, a scientist notices that plants in one part of the forest are not thriving. She sees broken plants and compares the height of the plants in one area with the height of those in another.

An **experiment** is an organized procedure during which all factors but the one being studied are controlled. For example, the scientist thinks the reason some plants in the forest are not thriving may be that deer are eating the flowers off the plants. An experiment she might try is to mark two similar parts of an area where the plants grow and then build a fence around one part so the deer can't get to the plants there. The fence must be constructed so the same amounts of light, air, and water reach the plants. The only factor that changes is contact between plants and the deer.

Close observation of the Colorado potato beetle led scientists to a biological pesticide that can help farmers control this insect pest.

Forming hypotheses and making predictions are two other skills involved in scientific investigations. A **hypothesis** is a tentative explanation for an observation or a scientific problem that can be tested by further investigation. For example, since at least 1900, Colorado potato beetles were known to be resistant to chemical insecticides. Yet the numbers of beetles were not as large as expected. It was hypothesized that bacteria living in the beetles' environment were killing many beetles. A **prediction** is an expectation of what will be observed or what will happen and can be used to test a hypothesis. It was predicted that certain bacteria would kill Colorado potato beetles. This prediction was confirmed when a bacterium called *Bt* was discovered to kill Colorado potato beetles and other insect pests.

Interpret Results

As scientists investigate, they analyze their evidence, or data, and begin to draw conclusions. **Analyzing data** involves looking at the evidence gathered through observations or experiments and trying to identify any patterns that might exist in the data. Often scientists need to make additional observations or perform more experiments before they are sure of their conclusions. Many times scientists make new predictions or revise their hypotheses.

Computers help scientists analyze the sequence of base pairs in the DNA molecule.

Share Results

An important part of scientific investigation is sharing results of experiments. Scientists read and publish in journals and attend conferences to communicate with other scientists around the world. Sharing data and procedures gives them a way to test one another's results. They also share results with the public through newspapers, television, and other media.

Living things contain complex molecules such as RNA and DNA. To study them, scientists often use models like the one shown here.

The Nature of Technology

Imagine what life would be like without cars, computers, and cell phones. Imagine having no refrigerator or radio. It's difficult to think of a world without these items we call technology. Technology, however, is more than just machines that make our daily activities easier. Like science, technology is also a process. The process of technology uses scientific knowledge to design solutions to real-world problems.

Science and Technology

Science and technology go hand in hand. Each depends upon the other. Even designing a device as simple as a toaster requires knowledge of how heat flows and which materials are the best conductors of heat. Scientists also use a number of devices to help them collect data. Microscopes, telescopes, spectrographs, and computers are just a few of the tools that help scientists learn more about the world. The more information these tools provide, the more devices can be developed to aid scientific research and to improve modern lives.

The Process of Technological Design

Heart disease is among the leading causes of death today. Doctors have successfully replaced damaged hearts with hearts from donors. Medical engineers have developed pacemakers that improve the ability of a damaged heart to pump blood. But none of these solutions is perfect. Although it is very complex, the heart is really a pump for blood, thus, using technology to build a better replacement pump should be possible. The process of technological design involves many choices. In the case of an artificial heart, choices about how and what to develop involve cost, safety, and patient preference. What kind of technology will result in the best quality of life for the patient?

Identify a Need

Developers of technology must first establish exactly what needs their technology must meet. A healthy heart pumps blood at the rate of 5–30 liters per minute. What type of artificial pump could achieve such rates, responding to changes in activity level? Could such a pump be small enough to implant into a person? How would such a heart be powered? What materials would not be rejected by the human body?

Design and Develop

Several designs for artificial hearts have been proposed. The Jarvik-7 was the first intended to be a long-term replacement for a human heart. The Jarvik-7 did not work very well. Although it lengthened the lives of some patients, their quality of life was poor. Doctors and engineers knew they needed to refine the design further. For example, the heart needed to be smaller, and it needed to have a better power system. The heart also needed to be made out of a better material so that it would not cause blood clots when implanted into a patient.

Test and Improve

The new AbioCor heart may hold the solutions to many of these problems. This fully self-contained implantable device makes the goal of replacing a damaged heart seem not so far away. Still, many improvements will be needed before the AbioCor is routinely put into human beings. Tests of the AbioCor are still in progress.

Using McDougal Littell Science

Reading Text and Visuals

This book is organized to help you learn. Use these boxed pointers as a path to help you learn and remember the **Big Ideas** and **Key Concepts**.

Read the Big Idea.

As you read **Key Concepts** for the chapter, relate them to **the Big Idea**.

Take notes.

Use the strategies on the **Getting Ready to Learn** page.

CHAPTER

1 The

the BIG idea

All living things are made up of cells.

Key Concepts

SECTION
1.1 The cell is the basic unit of living things.
Learn why cells are important to the study of life.

SECTION
1.2 Microscopes allow us to see inside the cell.
Learn what microscopes have shown about the inner structure of cells.

SECTION
1.3 Different cells perform various functions.
Learn about different types of cells in both unicellular and multicellular organisms.

Internet Preview

CLASSZONE.COM

Chapter 1 online resources: Content Review, two Simulations, two Resource Centers, Math Tutorial, Test Practice

---

CHAPTER 1

Getting Ready to Learn

◄ CONCEPT REVIEW

- Living things share certain characteristics that distinguish them from nonliving things.
- Living things have common needs, including energy, matter, and living space.

◄ VOCABULARY REVIEW

See Glossary for definitions.

cell
DNA
genetic material
theory

CONTENT REVIEW
CLASSZONE.COM
Review concepts and vocabulary.

► TAKING NOTES

MAIN IDEA WEB

Write each new blue heading, or main idea, in the top box. In the boxes around it, take notes about important terms and details that relate to the main idea.

VOCABULARY STRATEGY

Write each new vocabulary term in the center of a **four square** diagram. Write notes in the squares around each term. Include a definition, some characteristics, and some possible examples of the term. If possible, write some things that are not examples of the term.

See the Note-Taking Handbook on pages R45–R51.

SCIENCE NOTEBOOK

All living things are made of cells.

| The cell is the smallest unit that performs the activities of life. | Multicellular organisms have many different types of cells working together. | In a unicellular organism a single cell carries out the activities of life. |

Definition	Characteristics
Any living thing	Needs energy, materials from the environment, and living space.
	Grows, develops, responds to environment, reproduces.
	Is made up of one or more cells.

ORGANISM

Examples	Nonexamples
Dogs, cats, birds, insects, moss, trees, bacteria	Rocks, water, dirt

Read each heading.

See how it fits in the outline of the chapter.

KEY CONCEPT

1.1 The cell is the basic unit of living things.

BEFORE, you learned	NOW, you will learn
• Living things have common characteristics	• How living things are different from nonliving things
• Living things have common needs	• How the microscope led to the discovery of cells
• A theory is something that explains what is observed in nature	• About the cell theory

Remember what you know.

Think about concepts you learned earlier and preview what you'll learn now.

VOCABULARY

organism p. 9
unicellular p. 11
multicellular p. 11
microscope p. 12
bacteria p. 14

EXPLORE Activity and Life

Does a candle show signs of life?

PROCEDURE

1. Carefully light one candle.

2. Sit quietly and observe the candle. Note its behavior. What does the flame do? What happens to the wax?

MATERIALS
• small candle
• candleholder
• matches

WHAT DO YOU THINK?
• How does a lit candle seem alive?
• How do you know for sure that it is not?

Try the activities.

They will introduce you to science concepts.

Living things are different from nonliving things.

MAIN IDEA WEB
Make a main idea web about living things, including how they differ from nonliving things.

You know life when you see it. Perhaps your class takes a field trip to a local state park to collect water samples. You are surrounded by trees. There is a stream, with rocks covered with moss and green algae. There are fish and frogs; there are birds and insects. You are surrounded by life. But how would you define it?

One way to answer the question is to think about what makes a living thing different from a nonliving thing. You might ask if a thing uses energy. Or maybe you would observe it to see if it moves. You could investigate whether it consumes food and water. These are characteristics of living things, or organisms. Any individual form of life that uses energy to carry out its activities is an **organism.** Most organisms move. All organisms get water and other materials from the environment.

Learn the vocabulary.

Take notes on each term.

Chapter 1: **The Cell 9** A

Reading Text and Visuals

Cells come from other cells.

The studies of Hooke and Leeuwenhoek made people ask if all living things have cells. People continued to observe samples taken from all sorts of living matter. They continued to find cells, although often these cells looked very different from one another. Still, it was clear that all living matter was made of cells.

There was another important question scientists were trying to answer: Where do cells come from? The answer to this question was settled by the 1850s. People studying all types of living cells observed the same thing—that cells divide. One living cell divides into two living cells. Here, under the microscope, was evidence of where cells come from. Life comes from life—that is, one cell comes from another cell.

CHECK YOUR READING What do scientists mean when they say that life comes from life? Your answer should include the word *cells*.

The observations and evidence gathered over a long time by many scientists are summarized in the three concepts of the cell theory:

1 Every living thing is made of one or more cells.

2 Cells carry out the functions needed to support life.

3 Cells come only from other living cells.

Read one paragraph at a time.

Look for a topic sentence that explains the main idea of the paragraph. Figure out how the details relate to that idea. One paragraph might have several important ideas; you may have to reread to understand.

Answer the questions.

Check Your Reading questions will help you remember what you read.

Study the visuals.

- Read the title.
- Read all labels and captions.
- Figure out what the picture is showing. Notice the information in the captions.

The Cell Theory

The importance of the cell to life is summarized in the cell theory.

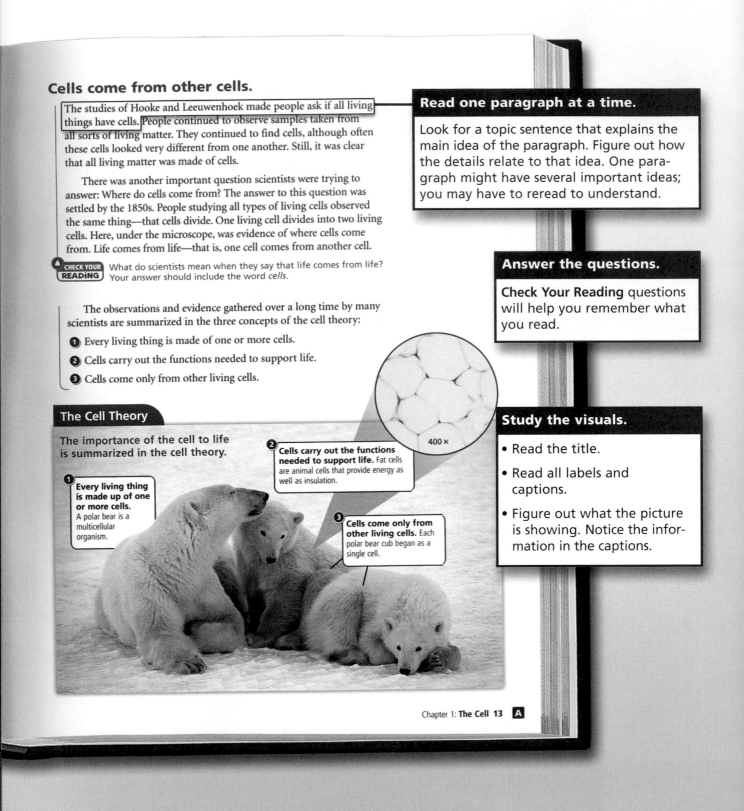

1 Every living thing is made up of one or more cells. A polar bear is a multicellular organism.

2 Cells carry out the functions needed to support life. Fat cells are animal cells that provide energy as well as insulation.

400×

3 Cells come only from other living cells. Each polar bear cub began as a single cell.

Chapter 1: **The Cell 13** **A**

Doing Labs

To understand science, you have to see it in action. Doing labs helps you understand how things really work.

① Read the entire lab first.

② Form a hypothesis.

③ Follow the procedure.

④ Record the data.

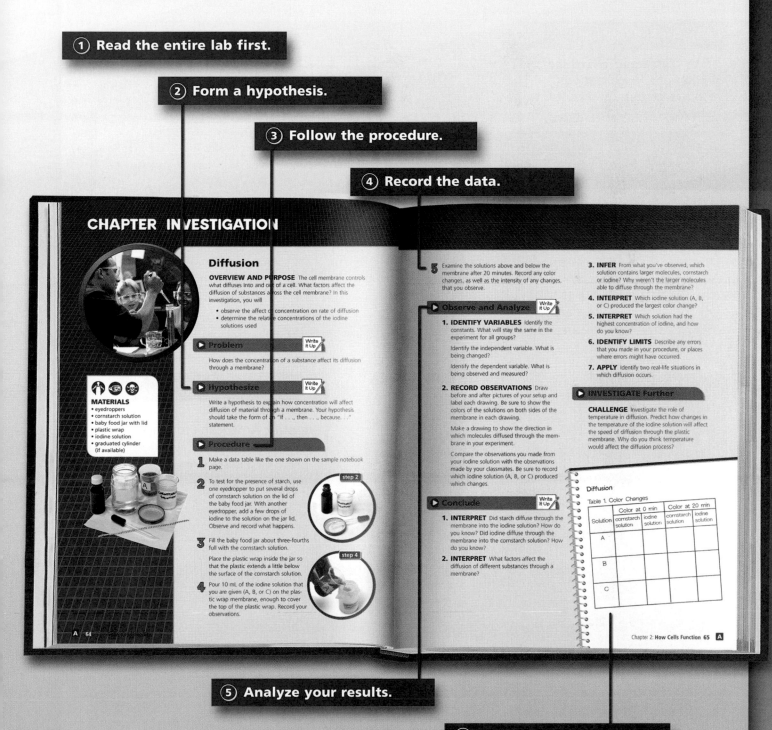

CHAPTER INVESTIGATION

Diffusion

OVERVIEW AND PURPOSE The cell membrane controls what diffuses into and out of a cell. What factors affect the diffusion of substances across the cell membrane? In this investigation, you will

- observe the affect of concentration on rate of diffusion
- determine the relative concentrations of the iodine solutions used

▶ **Problem** *Write It Up*

How does the concentration of a substance affect its diffusion through a membrane?

▶ **Hypothesize** *Write It Up*

Write a hypothesis to explain how concentration will affect diffusion of material through a membrane. Your hypothesis should take the form of an "If . . . , then . . . , because. . ." statement.

MATERIALS
- eyedroppers
- cornstarch solution
- baby food jar with lid
- plastic wrap
- iodine solution
- graduated cylinder (if available)

▶ **Procedure**

1 Make a data table like the one shown on the sample notebook page.

2 To test for the presence of starch, use one eyedropper to put several drops of cornstarch solution on the lid of the baby food jar. With another eyedropper, add a few drops of iodine to the solution on the jar lid. Observe and record what happens.

3 Fill the baby food jar about three-fourths full with the cornstarch solution.

Place the plastic wrap inside the jar so that the plastic extends a little below the surface of the cornstarch solution.

4 Pour 10 mL of the iodine solution that you are given (A, B, or C) on the plastic wrap membrane, enough to cover the top of the plastic wrap. Record your observations.

A 64

5 Examine the solutions above and below the membrane after 20 minutes. Record any color changes, as well as the intensity of any changes, that you observe.

▶ **Observe and Analyze** *Write It Up*

1. **IDENTIFY VARIABLES** Identify the constants. What will stay the same in the experiment for all groups?

   Identify the independent variable. What is being changed?

   Identify the dependent variable. What is being observed and measured?

2. **RECORD OBSERVATIONS** Draw before and after pictures of your setup and label each drawing. Be sure to show the colors of the solutions on both sides of the membrane in each drawing.

   Make a drawing to show the direction in which molecules diffused through the membrane in your experiment.

   Compare the observations you made from your iodine solution with the observations made by your classmates. Be sure to record which iodine solution (A, B, or C) produced which changes.

▶ **Conclude** *Write It Up*

1. **INTERPRET** Did starch diffuse through the membrane into the iodine solution? How do you know? Did iodine diffuse through the membrane into the cornstarch solution? How do you know?

2. **INTERPRET** What factors affect the diffusion of different substances through a membrane?

3. **INFER** From what you've observed, which solution contains larger molecules, cornstarch or iodine? Why weren't the larger molecules able to diffuse through the membrane?

4. **INTERPRET** Which iodine solution (A, B, or C) produced the largest color change?

5. **INTERPRET** Which solution had the highest concentration of iodine, and how do you know?

6. **IDENTIFY LIMITS** Describe any errors that you made in your procedure, or places where errors might have occurred.

7. **APPLY** Identify two real-life situations in which diffusion occurs.

▶ **INVESTIGATE Further**

CHALLENGE Investigate the role of temperature in diffusion. Predict how changes in the temperature of the iodine solution will affect the speed of diffusion through the plastic membrane. Why do you think temperature would affect the diffusion process?

Diffusion

Table 1. Color Changes

Solution	Color at 0 min		Color at 20 min	
	cornstarch solution	iodine solution	cornstarch solution	iodine solution
A				
B				
C				

Chapter 2: **How Cells Function** 65 A

⑤ Analyze your results.

⑥ Write your lab report.

Using Technology

The Internet is a great source of information about up-to-date science. The ClassZone Web site and NSTA SciLinks have exciting sites for you to explore. Video clips and simulations can make science come alive.

Look for red banners.

Go to **ClassZone.com** to see simulations, visualizations, resource centers, and content review.

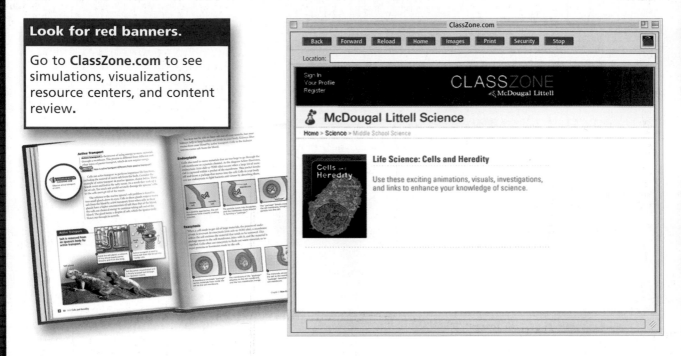

CLASSZONE
McDougal Littell

McDougal Littell Science

Home > Science > Middle School Science

Life Science: Cells and Heredity

Use these exciting animations, visuals, investigations, and links to enhance your knowledge of science.

Watch the video.

See science at work in the **Scientific American Frontiers** video.

FRONTIERS in Science

Genes
that **MAP**
the **Body**

Look up SciLinks.

Go to **scilinks.org** to explore the topic.

NSTA
scilinks.org
SCiLINKS

Heredity **Code: MDL034**

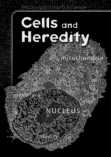

Cells and
Heredity

Cells and Heredity
Contents Overview

Genes that MAP the Body

What signals a monkey to grow a tail and a fish to grow fins? The answer is in their genes.

SCIENTIFIC AMERICAN FRONTIERS

Learn about genes that affect aging. See the video "Genes for Youth."

What's in a Gene?

Humans and fish are about as different as one animal can be from another. Yet both organisms have a similar body pattern: front and back, top and bottom, left side and right side. The head is at one end and limbs extend from the body—fins in a fish, arms and legs in a human. Inside are similar structures—brains, hearts, and stomachs—and cells that function in similar ways.

DNA is the genetic material found in all living things. DNA determines how cells grow, develop, and function. Within the DNA are genes, segments of DNA, that determine whether a cell becomes a brain cell or a heart cell. Both a fish and a human start out life as a single cell. As the cell divides again and again, each organism grows into its familiar shape. Scientists are studying what it is that maps out the head-to-tail development that gets every part of a body in the right place.

One group of genes, called *Hox* genes, are critical in the early development of an animal's body. These genes are found in the DNA of every animal—from humans to fruit flies. The position of *Hox* genes, from top to bottom along the DNA, matches up to the particular parts they control of an organism's body.

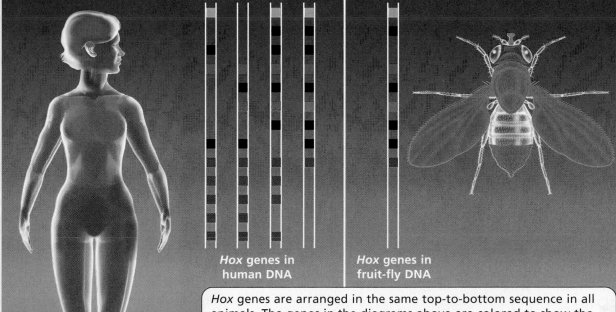

Hox genes in human DNA

Hox genes in fruit-fly DNA

Hox genes are arranged in the same top-to-bottom sequence in all animals. The genes in the diagrams above are colored to show the parts of the body they are associated with.

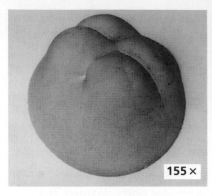
155×

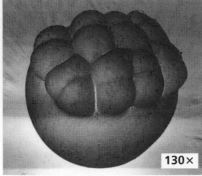
130×

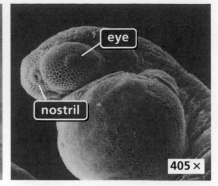
eye
nostril
405×

The egg of a zebrafish starts to divide after fertilization.
SOURCE for three images, Dr. Richard Kessel and Dr. Gene Shih/Visuals Unlimited

The egg now has 16 cells, all of which are similar in size and shape.

Many hours later, the cells have started to develop into different parts of the body.

How *Hox* Genes Work

Hox genes act like switches. A particular *Hox* gene turns on the development of a particular structure in an animal's body. One type of *Hox* gene switches on the development of structures in the head—for example, eyes and ears. Another switches on the development of limbs—the arms, legs, fins, or wings of an animal. The position of the genes within an animal's DNA matches to the part of the body it controls. *Hox* genes at the top control development of parts of the head. Those toward the middle control development of the main part of the body and the limbs.

How a Limb Develops

What happens if a *Hox* gene gets out of position? If the *Hox* gene that controls the development of legs in a fruit fly is placed in with the *Hox* genes that control development of the head, the fruit fly will grow legs from its head. The gene functions as it should, it's just that it's not doing its job in the right place.

Another interesting thing about *Hox* genes is that they are active only for a certain period of time. They "switch off" when the part of the body they control has developed. Studies of the zebrafish have provided clues as to how this happens.

SCIENTIFIC AMERICAN FRONTIERS

View the "Genes for Youth" segment of your Scientific American Frontiers video to learn about the role of genes in aging.

IN THIS SCENE FROM THE VIDEO ▶ biologist Cynthia Kenyon observes the activity level of some unusual worms that remain active much longer than other worms.

UNDERSTANDING AGING A multicellular organism starts life as a single cell. As an organism grows, it goes through different stages of development. Think of the differences between a baby, a teenager, a young adult, and an older person.

Kenyon is interested in what controls aging in worms. She studies how the genes in long-living worms affect the activity of their cells. She looks for differences between the cells of unusual worms and those of normal worms. Because cells of animals function in similar ways, she is interested in how what she learns about aging in worms might apply to other animals. Even though a worm is far less complex an animal than a human, studying these worms may provide clues into how humans age.

The zebrafish egg provides a window into the early developmental stages of this animal.

A Window on Development

Zebrafish are tiny fish that hatch in about three days. Scientists can actually see through the fish egg to watch its body develop. Working with the *Hox* genes of zebrafish, one researcher studied the amount of time that the *Hox* gene that controls fin development was active. The gene "turned on" for a short period of time, the fin developed, then the gene "turned off."

This research led scientists to think about the length of time the same *Hox* gene is active in other animals. It's possible that limbs are longer in larger animals because their *Hox* genes are active for a longer period of time. Researchers are excited because what they learn about the *Hox* genes of a simple animal can provide clues into the development of larger, more complex animals.

UNANSWERED Questions

There are many unanswered questions about the role *Hox* genes play in the development of body plans:

• Which *Hox* genes control which stages of development and how long are the genes active?

• What is it that signals the genes to "turn on and off"?

• How can research on *Hox* genes be used by medical researchers to help them treat genetic diseases or disorders that affect how a body develops?

UNIT PROJECTS

As you study this unit, work alone or with a group on one of the projects below.

Design an Experiment

Use fast plants to observe differences among plants.

• Follow directions for growing fast plants.

• Observe the plants as they grow and identify different characteristics.

• Use your observations to form a question about genes and plant characteristics.

• Design an experiment to answer your question.

Living Cell

Work cooperatively to present a "living cell" demonstration. Model cell processes, such as photosynthesis and cellular respiration.

• Design a model that shows parts of the cell at work.

• Include structures such as membranes, the nucleus, chloroplasts, and mitochondria. Represent energy and materials that move into and out of a cell.

• Have one student narrate each process.

DNA Detective Work

Prepare an oral presentation about how DNA technology is used to solve crimes.

Explain the science behind police and detective work.

CAREER CENTER
CLASSZONE.COM

Learn more about careers in molecular biology.

The Cell

the BIG idea

All living things are made up of cells.

Key Concepts

SECTION

1.1 The cell is the basic unit of living things.
Learn why cells are important to the study of life.

SECTION

1.2 Microscopes allow us to see inside the cell.
Learn what microscopes have shown about the inner structure of cells.

SECTION

1.3 Different cells perform various functions.
Learn about different types of cells in both unicellular and multicellular organisms.

Internet Preview

CLASSZONE.COM

Chapter 1 online resources: Content Review, two Simulations, two Resource Centers, Math Tutorial, Test Practice

The cell is the smallest unit of a living thing. What structures can you see in this plant cell?

Seeing and Understanding

Cut out a color photograph or drawing from a magazine or newspaper and place it on a flat surface. Use a magnifying glass to look at the image. Start with the magnifying glass right on top of the image and then slowly move the magnifying glass away, studying the photograph as you do.

Observe and Think What happens as you move the magnifying glass away from the image? How can a simple magnifying tool help you understand better how the image was printed?

Bits and Pieces

Find a sentence approximately ten words long in a newspaper or magazine and cut it out. Then cut the sentence into words. Ask a friend to put the words back together into a sentence.

Observe and Think What clues can your friend use to put the sentence back together? How can the parts of something help you understand how the whole works?

Internet Activity: Cells

Go to **ClassZone.com** to take a virtual tour of a cell.

Observe and Think What functions do the different parts of the cell perform?

NSTA
scilinks.org
SCILINKS

Cell Theory Code: MDL031

Getting Ready to Learn

◀ CONCEPT REVIEW

- Living things share certain characteristics that distinguish them from nonliving things.
- Living things have common needs, including energy, matter, and living space.

◀ VOCABULARY REVIEW

See Glossary for definitions.

cell

genetic material

organism

theory

 **CONTENT REVIEW**
CLASSZONE.COM
Review concepts and vocabulary.

▶ TAKING NOTES

MAIN IDEA WEB

Write each new blue heading, or main idea, in the top box. In the boxes around it, take notes about important terms and details that relate to the main idea.

VOCABULARY STRATEGY

Write each new vocabulary term in the center of a **four square** diagram. Write notes in the squares around each term. Include a definition, some characteristics, and some possible examples of the term. If possible, write some things that are not examples of the term.

See the Note-Taking Handbook on pages R45–R51.

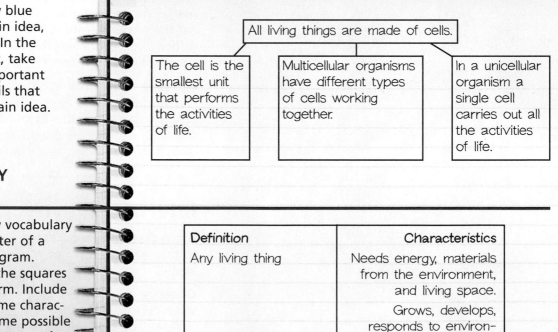

SCIENCE NOTEBOOK

All living things are made of cells.

| The cell is the smallest unit that performs the activities of life. | Multicellular organisms have different types of cells working together. | In a unicellular organism a single cell carries out all the activities of life. |

Definition	Characteristics
Any living thing	Needs energy, materials from the environment, and living space.
	Grows, develops, responds to environment, reproduces.
	Is made up of one or more cells.

ORGANISM

Examples	Nonexamples
Dogs, cats, birds, insects, moss, trees, bacteria	Rocks, water, dirt

KEY CONCEPT
1.1 The cell is the basic unit of living things.

◀ BEFORE, you learned

- Living things have common characteristics
- Living things have common needs
- A theory is something that explains what is observed in nature

▶ NOW, you will learn

- How living things are different from nonliving things
- How the microscope led to the discovery of cells
- About the cell theory

VOCABULARY

unicellular p. 11
multicellular p. 11
microscope p. 12
bacteria p. 14

EXPLORE Activity and Life

Does a candle show signs of life?

PROCEDURE

1 Carefully light one candle.

2 Sit quietly and observe the candle. Note its behavior. What does the flame do? What happens to the wax?

WHAT DO YOU THINK?

- How does a lit candle seem alive?
- How do you know for sure that it is not?

MATERIALS
- small candle
- candleholder
- matches

Living things are different from nonliving things.

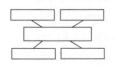

MAIN IDEA WEB
Make a main idea web about living things, including how they differ from nonliving things.

You know life when you see it. Perhaps your class takes a field trip to a local state park to collect water samples. You are surrounded by trees. There is a stream, with rocks covered with moss and green algae. There are fish and frogs; there are birds and insects. You are surrounded by life. But how would you define it?

One way to answer the question is to think about what makes a living thing different from a nonliving thing. You might ask if a thing uses energy. Or maybe you would observe it to see if it moves. You could investigate whether it consumes food and water. These are characteristics of living things, or organisms. Any individual form of life that is capable of growing and reproducing is an organism. All organisms get water and other materials from the environment.

Characteristics of Life

Living things have these characteristics:

- organization
- the ability to develop and grow
- the ability to respond to the environment
- the ability to reproduce

An organism's body must be organized in a way that enables it to meet its needs. Some organisms, like bacteria, are very simple. A more complex organism, such as the kingfisher shown in the photograph below, is organized so that different parts of its body perform different jobs, called functions. For example, a kingfisher has wings for flying, a heart for pumping blood, and eyes for seeing.

Another characteristic of organisms is that they grow and, in most cases, develop into adult forms. Some organisms change a great deal in size and appearance throughout their lifetimes, whereas others grow and change very little. Organisms also respond to the world outside them. Think of how the pupils of your eyes get smaller in bright light. Finally, organisms can reproduce, producing new organisms that are similar to themselves.

 CHECK YOUR READING What four characteristics are common to all living things?

Needs of Life

Organisms cannot carry out the activities that characterize life without a few necessities: energy, materials, and living space. What does it mean to need energy? You know that if you want to run a race, you need energy. But did you know that your body also needs energy to sleep or to breathe or even to think? All organisms require a steady supply of energy to stay alive. Where does this energy come from, and how does an organism get it?

APPLY Identify three living things in this photograph. How do they meet their needs?

Food is a source of **energy** and **materials**.

Water provides **materials** and **living space**.

The energy used by almost all forms of life on Earth comes from the Sun. Some organisms, like plants and some bacteria, are able to capture this energy directly. Your body, like the bodies of other animals, uses food as a source of energy. The food animals eat comes from plants or from organisms that eat plants. Food also provides the materials necessary for growth and reproduction. These materials include substances such as carbon dioxide, nitrogen, oxygen, and water. Finally, all organisms need space to live and grow. If any one of these requirements is missing, an organism will die.

All living things are made of cells.

The cell is the smallest unit of a living thing. Some organisms are made of a single cell. These organisms are **unicellular** and usually too small for you to see directly. Pond water is full of tiny unicellular organisms. Most of the organisms you can see, such as a frog or a water lily, are made up of many cells. Organisms made up of many cells are called **multicellular** organisms.

The needs and characteristics of a single cell in a unicellular organism are the same as those for any organism. Each of the tiny single-celled organisms found in a drop of pond water performs all the activities that characterize life. Multicellular organisms, like a frog or a water lily, have bodies that are more complex. Different parts of the body of a multicellular organism perform different functions. A water lily's roots hold it in the soil and its leaves capture energy from the Sun. A frog moves with its arms and legs and eats with its mouth.

Multicellular organisms have different types of cells that make up their body parts and help the organisms meet their needs. Roots are made of root cells, which are different from leaf cells. Muscle cells have special parts that allow them to move. In a multicellular organism, many cells work together to carry out the basic activities of life.

VOCABULARY
Add four squares for *unicellular* and *multicellular* to your notebook. You may want to add to your lists of characteristics and examples as you read through the chapter.

Multicellular and Unicellular Organisms

Both multicellular and unicellular organisms live in this pond.

There are many **unicellular organisms** in this drop of pond water, magnified 75×.

The frog and water lilies are **multicellular organisms**.

READING VISUALS What are some differences between the multicellular and unicellular organisms in this photograph? some similarities?

The microscope led to the discovery of cells.

Most cells are microscopic, too small to see without the aid of a microscope. A **microscope** is an instrument which makes an object appear bigger than it is. It took the invention of this relatively simple tool to lead to the discovery of cells. In the 1660s, Robert Hooke began using microscopes to look at all sorts of materials. Anton van Leeuwenhoek took up similar work in the 1670s. They were among the first people to describe cells.

Robert Hooke gave the cell its name. While looking at a sample of cork, a layer of bark taken from an oak tree, he saw a group of similarly shaped compartments that looked to him like tiny empty rooms, or cells. You can see from his drawing, shown at right, how well these cells fit Hooke's description. Hooke used a microscope that magnified objects 30 times (30×). In other words, objects appeared thirty times larger than their actual size.

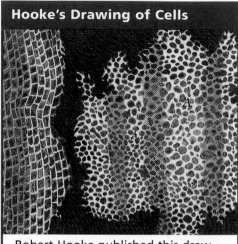

Hooke's Drawing of Cells

Robert Hooke published this drawing of dead cork cells in 1665. The microscope he used, shown at left, has two lenses.

The bark cells Hooke saw were actually dead cells, which is why they appeared empty. Anton van Leeuwenhoek was one of the first people to describe living cells. He looked at a drop of pond water under a microscope. Imagine his surprise when he saw that a drop of water was full of living things! Using lenses that could magnify an object almost 300×, he observed tiny unicellular organisms like those shown on page 11.

CHECK YOUR READING How did the invention of the microscope change the study of biology?

You can understand how powerful a microscope is if you think of how big a penny would be if it were increased in size 30 ×. It would be a little bigger than the tire of a ten-speed bicycle. Enlarged 300 ×, that penny would be so big that you would need a tractor-trailer to move it. Magnify your best friend 30 × (supposing a height of 1.5 meters, or almost 5 ft), and your friend would appear to be 45 meters (147 ft) tall. That's almost the height of Niagara Falls. Change the magnification to 300 ×, and your friend would appear to be 450 meters (1470 ft) tall—taller than the Empire State Building.

Cells come from other cells.

The studies of Hooke and Leeuwenhoek made people ask if all living things have cells. People continued to observe samples taken from all sorts of living matter. They continued to find cells, although often these cells looked very different from one another. Still, it was clear that all living matter was made of cells.

There was another important question scientists were trying to answer: Where do cells come from? The answer to this question was settled by the 1850s. People studying all types of living cells observed the same thing—that cells divide. One living cell divides into two living cells. Here, under the microscope, was evidence of where cells come from. Life comes from life—that is, one cell comes from another cell.

CHECK YOUR READING What do scientists mean when they say that life comes from life? Your answer should include the word *cells*.

The observations and evidence gathered over a long time by many scientists are summarized in the three concepts of the cell theory:

❶ Every living thing is made of one or more cells.

❷ Cells carry out the functions needed to support life.

❸ Cells come only from other living cells.

The Cell Theory

The importance of the cell to life is summarized in the cell theory.

❶ **Every living thing is made up of one or more cells.** A polar bear is a multicellular organism.

❷ **Cells carry out the functions needed to support life.** Fat cells are animal cells that provide energy as well as insulation.

400 ×

❸ **Cells come only from other living cells.** Each polar bear cub began as a single cell.

The cell theory is important to the study of biology.

The three ideas on page 13 are so important that they are grouped together using the word *theory*. A scientific theory is a widely accepted explanation of things observed in nature. A theory must be supported by evidence, including experimental evidence and observations. A theory proves its value when it explains new discoveries and observations.

 CHECK YOUR READING What are two characteristics of a scientific theory?

Theories are important for a number of reasons. Certainly they satisfy scientists' desire to understand the natural world, and they serve as foundations for further research and study. Theories can also lead to research that has some practical benefit for society.

Louis Pasteur

The work of the French scientist Louis Pasteur shows how an understanding of cell theory can have practical uses. Pasteur lived in the 1800s, when there was no mechanical refrigeration in homes. People were used to having foods spoil, like milk going sour. During this time, many people died from diseases such as typhoid fever, tuberculosis, and diphtheria. Pasteur's work showed that microscopic organisms were involved both in the spoilage of food and in disease.

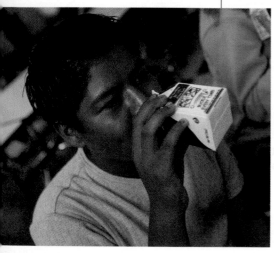

The milk that you get from the school cafeteria has been pasteurized so that it will stay fresh longer.

Pasteur observed that milk that turned sour contained large numbers of tiny single-celled organisms called **bacteria** (bak-TEER-ee-uh). He developed a process, now known as pasteurization, in which heat is used to kill the bacteria. Killing the bacteria keeps milk fresh longer. The fact that bacteria cause milk to sour or "sicken" made Pasteur wonder whether microscopic organisms could also be the cause of sickness in humans and animals.

Bacteria and Spontaneous Generation

Using a microscope to study air, water, and soil, Pasteur found microorganisms everywhere. He found bacteria in the blood of animals, including people who were sick. Pasteur referred to the microorganisms he observed as "germs." He realized that an understanding of germs might help prevent disease. Pasteur's work led to the first animal vaccinations for cholera and anthrax and to a treatment for rabies in humans.

At the time that Pasteur was doing his research, there were scientists who thought that bacteria grew from nonliving materials, an idea called spontaneous generation. Pasteur conducted a now-

Pasteur's Experiments

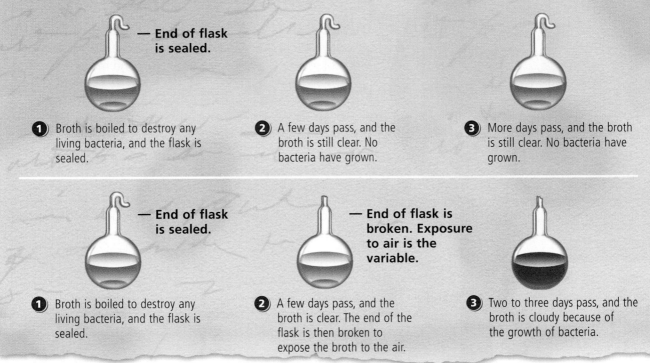

Pasteur's experiments showed that bacteria are present in the air. They do not appear spontaneously.

— End of flask is sealed.

1 Broth is boiled to destroy any living bacteria, and the flask is sealed.

2 A few days pass, and the broth is still clear. No bacteria have grown.

3 More days pass, and the broth is still clear. No bacteria have grown.

— End of flask is sealed.

— End of flask is broken. Exposure to air is the variable.

1 Broth is boiled to destroy any living bacteria, and the flask is sealed.

2 A few days pass, and the broth is clear. The end of the flask is then broken to expose the broth to the air.

3 Two to three days pass, and the broth is cloudy because of the growth of bacteria.

famous series of experiments that did not support the idea of spontaneous generation and confirmed the cell theory. He showed that cells come only from other cells. Two of Pasteur's experiments are shown above. Both began with a sealed flask containing boiled broth. In the first experiment, the flask remained sealed, while in the second experiment, the top of the flask was broken to expose the contents to air. Bacteria grew only in the second flask.

1.1 Review

KEY CONCEPTS

1. Name four characteristics of living things.
2. How did the microscope change human understanding of life?
3. Explain the three concepts that make up the cell theory.

CRITICAL THINKING

4. **Analyze** Relate the characteristics of a scientific theory to the cell theory.
5. **Compare and Contrast** Draw a Venn diagram to compare and contrast multicellular and unicellular organisms.

⬤ CHALLENGE

6. **Synthesize** Explain how Pasteur's experiment supported the cell theory and failed to support the theory of spontaneous generation.

CHAPTER INVESTIGATION

Using a Microscope

OVERVIEW AND PURPOSE The smallest forms of life are not visible to the human eye. You will use a light microscope as a tool to observe very small unicellular and multicellular organisms. Then you will compare the organisms you see under the microscope to the Identification Key. Refer to pages R14 and R15 of the Lab Handbook for more information about using a microscope and preparing a slide.

▶ Procedure

1 Make a data table like the one shown on page 17. To observe the microscopic organisms, you need to make a wet-mount slide. Obtain a slide and use the eyedropper to place 2–3 drops of pond water in the center of the slide.

2 Obtain a cover slip for your slide. Place one edge of the cover slip on the slide, at the left edge of the pond water. Slowly lower the cover slip as if you were closing the cover of a book. The cover slip should lie flat on the slide. If you see air bubbles, pick up the cover slip and lower it again.

step 2

3 Clean the lenses of the microscope with lens paper. Choose the lowest magnification, then place the slide on the stage. Start with the objective at its lowest point and raise the objective to focus. First focus with the coarse adjustment, which is usually the larger knob. Begin your search for living organisms. Use the fine adjustment to make the image clearer. Be patient when looking for life on your slide. It may take some time.

4 When you find something interesting, carefully switch to a higher magnification. Turn the nose of the microscope until another objective snaps into place. Use only the fine adjustment when viewing at high power, to avoid scratching the microscope or the slide. Move the slide gently from side to side as you look through the microscope. Search different parts of the sample for different organisms.

step 4

MATERIALS
- slides
- eyedropper
- pond water
- cover slip
- light microscope
- lens paper
- Identification Key

lens

coarse adjustment

fine adjustment

objective

slide

nose

stage

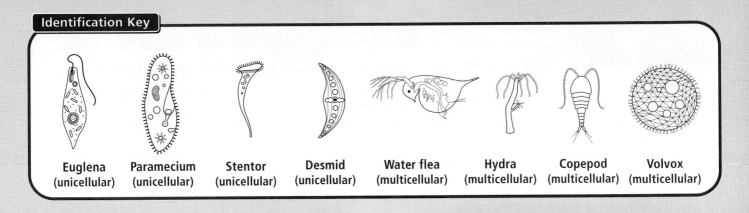

Identification Key

| Euglena (unicellular) | Paramecium (unicellular) | Stentor (unicellular) | Desmid (unicellular) | Water flea (multicellular) | Hydra (multicellular) | Copepod (multicellular) | Volvox (multicellular) |

5 Make a sketch of each of the different organisms that you see. Record any movement or behavior you observe. Include the magnification of the objective lens that you used.

 **Observe and Analyze** Write It Up

1. **CLASSIFY** Use the Identification Key above to identify the organism. If you cannot make an identification, write *unknown*.

Conclude Write It Up

1. **COLLECT DATA** Compare your sketches with those of your classmates. How many different organisms in total did your class find? How many were identified as unicellular? How many were identified as multicellular?

2. **COMMUNICATE** Why is the microscope an important tool for studying cells and entire organisms?

3. **INTERPRET** Using what you learned in this chapter and in this investigation, explain the ways in which you would use the different objectives on a microscope.

4. **APPLY** Many diseases, such as strep throat, are caused by microscopic organisms. Why might a microscope be an important tool for a doctor?

5. **APPLY** How might the way a biologist uses a microscope be different from the way a doctor uses a microscope?

INVESTIGATE Further

Collect a small sample of soil from outside the school or your home. Mix the soil with enough tap water to make it liquid. Then take a sample of the soil mixture and examine it under the microscope. Sketch some of the organisms you see. Are they similar to those in the pond-water sample? Why do you think different types of organisms live in different environments?

Using a Microscope

Table 1. Identifying Microorganisms

Organism 1
  Magnification used:
  Movement/behavior:
  Sketch:

  Name:

Organism 2
  Magnification used:
  Movement/behavior:
  Sketch:

  Name:

1.2 Microscopes allow us to see inside the cell.

◀ **BEFORE,** you learned

- Some organisms are unicellular and some are multicellular
- A microscope is necessary to study most cells
- The cell theory describes the cell as the fundamental unit of life

▶ **NOW,** you will learn

- About different types of microscopes
- About prokaryotic and eukaryotic cells
- How plant and animal cells are similar and different

VOCABULARY

cell membrane p. 20
cytoplasm p. 20
nucleus p. 20
eukaryotic cell p. 20
prokaryotic cell p. 20
organelle p. 20
cell wall p. 21
chloroplast p. 23
mitochondria p. 23

THINK ABOUT

How small are cells?

Because cells are so small, describing them requires a very small unit of measure: the micrometer (µm). A micrometer is one millionth of a meter. Most cells range in size from about 1 micrometer (some bacteria) to 1000 micrometers (some plant and animal cells). To get a sense of the sizes of cells, consider that it would take about 17,000 tiny bacterial cells lined up to reach across a dime. How many of these cells might fit on your fingertip?

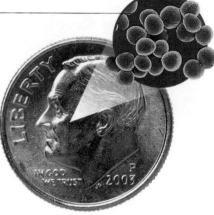

The microscope is an important tool.

MAIN IDEA WEB
Make a main idea web that explains the importance of the microscope.

The invention of the light microscope led to the discovery of cells and to the development of cell theory. In light microscopes, lenses are used to bend light and make objects appear bigger than they are. Modern light microscopes can magnify objects up to 1000 times.

The light microscope is still used today to study cells. Over many years scientists have found ways to make light microscopes more useful. Cell samples are treated with dyes to make structures in the cells easier to see. Scientists use video cameras and computer processing to observe the movement of cell parts and materials within cells. One important advantage of light microscopes is that scientists can observe living cells with them.

Two other types of microscopes are important in the study of cells. The scanning electron microscope (SEM) and the transmission electron microscope (TEM) can produce images of objects as small as 0.002 micrometers. The light microscope can be used only for objects that are larger than 0.2 micrometers. Therefore, although a light microscope can be used to see many of the parts of a cell, only the SEM and TEM can be used for looking at the details of those parts.

In both the SEM and the TEM, tiny particles called electrons, not light, are used to produce images. The advantage of these microscopes is that they can magnify objects up to a million times. The disadvantage is that they cannot be used to study live specimens.

SIMULATION
CLASSZONE.COM
View cells through different types of microscopes.

CHECK YOUR READING Compare light microscopes with electron microscopes. What are the advantages and disadvantages of each?

To be viewed with an SEM, a cell sample is coated in a heavy metal, such as gold. Then a beam of electrons is run back and forth over the surface of the cell. The electrons bounce off the coating and are read by a detector that produces a three-dimensional image of the surface.

A cell viewed with a TEM is sliced extremely thin. Electrons pass through a section. Images produced by a TEM appear two-dimensional.

Electron Microscopes

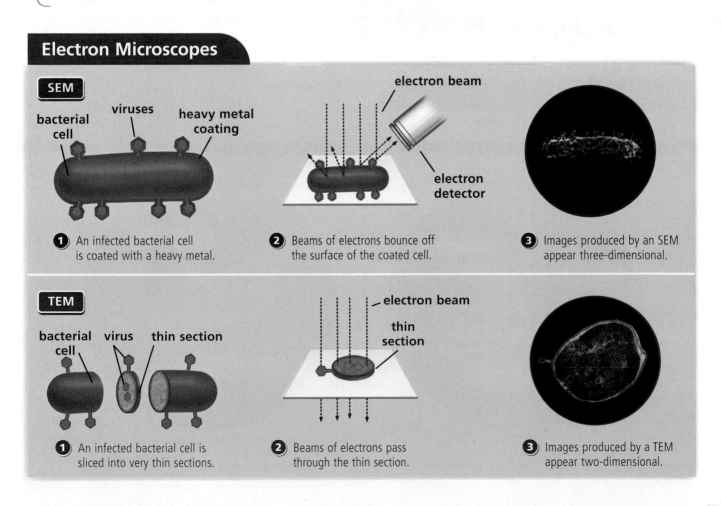

SEM

bacterial cell   viruses   heavy metal coating

electron beam

electron detector

1 An infected bacterial cell is coated with a heavy metal.

2 Beams of electrons bounce off the surface of the coated cell.

3 Images produced by an SEM appear three-dimensional.

TEM

bacterial cell   virus   thin section

electron beam

thin section

1 An infected bacterial cell is sliced into very thin sections.

2 Beams of electrons pass through the thin section.

3 Images produced by a TEM appear two-dimensional.

Cells are diverse.

Very early on, the people studying cells knew that cells have a great diversity of sizes and shapes. As microscopes were improved, scientists could see more and more details of cells. What they saw was that the inside of one cell can be very different from that of another cell.

Every cell has a boundary that separates the inside from the outside. That boundary is the **cell membrane,** a protective covering that encloses the entire cell. Any material coming into or out of the cell must pass through the cell membrane. Contained inside the cell membrane is a gelatin-like material called **cytoplasm** (SY-tuh-PLAZ-uhm). Most of the work of the cell is carried out in the cytoplasm.

Scientists separate cells into two broad categories based on one key difference: the location of the genetic material cells need to reproduce and function. In a **eukaryotic cell** (yoo-KAR-ee-AHT-ihk) the genetic material is in a structure called the **nucleus** (NOO-klee-uhs), a structure enclosed by its own membrane. Scientists use the word **organelle** (AWR-guh-NEHL) to describe any part of a cell that is enclosed by membrane.

In a **prokaryotic cell** (proh-KAR-ee-AWT-ihk) there is no separate compartment for the genetic material. Instead, it is in the cytoplasm. There are no organelles. Most unicellular organisms are prokaryotic cells. Almost all multicellular organisms are eukaryotic.

VOCABULARY
Add a four square for *cell membrane* to your notebook. Try to include the word *cytoplasm* in your diagram.

Eukaryotic and Prokaryotic Cells

Eukaryotic cells have a nucleus while prokaryotic cells do not. On average, eukaryotic cells are about 100 times larger than prokaryotic cells.

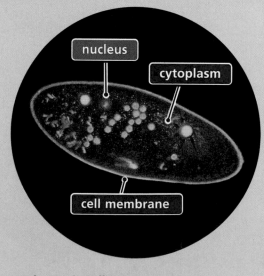

nucleus

cytoplasm

cell membrane

cytoplasm

cell membrane

A **eukaryotic cell** has a nucleus. The paramecium shown here is magnified 133×.

A **prokaryotic cell** does not have a nucleus. The bacterium shown here is magnified 12,000×.

INVESTIGATE Plant and Animal Cells

How do plant and animal cells compare?

PROCEDURE

1. Choose the objective lens with the lowest magnification. Place the plant-cell slide on the stage and turn on the light source. Handle the slide carefully.

2. Observe the cells at low magnification. Make a drawing of one of the cells.

3. Observe the cells at high magnification. Fill in details. Return to the low-magnification lens before removing the slide.

4. Repeat steps 1–3 with the animal-cell slide.

WHAT DO YOU THINK?

- Compare the drawings you made. How are the plant and animal cells alike, and how are they different?

- Compare the thickness of plant cell's cell membrane and cell wall with the thickness of the animal cell's cell membrane.

CHALLENGE Placing a ruler on top of the slides, view each slide at low power. Estimate and compare the sizes of the two cells.

Plants and animals have eukaryotic cells.

Plant and animal cells, like all eukaryotic cells, are divided into two main compartments. The nucleus, usually the largest organelle, is the compartment that stores the instructions a cell needs to function. You will learn more about how cells use this information in Chapter 5.

Surrounding the nucleus is the cytoplasm. The cell membrane is the boundary between the cytoplasm and the outside of the cell. Plant cells also have cell walls. A **cell wall** is a tough outer covering that lies just outside the cell membrane. The cell wall supports and protects the cell. Having a cell wall is one important way in which plant cells differ from animal cells.

RESOURCE CENTER
CLASSZONE.COM

Find out more about cell structures.

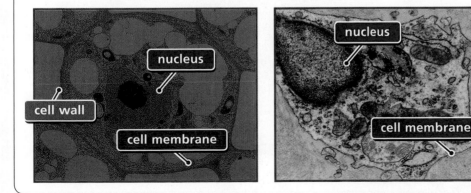

Both a plant cell (shown at left magnified 1750×) and an animal cell (shown at right magnified 12,000×) have a nucleus and a cell membrane. Plant cells also have a cell wall.

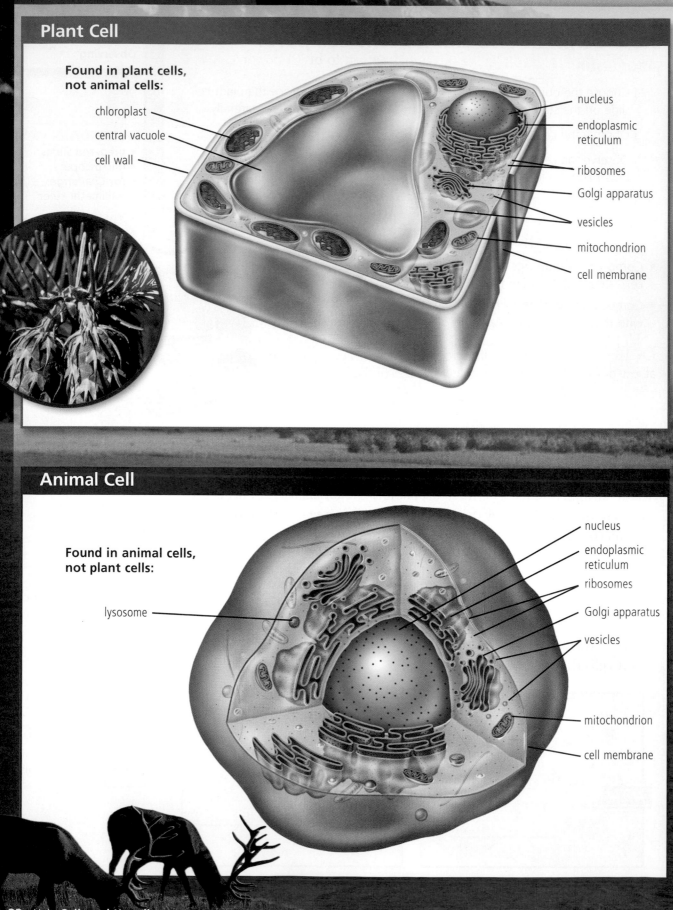

Plant Cell

Found in plant cells, not animal cells:

- chloroplast
- central vacuole
- cell wall

- nucleus
- endoplasmic reticulum
- ribosomes
- Golgi apparatus
- vesicles
- mitochondrion
- cell membrane

Animal Cell

Found in animal cells, not plant cells:

- lysosome

- nucleus
- endoplasmic reticulum
- ribosomes
- Golgi apparatus
- vesicles
- mitochondrion
- cell membrane

Structures That Process Information

The nucleus is often the largest organelle in a cell. It contains information a cell needs to function. Some of the information is translated by ribosomes, tiny structures located in the cytoplasm and the endoplasmic reticulum. Ribosomes use the information to build important molecules called proteins.

Organelles That Provide Energy

No cell can stay alive without energy. Cells need energy to perform all the activities of life. Plants get their energy directly from the Sun. Within plant cells are **chloroplasts** (KLAWR-uh-PLASTS), organelles in which the energy from sunlight is used to make sugar. Plants use some of the sugar immediately, to keep their cells functioning. The rest of the sugar is stored in the cells.

Animal cells do not contain chloroplasts. As a result, animals are not able to use the energy of the Sun directly. Instead, animals get their energy from food. Much of the food an animal uses for energy comes from the sugar that plant cells have stored. Animals can get this energy by eating plants or by eating animals that have eaten plants.

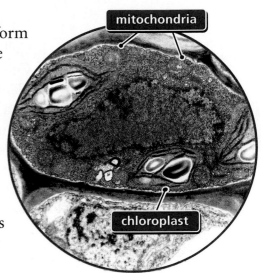

This plant cell is magnified 6000×.

CHECK YOUR READING How can a chloroplast, a structure found in plant cells but not in animal cells, provide energy for both plants and animals?

Both plant cells and animal cells must be able to use energy to do work. The energy is made available by organelles found in all eukaryotic cells. **Mitochondria** (MY-tuh-KAHN-dree-uh) are the organelles that use oxygen to get energy from processing food.

READING TIP

Mitochondria is plural. The singular form is *mitochondrion*.

Organelles That Process and Transport

You know that plant and animal cells get their energy from the sugars that the organisms make or consume. Sugars are also an important part of the starting materials that cells use to maintain themselves and grow. The job of making cell parts from the starting materials that enter a cell is divided among a number of structures in the cytoplasm.

In the illustrations on page 22, you can see that the endoplasmic reticulum is a system of twisting and winding membranes. Some of the endoplasmic reticulum contains ribosomes, which manufacture proteins. The endoplasmic reticulum manufactures parts of the cell membrane.

The endoplasmic reticulum is also part of the cellular transport system. Portions of endoplasmic reticulum break off to form small packages called vesicles. The vesicles transport processed materials to an organelle called the Golgi apparatus. The folded membranes of the Golgi apparatus make it look something like a stack of pancakes. The Golgi apparatus takes the materials manufactured by the endoplasmic reticulum and finishes processing them.

Organelles for Storage, Recycling, and Waste

Cells store water, sugar, and other materials, which they use to function. Cells must also store waste materials until they can be removed. Inside plant and fungus cells are sacs called vacuoles. Vacuoles are enclosed by a membrane and can hold water, waste, and other materials. Vacuoles function with the cell membrane to move materials either into or out of the cell. A plant cell has a large central vacuole in which water and other materials can be stored. Water in the vacuole provides support for smaller plants.

Animal cells do not have central vacuoles. What animal cells do have are similar structures called lysosomes. Lysosomes are vesicles that contain chemicals that break down materials taken into the cell, as well as old cell parts. Remember that animals, unlike plants, take in food. Nutrients brought into the cell need to be broken down, as well as wastes contained.

central vacuole

CHECK YOUR READING Compare and contrast lysosomes and central vacuoles.

1.2 Review

KEY CONCEPTS

1. What advantages and disadvantages does a light microscope have in comparison with an electron microscope?

2. What is the difference between a eukaryotic cell and a prokaryotic cell?

3. List three structures found in plant cells that are not in animal cells.

CRITICAL THINKING

4. **Synthesize** What organelles can be said to act like an assembly line within a cell? Explain.

5. **Compare and Contrast** Make a Venn diagram comparing and contrasting plant and animal cells.

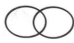

⬤ CHALLENGE

6. **Synthesize** Identify the type of microscope used to capture the image at the right, and indicate whether the cell is a plant cell or an animal cell. How do you know?

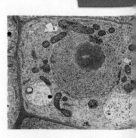
(magnified 27,900×)

SKILL: USING SCIENTIFIC NOTATION

MATH TUTORIAL
CLASSZONE.COM

Click on Math Tutorial for more help with scientific notation.

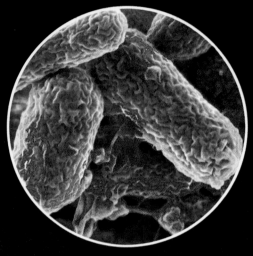

How many bacteria can fit on the head of a pin? The bacteria are magnified 50,000× in this photograph. The head of the pin below is magnified 7×.

Comparing Sizes

Measuring the sizes of very small things like atoms or very large things like planets requires numbers with many places. For example, the diameter of the nucleus of a cell is around 1/100,000 of a meter, while the diameter of Earth is 12,756,000 meters. How can you compare these sizes?

Example

(1) Express a large number as a number between 1 and 10 multiplied by a power of 10.

$12{,}756{,}000 = 1.2756 \times 10^7$

The exponent is the number of places following the first place.

(2) Express any number smaller than 1 as a negative power of 10.

$\dfrac{1}{100{,}000} = 0.00001 = 1 \times 10^{-5}$

The exponent is the number of places following the decimal point.

(3) Compare −5 and 7 to see that 7 is 12 more than −5.

ANSWER Earth's diameter is roughly 10^{12} times bigger than the diameter of a cell's nucleus.

Answer the following questions.

1. An oxygen atom measures 14/100,000,000,000 of a meter across. Write the width of the oxygen atom as a decimal number.

2. Write the width of the oxygen atom in scientific notation.

3. A chloroplast measures 5 millionths of a meter across. Write its width in standard form and in scientific notation.

4. A redwood tree stands 100 meters tall. There are 1000 millimeters in a meter. Express the height of the redwood tree in millimeters. Write the number in scientific notation.

5. A typical plant cell measures 1 millionth of a meter in width. Express the width in standard form and in scientific notation.

CHALLENGE The yolk of an ostrich egg is about 8 centimeters in diameter. The ostrich itself is about 2.4 meters tall. Write each of these lengths in the same unit, and express them in scientific notation. Then tell how many times taller the ostrich is than the yolk.

1.3 Different cells perform various functions.

◀ BEFORE, you learned

- Modern microscopes reveal details of cell structures
- Some cells are prokaryotic and some are eukaryotic
- Plant and animal cells have similarities and differences

▶ NOW, you will learn

- How organisms are classified into three domains
- About specialization in multi-cellular organisms
- How cells, tissues, and organs are organized

VOCABULARY

specialization p. 28
tissue p. 29
organ p. 30

EXPLORE Specialization

How do roots differ from leaves?

PROCEDURE

1. Soak the grass plant in a cup of water to clean away any dirt.

2. Compare the color of the roots with the color of the blades or leaves. Record your observations.

3. Wash your hands when you have finished.

WHAT DO YOU THINK?

- How does the color of the grass roots compare with that of the grass blades?
- Chloroplasts contain a chemical that gives leaves their green color. What does this suggest to you about the functions of the grass blades and roots?

MATERIALS

- grass plants
- cup
- water

Organisms can be classified by their cell type.

MAIN IDEA WEB
Make a web of the important terms and details about the main idea: *Organisms can be classified by their cell type.*

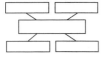

Look around you at this moment. The living organisms you see may number 10, 20, 100, or 1000, depending on where you are. What you are not seeing, but what is also there, is a huge number of unicellular organisms. For example, there are at least 2–3 million bacteria living on each square centimeter of your skin.

Most of the organisms alive on Earth today are made of a single cell. One of the most interesting scientific discoveries made recently had to do with a group of unicellular organisms. These organisms were found living where no one expected to find any life at all.

Archaea and Bacteria

In the early 1980s, scientists discovered unicellular organisms living in rather extreme environments. Some were living deep in the ocean, at thermal vents where there is extreme heat and little oxygen. Others were found in the salty waters of the Great Salt Lake and in the hot sulfur springs of Yellowstone Park.

At first, these organisms were referred to as archaebacteria. The organisms were similar in appearance to bacteria. The prefix *archae* comes from a Greek word that means "ancient." Many of these organisms live in environments that scientists think are like the environments of ancient Earth.

thermal vent

archaea

Archaea are prokaryotic organisms that can live in extreme environments like these thermal vents. In a thermal vent, temperatures can reach 600 degrees Celsius.

It took a while for scientists to realize that these organisms that looked like bacteria were genetically very different from bacteria. Scientists decided to establish a separate category for them, a domain called Archaea (AHR-kee-uh). A domain is a broad category of living things that is based on characteristics of their cells. Scientists have identified three domains. Bacteria are classified in the domain Bacteria. A third domain includes organisms with eukaryotic cells.

Organisms that belong to the domains Bacteria and Archaea are similar in some important ways. They are prokaryotes, which are unicellular organisms with prokaryotic cells. Their cytoplasm contains ribosomes but no organelles, so the structure of a prokaryote is simple. Another feature of a prokaryote is a tough cell wall that protects the organism.

RESOURCE CENTER
CLASSZONE.COM

Learn more about unicellular organisms.

CHECK YOUR READING Why did scientists decide to establish separate domains for archaea and bacteria?

Eukarya

The third domain is the domain Eukarya. Organisms in this domain have cells with a nucleus. This domain includes almost all the multicellular organisms on Earth: plants, animals, and fungi. It also includes many unicellular organisms called protists. The cells of unicellular eukaryotes are more complex in structure and larger than the cells of prokaryotes.

CHECK YOUR READING How are eukaryotes different from prokaryotes?

The paramecium is one of the most complex of all unicellular eukaryotes. Its body is lined with hairlike strands, called cilia (SIHL-ee-uh), that allow it to move. It has dartlike structures that carry a substance used in healing and, perhaps, defense. Along the outside of the cell is a long oral groove lined with cilia that leads to a mouth pore. In addition to a nucleus, the cell of a paramecium has organelles that enable it to digest food and remove water and wastes. The paramecium has all it needs to live as a single cell. By comparison, in most multicellular eukaryotes, no individual cell can survive on its own.

paramecium 1000×

mouth pore

oral groove

cilia

Cells in multicellular organisms specialize.

Most multicellular organisms consist of many different types of cells that do different jobs. For example, most animals have blood cells, nerve cells, and muscle cells. The cells are specialized. **Specialization** of cells means that specific cells perform specific functions. This specialization is why a single cell from a multicellular organism cannot survive on its own. A blood cell can help you fight infection or deliver oxygen to your muscles, but it cannot cause your body to move as a muscle cell can. Plants have cells that function in photosynthesis, and other cells that draw water from the soil, and still others that function mainly to support the plant's weight.

CHECK YOUR READING What does it mean for a cell to be specialized?

Specialization

A fully grown salamander has many specialized cells.

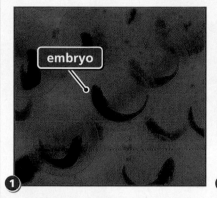
① A salamander, like all multicellular organisms, begins life as an egg. After fertilization, the egg develops into an embryo.

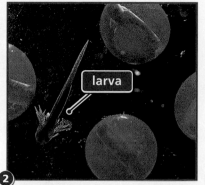
② As the cells divide, they begin to specialize. The amount of specialization depends on the complexity of the organism.

③ A salamander's body has many specialized cells. These include skin cells, blood cells, bone cells, muscle cells, and nerve cells.

A multicellular organism is a community of cells.

Cells in a multicellular organism are specialized. The ways in which the cells work together and interact depend on the organism. You can think of the cells of an organism as members of a community. The size and complexity of the community differ from organism to organism.

A sponge is an animal that is fairly simple in its organization. It spends its life attached to the ocean floor, filtering food and other nutrients from the water. Like all animals, the sponge is organized at a cellular level. Different types of cells in its body perform different functions. For example, certain cells take in food, and other cells digest it. However, cells in a sponge are not very highly specialized. A piece broken from a living sponge will actually regenerate itself as new cells replace the lost ones.

In more complex organisms, such as plants and animals, cells are not only specialized but grouped together in tissues. A **tissue** is a group of similar cells that are organized to do a specific job. If you look at your hand, you will see the top layer of tissue in your skin. Humans have two layers of skin tissue, layered one on top of the other. Together these skin tissues provide protection and support.

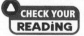 In what way is a tissue an organization of cells?

Levels of Organization

Levels of organization in multicellular organisms include cells, tissues, organs, organ systems, and the organism itself.

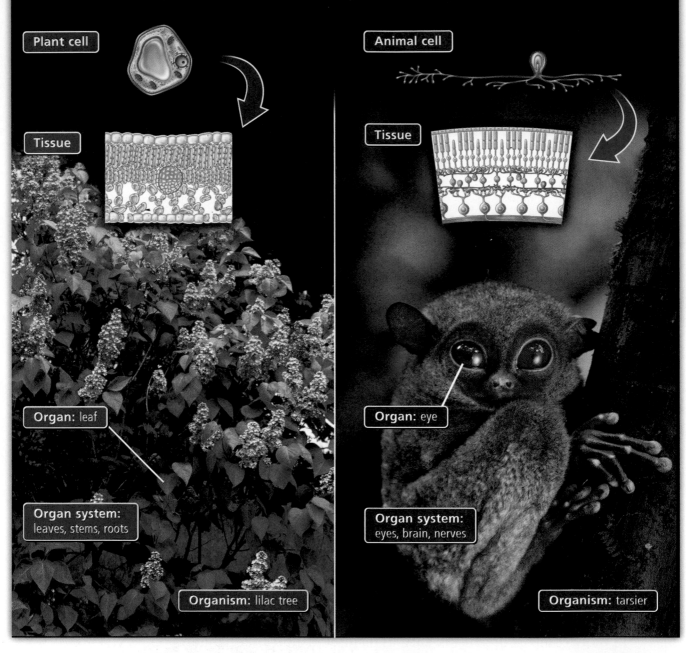

Plant cell

Tissue

Organ: leaf

Organ system: leaves, stems, roots

Organism: lilac tree

Animal cell

Tissue

Organ: eye

Organ system: eyes, brain, nerves

Organism: tarsier

Different tissues working together to perform a particular function represent another level of organization, the **organ.** The eye is an organ that functions with the tarsier's brain to allow sight. A leaf is an organ that provides a plant with energy and materials. It has tissue that brings in water and nutrients, tissue that uses the Sun's energy to make sugar, and tissue that moves sugar to other parts of the plant.

CHECK YOUR READING What is the relationship between tissues and organs?

Different organs and tissues working together form an organ system. An organism may have only a few organ systems. The organ systems of plants include roots, stems, and leaves. Other organisms have many organ systems. Humans have 11 major organ systems, made up of about 40 organs and over 200 types of tissue. The human nervous system, for example, includes the brain, the spinal cord, nerves, and sensory organs, such as the ears and eyes.

An organism itself represents the highest level of organization. It is at this level that we see all the characteristics we associate with life. If an organism is a complex organism—a human, for example— it will consist of trillions of cells grouped into tissues, organs, and organ systems. However, a simple organism, like a sponge, meets its needs with a body made up of only a few types of specialized cells.

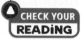 **CHECK YOUR READING** What level of organization is an organism? What do we see at this level of organization?

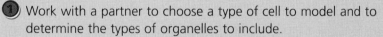

INVESTIGATE Cell Models

What are some of the limitations of using a model to represent a cell?

PROCEDURE

1. Work with a partner to choose a type of cell to model and to determine the types of organelles to include.

2. Using the poster board as a base, construct the model from available supplies. Make the model as accurate as you can.

3. Use a marker to label each organelle, and include a description of its function.

4. Compare your cell model with those made by your classmates.

WHAT DO YOU THINK?

- What are some of the limitations of using a model to represent a cell?

- What are some of the benefits of making a three-dimensional model of a cell?

CHALLENGE Think of something to which you might compare the activities of a cell—perhaps the activities of a factory or a school. Add labels to your model to show how the comparison applies to each of the cell's structures.

SKILL FOCUS
Making models

MATERIALS
- craft supplies
- scissors
- glue
- poster board
- markers

TIME
30 minutes

Scientists use models to study cells.

Any drawing or photograph on a flat page is two-dimensional. In addition, diagrams of cells are often simplified to make them easier to understand. If you look at plant or animal cells under a microscope, you will notice some differences between real cells and the diagrams on page 22. In order to study cell structures and their functions, scientists use many types of models, including three-dimensional models. One of the most important discoveries in science involved the use of models.

DNA is the genetic material common to all cells. (You will read more about the structure and function of DNA later in this unit.) In the early 1950s, scientists had a good idea what DNA was made up of. The problem was that they could not figure out how all the pieces of the molecule fit together.

A scientist named Rosalind Franklin used x-rays to produce images of DNA. The x-ray provided an important clue as to the shape of the molecule. Two other scientists, James Watson and Francis Crick, were then able to put together a three-dimensional model of DNA and present it to the world in 1953.

Today's scientists have many different tools for making models. The images at the left show a computer model of DNA along with Watson and Crick's famous model.

Scientific Models

Scientists use several different types of models.

Watson and Crick used a model made from wire and tin.

1.3 Review

KEY CONCEPTS

1. What are the three domains, and what type of cells do the organisms in each domain have?

2. Define specialization in your own words.

3. Describe the levels of organization in a tree.

CRITICAL THINKING

4. **Synthesize** In what way does a specialized cell in a multicellular organism differ from the cell of a unicellular organism?

5. **Compare and Contrast** How is a model similar to the real object it represents? How is it different?

⬥ CHALLENGE

6. **Evaluate** The organism below is called *Chlamydomonas*. What domain does it belong to, and what do the internal structures tell you about it?

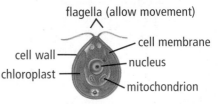

flagella (allow movement)

cell wall
chloroplast

cell membrane
nucleus
mitochondrion

Cells and Spacesuits

What do a space suit and a unicellular organism have in common? Both have to support life. And both can support life in difficult environments. What are some of the similarities—and differences—between the cell body of a unicellular organism and a space suit that supports an astronaut in outer space?

● Some Features of Spacesuits

FEATURE	FUNCTION
Strong outer material...	...protects the astronaut from space particles.
A special jet-propelled backpack...	...helps the astronaut move in the weightlessness of space.
Tanks of compressed air...	...provide oxygen for the astronaut to breathe.

● Some Features of Cells

FEATURE	FUNCTION
Tail-like flagella on the outside of some cells...	...help cells move.
An outer membrane...	...keeps harmful particles out.
Tiny openings in a cell's membrane...	...let oxygen move into the cell.

● Make Comparisons

On Your Own Match each cell feature with a similar spacesuit feature. What characteristics do the cell and spacesuit have in common? What is one key difference?

As a Group Use your comparisons to make a Venn diagram.

CHALLENGE An analogy uses a familiar thing to help explain or describe something new. Come up with your own analogies to describe the cell or some of its organelles.

flagella

This cell has flagella, which help it move.

Chapter Review

◀ KEY CONCEPTS SUMMARY

1.1 The cell is the basic unit of living things.

All living things are made up of one or more cells. **Organisms** share the following characteristics:

- organization
- ability to grow and develop
- ability to respond
- ability to reproduce

Multicellular organisms include this frog and these water-lily plants.

Many unicellular organisms live in pond water.

VOCABULARY
unicellular p. 11
multicellular p. 11
microscope p. 12
bacteria p. 14

1.2 Microscopes allow us to see inside the cell.

A **prokaryotic cell** is relatively simple in structure, with no nucleus or other organelles. A **eukaryotic cell** is more complex, with many different organelles inside it.

bacterium

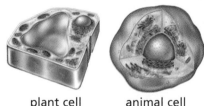

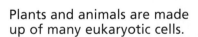
plant cell   animal cell

A bacterium consists of a single prokaryotic cell.

Plants and animals are made up of many eukaryotic cells.

VOCABULARY
cell membrane p. 20
cytoplasm p. 20
nucleus p. 20
eukaryotic cell p. 20
prokaryotic cell p. 20
organelle p. 20
cell wall p. 21
chloroplast p. 23
mitochondria p. 23

1.3 Different cells perform various functions.

- The single cell of a unicellular organism does all that is necessary for the organism to survive.
- A multicellular organism is a community of **specialized** cells.
- Scientific models make it easier to understand cells.

The tarsier has many levels of organization in its body.

tarsier

VOCABULARY
specialization p. 28
tissue p. 29
organ p. 30

Reviewing Vocabulary

1–5. *Use a vocabulary term to identify each numbered part of this plant cell.*

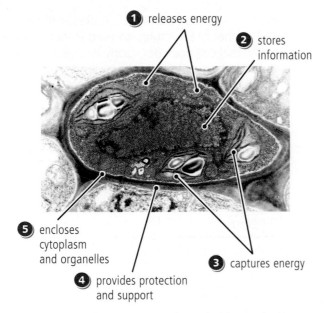

1 releases energy

2 stores information

3 captures energy

4 provides protection and support

5 encloses cytoplasm and organelles

In one or two sentences, describe how the terms in each of the following pairs are related. Underline each term in your answer.

6. unicellular, multicellular

7. cell, organelle

8. prokaryotic cell, eukaryotic cell

9. tissue, organ

Reviewing Key Concepts

Multiple Choice *Choose the letter of the best answer.*

10. Which statement about cells is part of the cell theory?
   a. Cells are found in most living things.
   b. Cells with cell walls do not have cell membranes.
   c. All cells capture energy from sunlight.
   d. Cells come only from other living cells.

11. What structure does a plant cell have that is not found in an animal cell and that allows a plant cell to capture energy from the Sun?
   a. cell wall
   b. chloroplast
   c. mitochondrion
   d. central vacuole

12. Which technology was important to the development of the cell theory?
   a. computer
   b. scientific model
   c. microscope
   d. refrigeration

13. Organisms can be divided into domains on the basis of the characteristics of their cells. What are these domains?
   a. Archaea, Bacteria, and Eukarya
   b. prokaryotes and eukaryotes
   c. plants, animals, and bacteria
   d. unicellular and multicellular

14. A complex multicellular organism has different levels of organization. What is the order of these levels?
   a. cell membrane, cytoplasm, nucleus
   b. tissues, organs, organ systems
   c. tissues, organs, specialized cells
   d. cell membrane, organelles, nucleus

15. What is the function of the genetic material in a cell?
   a. provides transport of materials from the nucleus to the cell membrane
   b. breaks down materials brought into the cell
   c. provides information a cell needs to function and grow
   d. controls what comes into a cell and what goes out

Short Answer *Write a short answer to each question.*

16. What are four characteristics common to all living things?

17. What are three needs common to all living things?

Thinking Critically

Questions 18–20 refer to polar bears and their cells as examples of animals and animal cells.

18. **PREDICT** Some polar bears go through long periods of sleep during the cold winter months. In what two ways might their fat cells help the bears survive during these periods?

19. **PROVIDE EXAMPLES** Animals do not get energy directly from the Sun as plants do. Give one or two examples of body systems in a polar bear that help it obtain and process food.

20. **COMPARE AND CONTRAST** Consider the fat cells in a polar bear and compare them with the single body cell of a bacterium. How are the cells alike, and how are they different?

21. **CONNECT** The cell theory applies to all organisms, including you. State the three parts of the cell theory and describe briefly how they relate to you.

22. **ANALYZE** Louis Pasteur designed the swan-necked flask to use in his experiments. In one experiment, he used two sealed flasks of nutrient broth. One flask he heated; the other he left untouched. Bacteria grew in the untouched flask. Nothing grew in the flask that had been heated, or sterilized. How did this experiment provide evidence against the theory of spontaneous generation?

Both ends of flasks are sealed.

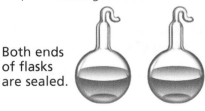

23. **PREDICT** What would happen if the neck of the sterilized swan-necked flask were broken?

24. **IDENTIFY CAUSE** Why does pasteurized milk eventually spoil?

25. **COMPARE AND CONTRAST** A plant cell has a number of structures and organelles that an animal cell does not. Copy the table below and place a check in the appropriate box of each row. The first two are done for you.

	Animal Cell	Plant Cell
Cell wall		✓
Cell membrane	✓	✓
Cytoplasm		
Nucleus		
Central vacuole		
Chloroplast		
Mitochondrion		

the BIG idea

26. **CLASSIFY** Look again at the photograph on pages 6–7. Can you identify any of the structures shown? Can you identify the type of microscope used to make the photograph? How do you know?

27. **CONNECT** What are three ways that an understanding of cells has changed the way people live? **Hint:** Think about Pasteur and his work.

UNIT PROJECTS

If you are doing a unit project, make a folder for your project. Include in your folder a list of the resources you will need, the date on which the project is due, and a schedule to track your progress. Begin gathering data.

The Euglena Puzzle

*Read the following description of euglenas and how scientists classify them.
Then answer the questions below.*

Plants and animals are typically multicellular organisms. For a long time, scientists tried to classify any unicellular organism that had a nucleus as either a single-celled plant or a single-celled animal. One group of unicellular organisms, *Euglenas,* was particularly difficult to classify. These tiny organisms can be found living in most ponds. What is puzzling about *Euglenas* is that they have characteristics of both plants and animals.

Some scientists argued that *Euglenas* are more like plants because many of them have chloroplasts. Chloroplasts are cellular structures that enable both plants and *Euglenas* to capture energy from the Sun. Other scientists argued that *Euglenas* are more like animals because they can take in food particles from the water. *Euglenas* also have flagella, tail-like structures that enable them to swim. The *Euglena* even has an eyespot for sensing light.

1. What cellular structures enable plants and *Euglenas* to capture energy from the Sun?
   a. flagella
   b. chloroplasts
   c. nuclei
   d. eyespots

2. What cellular structures are common to plants, animals, and *Euglenas*?
   a. flagella
   b. chloroplasts
   c. nuclei
   d. eyespots

3. In what way are *Euglenas* different from both plants and animals?
   a. They have no nuclei.
   b. They are unicellular.
   c. They live in ponds.
   d. They get energy from food.

4. What does an eyespot do?
   a. senses light
   b. captures food
   c. provides energy
   d. senses movement

5. Having flagella makes *Euglenas* similar to animals because it allows *Euglenas* to do what?
   a. eat food
   b. get energy
   c. sense light
   d. move about

Extended Response

Answer the following questions in detail. Include some of the terms in the word box. In your answers, underline each term you use.

sunlight	energy	food
eyespot	flagellum	move

6. A jar of water containing *Euglenas* is placed in a sunny window. After a while, a noticeable cloud forms in the water, near where the light shines into the water. Over the course of the day, the position of the Sun changes. As it does, the cloud keeps moving toward the light. On the basis of your reading, what do you think is happening and why?

7. Suppose there is a small pond near your school. The pond is surrounded by many tall trees that tend to block sunlight around the edges of the pond. In this situation, explain why it is an advantage for *Euglenas* to have the characteristics they do. Which of these characteristics do you associate with plants? with animals?

2 How Cells Function

the **BIG** idea

All cells need energy
and materials for life
processes.

How do plants like these
sunflowers change energy
from the Sun?

Key Concepts

SECTION
2.1 Chemical reactions
take place inside cells.
Learn why water and four
types of large molecules are
important for cell functions.

SECTION
2.2 Cells capture and
release energy.
Learn about the process
of photosynthesis
and the two ways cells
release energy.

SECTION
2.3 Materials move
across the cell's
membranes.
Learn about the
different ways materials
move through cells.

Internet Preview

CLASSZONE.COM

Chapter 2 online resources:
Content Review, two
Visualizations, two Resource
Centers, Math Tutorial, and
Test Practice.

EXPLORE (the BIG idea)

Leaves Underwater

Put a dish, two plant leaves, and two baby food jars in a sink full of water. Fill one jar with water and both leaves, then turn the jar upside down on the dish. Fill the other jar with just water and do the same. Remove your set-up from the sink and place it in sunlight for two hours.

Observe and Think
What happened in the jars? Why do you think these things happened?

Just a Spoonful of Sugar

Pour a little warm water into each of two cups. Stir eight spoonfuls of sugar into one of the cups. Drop several raisins into each cup and wait for six hours. After six hours, compare the raisins in each cup.

Observe and Think How are the raisins different? How would you explain your observation?

Internet Activity: Photosynthesis

Go to **ClassZone.com** to examine how plants use sunlight to make sugar molecules.

Observe and Think
What are the starting materials of photosynthesis? What are the products?

NSTA
scilinks.org
SCiLINKS

Photosynthesis **Code: MDL032**

Getting Ready to Learn

◀ CONCEPT REVIEW

- Cells are the basic units of living things.
- Some cells have organelles that perform special functions for the cell.
- Animal cells and plant cells have similar structures, but plant cells have cell walls and chloroplasts.

◀ VOCABULARY REVIEW

cell membrane, p. 20

organelle, p. 20

chloroplast, p. 23

mitochondria, p. 23

 **CONTENT REVIEW**
CLASSZONE.COM
Review concepts and vocabulary.

▶ TAKING NOTES

OUTLINE

As you read, copy the headings on your paper in the form of an outline. Then add notes in your own words that summarize what you read.

VOCABULARY STRATEGY

Draw a **word triangle** diagram for each new vocabulary term. On the bottom line, write and define the term. Above that, write a sentence that uses the term correctly. At the top, draw a small picture to show what the term looks like.

See the Note-Taking Handbook on pages R45–R51.

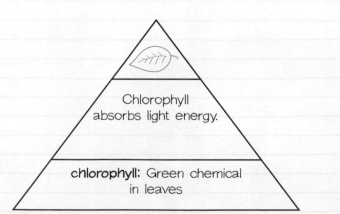

SCIENCE NOTEBOOK

OUTLINE

I. ALL CELLS ARE MADE OF THE SAME ELEMENTS.

  A. ALL MATTER IS MADE OF ELEMENTS.

     1. 6 make up most of human body

     2. elements interact to produce new materials

       a. smallest unit of element is atom

Chlorophyll absorbs light energy.

chlorophyll: Green chemical in leaves

KEY CONCEPT

2.1 Chemical reactions take place inside cells.

<table>
<tr><td>◀ **BEFORE, you learned**</td><td>▶ **NOW, you will learn**</td></tr>
<tr><td>

• All living things are made of cells

• Cells need energy to sustain life

• Plant and animal cells have similarities and differences

</td><td>

• About the types of elements found in all cells

• About the functions of large molecules in the cell

• Why water is important to the activities of the cell

</td></tr>
</table>

VOCABULARY

chemical reaction p. 42
carbohydrate p. 42
lipid p. 43
protein p. 43
nucleic acid p. 43

EXPLORE Food Molecules

How are different types of molecules important in your everyday life?

PROCEDURE

1. Examine the foods shown in the photograph. Protein, carbohydrates, and lipids (fats) are important substances in the food you eat. Locate at least one source of protein, carbohydrates, and lipids in the food.

2. Use your textbook and additional resource materials to find out a little more about these molecules in our food supply.

WHAT DO YOU THINK?
What foods do you eat that supply protein, carbohydrates, and lipids?

MATERIALS
• notebook
• reference materials

All cells are made of the same elements.

OUTLINE
Continue the outline begun on page 40.

I. Main idea
  A. Supporting idea
    1. Detail
    2. Detail
  B. Supporting idea

The microscope allowed people to observe the tiny cells that make up all living things. Even smaller, too small for a light microscope to show, is the matter that makes up the cell itself.

All matter in the universe—living and nonliving—can be broken down into basic substances called elements. About a hundred different elements are found on Earth. Each element has its own set of properties and characteristics. For example, the characteristics of oxygen include that it is colorless, odorless, and on Earth, it exists in the form of a gas.

Elements in the Human Body

Oxygen	65.0%
Carbon	18.5%
Hydrogen	9.5%
Nitrogen	3.3%
Calcium	1.5%
Phosphorus	1.0%
other 19 elements	1.2%

Source: CRC Handbook of Chemistry and Physics

Of all the elements found on Earth, about 25 are essential for life. As you can see from the table, just 6 elements account for about 99 percent of the mass of the human body. But very little of this matter exists as pure elements. Instead, most is in the form of compounds, which are substances made up of two or more different elements. For example, water is a compound made of hydrogen and oxygen.

The smallest unit of any element is called an atom. In a compound, atoms of two or more elements are joined together by chemical bonds. Most compounds in cells are made up of atoms bonded together in molecules. For example, a molecule of water is made of one atom of oxygen bonded to two atoms of hydrogen.

Most activities that take place within cells involve atoms and molecules interacting. In this process, called a **chemical reaction,** bonds between atoms are broken and new bonds form to make different molecules. Energy is needed to break bonds between atoms, and energy is released when new bonds form. Cells use chemical energy for life activities.

Large molecules support cell function.

RESOURCE CENTER
CLASSZONE.COM

Explore molecules in living things.

In living things, there are four main types of large molecules: (1) carbohydrates, (2) lipids, (3) proteins, and (4) nucleic acids. Thousands of these molecules work together in a cell. The four types of molecules in all living things share one important characteristic. They all contain carbon atoms. These large molecules are made up of smaller parts called subunits.

Carbohydrates

sugars

Carbohydrates are used for structure and energy storage. Carbohydrates, such as cellulose, are made of **sugars.**

Carbohydrates (KAHR-boh-HY-DRAYTS) provide the cell with energy. Simple carbohydrates are sugars made from atoms of carbon, oxygen, and hydrogen. Inside cells, sugar molecules are broken down. This process provides usable energy for the cell.

Simple sugar molecules can also be linked into long chains to form more complex carbohydrates, such as starch, cellulose, and glycogen. Starch and cellulose are complex carbohydrates made by plant cells. When a plant cell makes more sugar than it can use, extra sugar molecules are stored in long chains called starch. Plants also make cellulose, which is the material that makes up the cell wall. Animals get their energy by eating plants or other animals that eat plants.

Lipids

Lipids are the fats, oils, and waxes found in living things. Like carbohydrates, simple lipids are made of atoms of carbon, oxygen, and hydrogen and can be used by cells for energy and for making structures. However, the atoms in all lipids are arranged differently from the atoms in carbohydrates. Many common lipids consist of a molecule called glycerol bonded to long chains of carbon and hydrogen atoms called fatty acids. This structure gives lipids unique properties. One extremely important property of lipids is that they cannot mix with water.

Lipids make up the membranes surrounding the cell and organelles. Lipids are made of **fatty acids** and **glycerol**.

CHECK YOUR READING How do cells use carbohydrates and lipids?

Proteins

Proteins are made of smaller molecules called amino acids. Amino acids contain the elements carbon, oxygen, hydrogen, nitrogen, and sometimes sulfur. In proteins, amino acids are linked together into long chains that fold into three-dimensional shapes. The structure and function of a protein is determined by the type, number, and order of the amino acids in it.

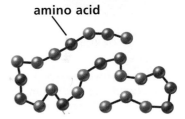

Proteins are made up of **amino acids**. Proteins carry out most of the chemical activity in cells.

Your body gets amino acids from protein in food, such as meat, eggs, cheese, and some beans. After taking in amino acids, your cells use them to build proteins needed for proper cell functioning. Some amino acids can be made by the body, but others must be taken in from an outside food source.

There are many types of proteins. Enzymes are proteins that control chemical reactions in the cells. Other proteins support the growth and repair of living matter. The action of proteins in your muscles allows you to move. Some of the proteins in your blood fight infections. Another protein in your blood delivers oxygen to all the cells in your body. Proteins are also important parts of cell membranes. Some proteins in the cell membrane transport materials into and out of the cell.

Nucleic Acids

Nucleic acids (noo-KLEE-ihk) are the molecules that hold the instructions for the maintenance, growth, and reproduction of a cell. There are two types of nucleic acids: DNA and RNA. Both DNA and RNA are made from carbon, oxygen, hydrogen, nitrogen, and phosphorus. The subunits of nucleic acids are called nucleotides.

Nucleic acids store and translate the genetic information a cell needs to function. Nucleic acids, such as DNA, are made up of **nucleotides**.

DNA provides the information used by the cell for making proteins a cell needs. This information takes the form of a code contained in the specific order of different nucleotides in the DNA.

The pattern of nucleotides in DNA is then coded into RNA, which delivers the information into the cytoplasm. Other RNA molecules in the cytoplasm produce the proteins.

CHECK YOUR READING What is the function of DNA and RNA?

About two thirds of every cell is water.

hydrogen

oxygen

Each **water** molecule is made of two **hydrogen** atoms bonded to one **oxygen** atom.

All of the chemical reactions inside the cell take place in water. Water is also in the environment outside the cell. For example, water inside cells makes up about 46 percent of your body's mass, and water outside the cells in body fluids accounts for another 23 percent.

A water molecule consists of two atoms of hydrogen bonded to one atom of oxygen. Because of its structure, a water molecule has a slight positive charge near the hydrogen atoms and a slight negative charge near the oxygen atom. Molecules that have slightly charged ends are said to be polar. Like a magnet, the ends of a polar molecule attract opposite charges and repel charges that are the same. Because water is a polar molecule, many substances dissolve in water. However, not all materials dissolve in water. If you have ever shaken a bottle of salad dressing, you've probably observed that oil and water don't mix.

INVESTIGATE Oil and Water

What happens when you combine oil and water?

PROCEDURE

1. Put a small amount of oil into one beaker and an equal amount of milk into another.

2. Put water into a third beaker and add enough food coloring to make the water darkly colored.

3. Add equal amounts of the colored water to the beaker of oil and the beaker of milk. Stir the liquids to mix them. Record your observations.

WHAT DO YOU THINK?

• Compare and contrast the behavior of the mixture of oil and water with that of the mixture of milk and water.

• Why does a mixture of oil and water behave differently from a mixture of milk and water?

CHALLENGE The outside of a cell is surrounded by water. Explain how the water-hating nature of lipids can keep a cell's inside separated from its outside.

SKILL FOCUS
Observing

MATERIALS
• vegetable oil
• milk
• water
• 3 beakers
• food coloring
• stirring stick

TIME
10 minutes

Cell Membrane

The cell membrane is made of a double layer of lipids.

Lipids have a water-loving head and a water-hating tail.

head

tail

cell membrane

inside of cell

outside of cell

Most lipids do not dissolve in water. A special type of lipid is the major molecule that makes up cell membranes. These special lipid molecules have two parts: a water-loving head and two water-hating tails. In other words, the head of the lipid molecule is polar, while the tails are nonpolar.

Why is it important that cell membranes contain lipids? Remember that cell membranes function as boundaries. That is, they separate the inside of a cell from the outside. Most of the material inside and outside the cell is water. As you can see in the diagram above, the water-hating tails in the lipids repel the water while the head clings to water.

READING TiP

As you read about the properties of cell, notice the arrangements of lipids in the diagram of the cell.

2.1 Review

KEY CONCEPTS

1. Explain how just a few elements can make up all living things.
2. What functions do proteins, carbohydrates, lipids, and nucleic acids perform?
3. What does it mean to describe water molecules as being polar?

CRITICAL THINKING

4. **Compare and Contrast** How are carbohydrates and lipids similar? How are they different?
5. **Draw Conclusions** What do the major types of molecules that make up living things have in common?

◆ CHALLENGE

6. **Model** Some people have compared the nucleic acids DNA and RNA to a blueprint for life. How are DNA and RNA like blueprints? How are they different?

TEXTILE DESIGNER

Natural Dyes and Cells

Where does the blue in your blue jeans come from? How about the red, yellow, green, or pink in your favorite wool or cotton sweater? Most fabrics are colored with dyes made up in labs, but some designers prefer to use natural dyes and natural cloth. All textile designers must understand the science of dyes and fibers to produce the colors they want.

Fibers

Natural fibers come either from plants or animals. Wool is an animal fiber. Silk, too, is made up of animal cells. Cotton, linen, and rayon are fibers made from plants. Plant fibers have thick cell walls, made mostly of cellulose. Animal fibers, on the other hand, contain mainly proteins.

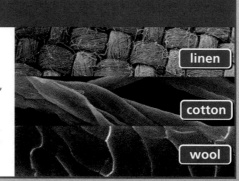

linen

cotton

wool

silk

Dyes

Most natural dyes come from plants, but sometimes insects are used too. The indigo plant is used for most blue, including the original blue jeans. Insects are most often used to make reds. All dyes are made of molecules—carbon, oxygen, hydrogen, and other atoms. The molecules of the dye bind to the molecules of the fibers, adding the dye's color to the fiber.

Color Fixers

A mordant is a chemical compound that combines with dye as a color fixer, or color keeper. The mordant must strengthen the bonds between natural dye molecules and fibers. A stronger bond means the color is less likely to fade or wash out of the fibers. Most mordants are liquid solutions containing metals, such as chromium.

EXPLORE

1. **EXPERIMENT** Design an experiment using onion skins, beets, or blackberries to color white wool and white cotton. The procedure should include chopping the plant and heating it with water to make the dye. Be sure that your experiment procedure includes only one variable. Your experiment should start with a question, such as How do the dyes differ? Or Which dye works best?

2. **CHALLENGE** Using different mordants with the same dye can give different colors. For example, dandelion leaf dye gives yellow-green, gray-green, tan, or gold with different mordants. Explain why this happens.

2.2 Cells capture and release energy.

BEFORE, you learned

- The cell is the basic unit of all living things
- Plant cells and animal cells have similarities and differences
- Plants and animals need energy and materials

NOW, you will learn

- Why cells need energy
- How energy is captured and stored
- How plants and animals get energy

VOCABULARY

chemical energy p. 47
glucose p. 47
photosynthesis p. 48
chlorophyll p. 48
cellular respiration p. 50
fermentation p. 52

THINK ABOUT

What do these cells have in common?

Both muscle cells and plant cells need energy to live. Your muscle cells need energy to help you move and perform other functions. Even though plant cells don't move in the same way that muscles move, they still need energy. How do human muscle cells and plant cells get energy?

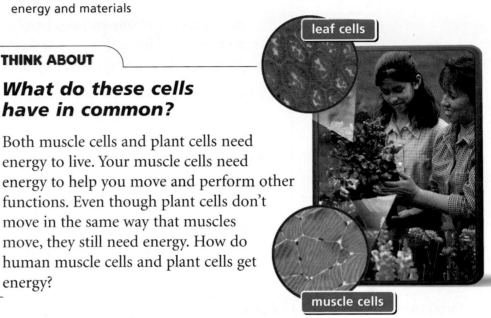

leaf cells

muscle cells

All cells need energy.

OUTLINE
Remember to include this heading in your outline of this section.

I. Main idea
  A. Supporting idea
    1. Detail
    2. Detail
  B. Supporting idea

To stay alive, cells need a constant supply of energy. Animal cells get energy from food, while plant cells get energy from sunlight. All cells use chemical energy. **Chemical energy** is the energy stored in the bonds between atoms of every molecule. To stay alive, cells must be able to release the chemical energy in the bonds.

A major energy source for most cells is stored in a sugar molecule called **glucose.** When you need energy, cells release chemical energy from glucose. You need food energy to run, walk, and even during sleep. Your cells use energy from food to carry out all of their activities.

Think about muscle cells. When you run, muscle cells release chemical energy from glucose to move your legs. The more you run, the more glucose your muscle cells need. You eat food to restore the glucose supply in muscles. But how do plant cells get more glucose? Plants transform the energy in sunlight into the chemical energy in glucose.

Some cells capture light energy.

The source of energy for almost all organisms ultimately comes from sunlight. Plants change the energy in sunlight into a form of energy their cells can use—the chemical energy in glucose. All animals benefit from the ability of plants to convert sunlight to food energy. Animals either eat plants, or they eat other animals that have eaten plants.

Photosynthesis (FOH-toh-SIHN-thih-sihs) is the process that plant cells use to change the energy from sunlight into chemical energy. Photosynthesis takes place in plant cells that have chloroplasts. Chloroplasts contain **chlorophyll** (KLAWR-uh-fihl), a light-absorbing pigment, or colored substance, that traps the energy in sunlight.

The process of photosynthesis involves a series of chemical steps, or reactions. The illustration on the next page shows an overview of how photosynthesis changes starting materials into new products.

READING TiP

As you read each numbered item here, find the number on the diagram on page 49.

❶ **The starting materials** of photosynthesis are carbon dioxide and water. The plant takes in carbon dioxide from the air and water from the soil.

❷ **The process** takes place when carbon dioxide and water enter the plant's chloroplasts. Chlorophyll captures energy from sunlight, which is used to change carbon dioxide and water into new products.

❸ **The products** of photosynthesis are oxygen and sugars such as glucose. The plant releases most of the oxygen to the air as a waste product and keeps the glucose for its energy needs.

⬭ **CHECK YOUR READING** Summarize photosynthesis. Remember that a summary includes only the most important information.

Plants do not immediately use all of the glucose they make. Some of the glucose molecules are linked together to build large carbohydrates called starch. Plants can store starch and later break it back down into glucose or other sugars when they need energy. Sugars and starches supply food for animals that eat plants.

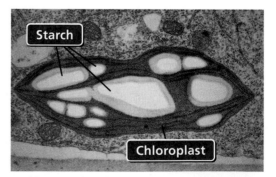

The starch in this plant cell stores energy.

Photosynthesis

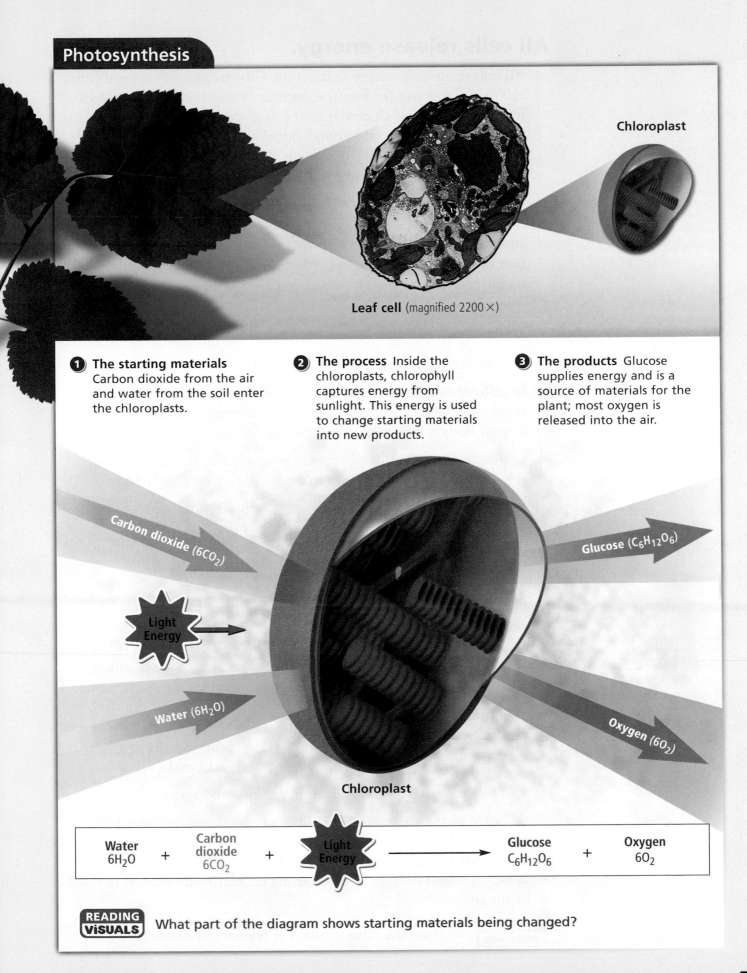

Chloroplast

Leaf cell (magnified 2200×)

1 **The starting materials** Carbon dioxide from the air and water from the soil enter the chloroplasts.

2 **The process** Inside the chloroplasts, chlorophyll captures energy from sunlight. This energy is used to change starting materials into new products.

3 **The products** Glucose supplies energy and is a source of materials for the plant; most oxygen is released into the air.

Carbon dioxide (6CO$_2$)

Glucose (C$_6$H$_{12}$O$_6$)

Light Energy

Water (6H$_2$O)

Oxygen (6O$_2$)

Chloroplast

| Water 6H$_2$O | + | Carbon dioxide 6CO$_2$ | + | Light Energy | $\longrightarrow$ | Glucose C$_6$H$_{12}$O$_6$ | + | Oxygen 6O$_2$ |

READING VISUALS What part of the diagram shows starting materials being changed?

All cells release energy.

All cells must have energy to function. Glucose and other sugars are cell food—they are the power source for cell activities in almost all living things. When glucose is stored as glycogen or taken in as starch, it must be broken down into individual sugar molecules before cells are able to use it. Chemical energy is stored in the bonds of sugars. When a sugar molecule is broken down, a usable form of energy is released for the cell's life functions.

Cells can release energy in two basic processes: cellular respiration and fermentation. Cellular respiration requires oxygen, but fermentation does not. In addition, cellular respiration releases much more usable energy than does fermentation.

 CHECK YOUR READING What is released when a sugar molecule is broken down?

Cellular Respiration

In **cellular respiration,** cells use oxygen to release energy stored in sugars such as glucose. In fact, most of the energy used by the cells in your body is provided by cellular respiration.

Just as photosynthesis occurs in organelles called chloroplasts, cellular respiration takes place in organelles called mitochondria. Remember that mitochondria are in both plant cells and animal cells, so both kinds of cells release energy through cellular respiration.

Like photosynthesis, cellular respiration is a process that changes starting materials into new products.

1 **The starting materials** of cellular respiration are sugars—such as glucose—and oxygen.

2 **The process** begins when glucose in the cytoplasm is broken down into smaller molecules. This releases a small amount of energy. These molecules then move into the mitochondria. At the same time, oxygen enters the cell and travels into the mitochondria. As the smaller molecules are broken down even further, hydrogen is released in a way that allows cells to capture energy in a usable form. The hydrogen combines with oxygen to make water.

3 **The products** are energy, carbon dioxide, and water.

Some of the energy released during cellular respiration is transferred to other molecules, which then carry the energy where it is needed for the activities of the cell. The rest of the energy is released as heat. Carbon dioxide formed during cellular respiration is released by the cell.

CHECK YOUR READING What are the three products of cellular respiration?

READING TiP

Reread step 2 to make sure you understand what happens to oxygen and glucose.

Cellular Respiration

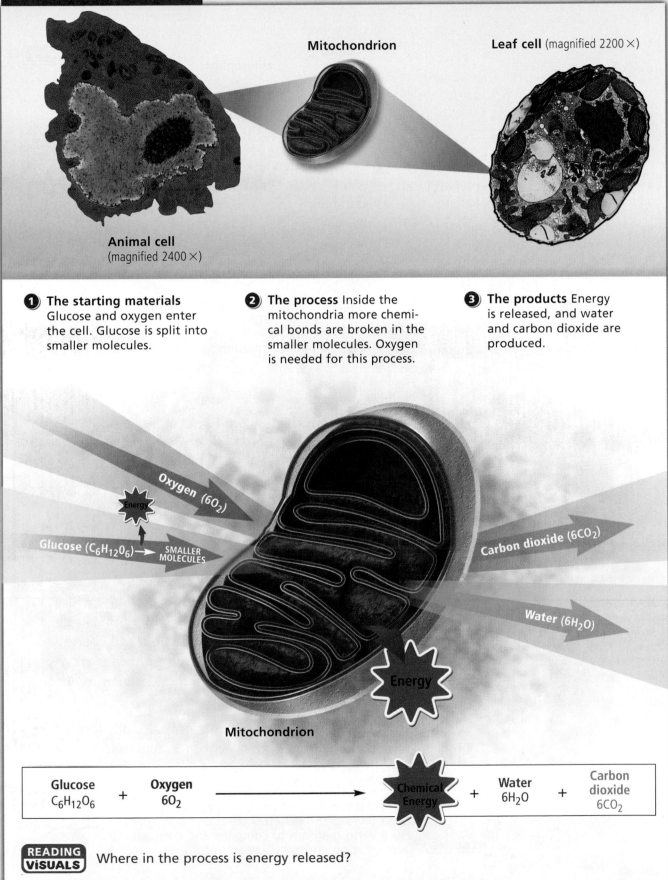

Mitochondrion

Leaf cell (magnified 2200×)

Animal cell
(magnified 2400×)

❶ The starting materials Glucose and oxygen enter the cell. Glucose is split into smaller molecules.

❷ The process Inside the mitochondria more chemical bonds are broken in the smaller molecules. Oxygen is needed for this process.

❸ The products Energy is released, and water and carbon dioxide are produced.

Oxygen ($6O_2$)

Energy

Glucose ($C_6H_{12}O_6$) → SMALLER MOLECULES

Carbon dioxide ($6CO_2$)

Water ($6H_2O$)

Energy

Mitochondrion

Glucose $C_6H_{12}O_6$	+	Oxygen $6O_2$	→	Chemical Energy	+	Water $6H_2O$	+	Carbon dioxide $6CO_2$

READING VISUALS Where in the process is energy released?

Photosynthesis and Respiration Cycle

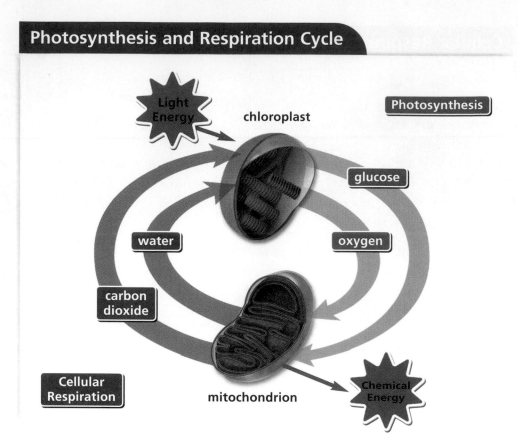

You may find it interesting to compare cellular respiration with photosynthesis. The diagram above highlights the cycle that occurs between photosynthesis and cellular respiration. Notice that the starting materials of one process are also the products of the other process. This cycle does not necessarily occur in the same cell, or even in the same organism.

Fermentation

Fermentation is the process by which cells release energy without oxygen. Recall that in cellular respiration the cell first breaks glucose into smaller molecules. This releases a small amount of energy. Without oxygen, cellular respiration cannot continue. In eukaryotic cells, instead of entering the mitochondria, these smaller molecules stay in the cytoplasm, where fermentation occurs.

There are two main types of fermentation: alcoholic fermentation and lactic acid fermentation. Both types of fermentation break sugars down to small molecules. In the absence of oxygen, different reactions occur that produce either alcohol and carbon dioxide or lactic acid. In both cases, a small amount of energy is released.

 Use a Venn diagram to compare and contrast fermentation and cellular respiration.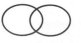

The production of many foods that people eat every day involve either alcoholic fermentation or lactic acid fermentation. Three important foods are bread, yogurt, and cheese.

Bread is often made by mixing flour, milk, and sugar with a microorganism you know as yeast. Yeast runs out of oxygen and uses fermentation to convert the sugar into alcohol and carbon dioxide. Bubbles of carbon dioxide gas forming inside the dough cause it to rise. When the dough is baked, the small amount of alcohol evaporates, the yeast is killed, and the carbon dioxide bubbles give the bread a light, spongy structure.

Some bacteria release energy through lactic acid fermentation. These bacteria convert the sugar found in milk into lactic acid and are used to make yogurt, cheese, and sourdough bread. Lactic acid changes the acidity of a bread mixture to give it a slightly sour flavor. In yogurt and cheese, the buildup of lactic acid causes the milk to partially solidify, producing the creamy texture of yogurt. If fermentation continues for a long time, the milk eventually turns into cheese.

INVESTIGATE Fermentation

How can you tell if fermentation releases material?

PROCEDURE

1. Add 1/2 teaspoon of yeast to the empty water bottle.
2. Fill the bottle about three-quarters full with the sugar solution.
3. Place the balloon tightly around the mouth of the bottle.
4. Gently swirl the bottle to mix the yeast and sugar solution.
5. After 20 minutes, observe the balloon and record your observations.

WHAT DO YOU THINK?

- What changes did you observe? What do you think is the source of energy that caused these changes?
- What accounts for the change in the amount of gas inside the balloon?

CHALLENGE Design an experiment to answer the following question. How might the temperature of the sugar solution affect the process?

SKILL FOCUS
Observing

MATERIALS
- dry yeast
- spoon
- small water bottle
- warm sugar solution
- balloon

TIME
30 minutes

Energy and Exercise

Your muscle cells, like some organisms, are able to release energy by both cellular respiration and fermentation. While you are at rest, your muscle cells use specialized molecules to store both energy and oxygen.

During hard or prolonged exercise, your muscle cells may use up all their stores of energy and oxygen. Then your muscle cells rely on fermentation to break down sugars. There is much less energy available to cells that use fermentation, which is why you cannot continue to run rapidly for long distances. When your cells use fermentation to release energy, one of the waste products is lactic acid, which can cause a burning sensation in your muscles.

APPLY Why might these students feel a burning sensation in their arm muscles while doing pull-ups?

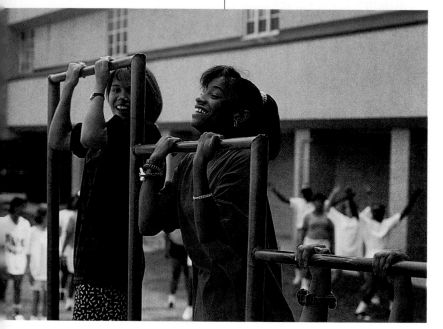

When you stop after this type of exercise, your muscles continue to hurt and you continue to breathe hard for many minutes. During this time, your muscles are playing catch-up. They use the oxygen brought into your blood by your heavy breathing to finish breaking down the byproducts of fermentation. As the lactic acid is converted into carbon dioxide and water, the burning sensation in your muscles goes away. Your muscles build back up their stores of energy and oxygen until the next time they are needed.

2.2 Review

KEY CONCEPTS

1. Which form of energy is especially important for living things? Why?

2. How is photosynthesis important to life on Earth?

3. What starting materials do cells need for cellular respiration?

CRITICAL THINKING

4. **Compare and Contrast** How are photosynthesis and cellular respiration similar? How are they different?

5. **Predict** Suppose that in a lab you could remove all the oxygen from a terrarium. What would happen to the plants? Why?

● CHALLENGE

6. **Synthesize** In everyday language, the word *respiration* refers to breathing. How is breathing related to *cellular respiration*? Hint: The air we breathe out contains more carbon dioxide than the air we breathe in.

MATH in SCIENCE

MATH TUTORIAL
CLASSZONE.COM
Click on Math Tutorial for more help with interpreting line graphs.

Carbon Dioxide Levels in Biosphere 2

Biosphere 2 is a research and education center in Arizona that can house people, plants, and animals. It was built to find out whether people could get the food and breathable air needed to survive in a small sealed environment over a two-year period.

Example

Data on carbon dioxide levels in the air of Biosphere 2 were collected at 15-minute intervals for several weeks. The graph below shows the amounts of carbon dioxide (CO_2) in the air on January 20, 1996.

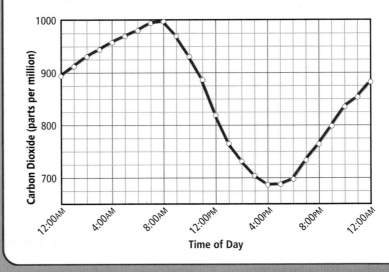

Answer the following questions.

1. What intervals are shown on the *x*-axis? What is shown on the *y*-axis?

2. At what time of day does the carbon dioxide concentration reach its highest point? About how many parts per million of CO_2 are in the air at that time?

3. Between what hours is the CO_2 level decreasing?

CHALLENGE The data in the graph were collected on a sunny day. How might the graph look different if the day had been overcast?

2.3 Materials move across the cell's membranes.

◀ **BEFORE, you learned**

- All cells have an outer covering called the cell membrane
- Cells need starting materials for life-sustaining processes
- Cells need to get rid of waste products

▶ **NOW, you will learn**

- How materials move into and out of the cell through the cell membrane
- How energy is involved in transporting some materials into and out of cells
- How surface area affects transport in cells

VOCABULARY

diffusion p. 56
passive transport p. 58
osmosis p. 59
active transport p. 60

EXPLORE Diffusion

How do particles move?

PROCEDURE

1. Fill the beaker with tap water.
2. Add 3 drops of food coloring to the water.
3. For 10 minutes, observe what happens. Write down your observations.

WHAT DO YOU THINK?
- What changes did you observe?
- What might have caused the changes?

MATERIALS
- beaker
- water
- food coloring

VOCABULARY
Add a word triangle for *diffusion* to your notebook. Your triangle could include a sketch of the sun.

Some materials move by diffusion.

When you walk toward the shampoo section in a store, you can probably smell a fragrance even before you get close. The process by which the scent spreads through the air is an example of diffusion. **Diffusion** (dih-FYOO-zhuhn) is the process by which molecules spread out, or move from areas where there are many of them to areas where there are fewer of them.

Diffusion occurs because the molecules in gases, liquids, and even solids are in constant motion in all directions. This random movement of molecules tends to spread molecules out until they are evenly distributed. But diffusion does more than just spread a scent around a room. Cells use diffusion to carry out important life functions. Diffusion helps cells maintain conditions necessary for life. For example, the oxygen needed for respiration enters cells by diffusion. Similarly, the carbon dioxide produced by respiration leaves cells by diffusion.

Concentration

Diffusion occurs naturally as particles move from an area of higher concentration to an area of lower concentration. The concentration of a substance is the number of particles of that substance in a specific volume. For example, if you dissolved 9 grams of sugar in 1 liter of water, the concentration of the sugar solution would be 9 g/L. When there is a difference in the concentration of a substance between two areas, diffusion occurs.

Generally, the greater the difference in concentration between two areas, the more rapidly diffusion occurs. As the difference in concentration decreases, diffusion slows down. The number of particles moving to one area is balanced by the number moving in the other direction. Particles are still moving in all directions, but these movements do not change the concentrations.

CHECK YOUR READING Summarize what happens during diffusion. (Remember, a summary includes only the most important information.)

Concentration and Diffusion

A sugar cube dissolving in water provides an example of diffusion.

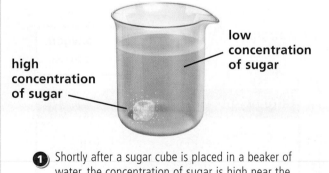

high concentration of sugar

low concentration of sugar

equal concentrations of sugar throughout

① Shortly after a sugar cube is placed in a beaker of water, the concentration of sugar is high near the sugar cube and very low elsewhere in the beaker.

② Over time, diffusion causes the concentration of sugar to become the same throughout the beaker. Particles are still moving.

Diffusion in Cells

Diffusion is one way by which materials move in and out of cells. Small molecules such as oxygen can pass through tiny gaps in the cell membrane by diffusion. For example, consider the conditions that result from photosynthesis in a leaf cell.

RESOURCE CENTER
CLASSZONE.COM

Learn more about diffusion.

• Photosynthesis produces oxygen inside the cell.

• The concentration of oxygen molecules becomes higher inside the cell than outside.

• Oxygen molecules move out of the cell by diffusion.

In a plant cell, some of the oxygen produced by photosynthesis is used in cellular respiration. The remaining oxygen diffuses out of the cell. Much of it escapes to the air. Some of it diffuses to other cells where there is a lower concentration of oxygen. This process of diffusion continues from one cell to the next.

Diffusion is a form of passive transport. In **passive transport,** materials move without using the cell's energy. Cells benefit from passive transport because some materials can move through various cell membranes without any input of energy. Whether or not a substance can diffuse across a cell membrane depends on how well the substance dissolves in the lipids that make up the cell membrane. A special form of passive transport allows polar substances, such as glucose, salts, and amino acids, to pass through cell membranes.

All cells need the food energy supplied by glucose. Yet glucose is produced in just some plant cells. Polar substances move into the cell through protein channels—or openings—in their membranes that are specific for each substance. This type of diffusion is still passive transport because it uses no energy.

CHECK YOUR READING What is passive transport? Your answer should mention energy.

VOCABULARY
Add a word diagram for *passive transport* to your notebook. You may want to use words instead of a sketch in part of your triangle.

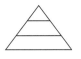

Passive Transport

Materials move across a cell membrane continuously.

= oxygen
= glucose

Different concentrations

More **oxygen** moves out of the cell than into the cell.

outside of cell

Special **proteins** allow passive transport of some molecules, such as glucose.

inside of cell

The concentration of oxygen is greater inside the cell than outside.

Equal concentrations

Equal amounts of **oxygen** move into and out of the cell.

The concentration of oxygen is the same inside and outside the cell.

Osmosis

You have read about the importance of water. Water molecules move through cell membranes by diffusion. The diffusion of water through a membrane is given a special name, **osmosis** (ahz-MOH-sihs). If the concentration of water is higher outside a cell than inside, water moves into the cell. If the concentration of water is lower outside a cell, water moves out of the cell.

You can easily observe the effect of osmosis on plants. If you forget to water a plant, it wilts. Why? The soil dries out, and the plant's roots have no water to absorb. As a result, water leaves the plant cells by osmosis and they shrink. If you water the plant, water becomes available to enter the shrunken cells by osmosis. The leaves will return to normal as water moves into the cells.

Without water, a plant droops. The cells have little water in their vacuoles, shown in blue. (magnified 1200×)

Water moves into leaf cells by osmosis and fills the vacuoles, shown in blue. (magnified 1200×)

Some transport requires energy.

Not all materials that move in and out of a cell can do so by diffusion. For cells to carry out life functions, materials must often move from areas of low concentration into areas of high concentration. This process of moving materials against a concentration requires energy.

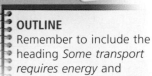

OUTLINE
Remember to include the heading *Some transport requires energy* and notes on the red headings in your outline.

Active Transport

Active transport is the process of using energy to move materials through a membrane. This process is different from diffusion and other types of passive transport, which do not require energy.

⬤ **CHECK YOUR READING** How is active transport different from passive transport?

VISUALIZATION
CLASSZONE.COM
Observe active transport at work.

Cells use active transport to perform important life functions, including the removal of excess salt from the body. Consider the example of active transport in marine iguanas, shown below. These lizards swim and feed in the salty ocean. As a result they soak up a lot of salt. Too much salt would seriously damage the iguanas' cells, so the cells must get rid of the excess.

The solution to the marine iguana's salt problem is found in two small glands above its eyes. Cells in these glands remove excess salt from the blood by active transport. Even when cells in these glands have a higher concentration of salt than that of the blood, the cells use chemical energy to continue taking salt out of the blood. The gland forms a droplet of salt, which the iguana easily blows out through its nostrils.

Active Transport

Salt is removed from an iguana's body by active transport.

Salt gland

salt gland cell
blood vessel
to nostril

1 Inside the salt gland, a network of tiny blood vessels carries blood to and from the body.

energy
inside cell
salt

2 Active transport is used to move salt from the blood into nearby cells.

3 Salt becomes concentrated and is finally sneezed out through the iguana's nostrils.

You may not be able to blow salt out of your nostrils, but your kidneys help to keep healthy salt levels in your body. Kidneys filter wastes from your blood by active transport. Cells in the kidneys remove excess salt from the blood.

Endocytosis

Cells also need to move materials that are too large to go through the cell membrane or a protein channel. As the diagram below illustrates, endocytosis (EHN-doh-sy-TOH-sihs) occurs when a large bit of material is captured within a pocket of the membrane. This pocket breaks off and forms a package that moves into the cell. Cells in your body can use endocytosis to fight bacteria and viruses by absorbing them.

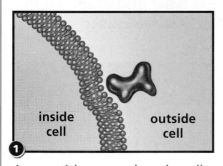

1 As a particle approaches, the cell membrane folds inward, creating a pocket.

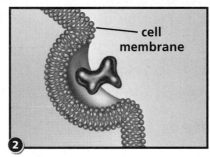

2 The particle moves into the pocket, and the membrane closes around it, forming a "package."

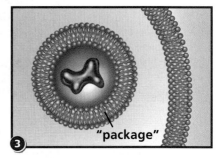

3 The "package" breaks away from the cell membrane, bringing the particle into the cell.

Exocytosis

When a cell needs to get rid of large materials, the process of endocytosis is reversed. In exocytosis (EHK-soh-sy-TOH-sihs), a membrane within the cell encloses the material that needs to be removed. This package moves to the cell membrane, joins with it, and the material is expelled. Cells often use exocytosis to flush out waste materials or to expel proteins or hormones made by the cell.

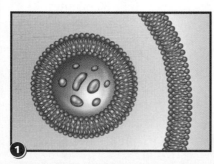

1 A membrane-enclosed "package" carries materials from inside the cell to the cell membrane.

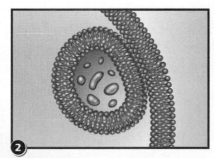

2 The membrane of the "package" attaches to the cell membrane, and the two membranes merge.

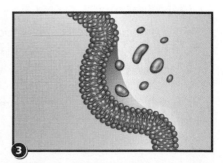

3 The materials are pushed out of the cell as the membrane of the "package" becomes part of the cell membrane.

Cell size affects transport.

Most cells are very small. In fact, most cells are too small to be seen without a microscope. The average cell in your body is about 50 micrometers (0.05 mm) in diameter. Most of the cells on this planet are bacteria, which are only 3 to 5 micrometers in diameter. How can something as important as a cell be so tiny? Actually, if cells were not so small, they could never do their jobs.

Everything the cell needs or has to get rid of has to go through the cell membrane. The amount of cell membrane limits the ability of cells to either get substances from the outside or transport waste and other materials to the outside. This ability is related to surface area. The relationship between surface area and volume controls cell size. As a cell gets larger, its volume increases faster than its surface area if the cell maintains the same shape. Why does this matter?

INVESTIGATE Cells

How does cell size affect transport?

Demonstrate how small size helps make it possible for cells to get resources.

PROCEDURE

1. Cut a large piece of egg white from the egg.

2. Use a knife to trim the egg white into one small cube, about 1 cm square, and one large cube, about 2 cm square.

3. Pour 100 mL of water into the beaker. Add 10 drops of blue food coloring and stir. Place both cubes into the solution. Let both stand in the colored water overnight.

4. Remove each gently from the water with a spoon. Place both on a paper towel. With the knife, cut each in half. Use the ruler to measure how far the blue water penetrated into the surface of each one.

WHAT DO YOU THINK?

- Record your observations. Which piece of egg was penetrated more, compared to its total diameter, by the blue water?

- Why was there a difference in water penetration?

CHALLENGE What do you predict would happen to an egg left in its shell?

SKILL FOCUS
Modeling

MATERIALS
- 2 hard-boiled, peeled eggs
- knife
- ruler
- 100 mL water
- glass beaker
- dark blue food coloring
- spoon
- paper towel

TIME
30 minutes

Surface Area and Volumes of Cubes

	Number of Cubes	Side Length	Surface Area	Volume
4 cm	1	4 cm	96 cm^2	64 cm^3
2 cm	8	2 cm	192 cm^2	64 cm^3
1 cm	64	1 cm	384 cm^2	64 cm^3

As the cell gets bigger, there comes a time when its surface area is not large enough to allow resources to travel to all parts of the cell. So the cell stops growing. Bird eggs and frog eggs are much larger than typical cells, but they have a storehouse of food and also rapidly divide to give rise to multicellular embryos. In fact, this multicellular embryo is a good illustration of another way cells get around the surface-area-to-volume problem: they divide. The ratio of surface area to volume in newly divided cells is much higher, giving more surface area for exchanging materials with the outside of cells.

A cell's shape also affects its surface area. For example, some single-celled organisms are thin and flat, providing increased surface area. Other cells, such as nerve cells and muscle cells, are long and skinny, which also gives them a higher ratio of surface area to volume.

READING TiP

Look at the chart above. Notice that the volumes are all the same, but the surface area changes.

2.3 Review

KEY CONCEPTS

1. How are the processes of diffusion and osmosis alike?

2. What is the difference between active and passive transport? Use the term *energy* in your answer.

3. How does the surface area of a cell limit the growth of the cell?

CRITICAL THINKING

4. **Apply** If you put a bouquet of carnations in water, through what process does the water enter the stems?

5. **Predict** If a marine iguana were to spend a few days in a freshwater tank, would it continue to blow salt droplets from its nostrils? Why or why not?

○ CHALLENGE

6. **Predict** Freshwater protozoa, which are unicellular organisms, have a greater concentration of salt inside them than does the surrounding water. Does water diffuse into or out of the protozoa?

CHAPTER INVESTIGATION

Diffusion

OVERVIEW AND PURPOSE The cell membrane controls what diffuses into and out of a cell. What factors affect the diffusion of substances across the cell membrane? In this investigation, you will

- observe the effect of concentration on rate of diffusion
- determine the relative concentrations of the iodine solutions used

▶ Problem

Write It Up

How does the concentration of a substance affect its diffusion through a membrane?

▶ Hypothesize

Write It Up

Write a hypothesis to explain how concentration will affect diffusion of material through a membrane. Your hypothesis should take the form of an "If . . ., then . . ., because. . ." statement.

▶ Procedure

MATERIALS
- eyedroppers
- cornstarch solution
- baby food jar with lid
- plastic wrap
- iodine solution
- graduated cylinder (if available)

1 Make a data table like the one shown on the sample notebook page.

2 To test for the presence of starch, use one eyedropper to put several drops of cornstarch solution on the lid of the baby food jar. With another eyedropper, add a few drops of iodine to the solution on the jar lid. Observe and record what happens.

step 2

3 Fill the baby food jar about three-fourths full with the cornstarch solution.

Place the plastic wrap inside the jar so that the plastic extends a little below the surface of the cornstarch solution.

4 Pour 10 mL of the iodine solution that you are given (A, B, or C) on the plastic wrap membrane, enough to cover the top of the plastic wrap. Record your observations.

step 4

5 Examine the solutions above and below the membrane after 20 minutes. Record any color changes, as well as the intensity of any changes, that you observe.

Observe and Analyze

1. **IDENTIFY VARIABLES** Identify the constants. What will stay the same in the experiment for all groups?

   Identify the independent variable. What is being changed?

   Identify the dependent variable. What is being observed and measured?

2. **RECORD OBSERVATIONS** Draw before and after pictures of your setup and label each drawing. Be sure to show the colors of the solutions on both sides of the membrane in each drawing.

   Make a drawing to show the direction in which molecules diffused through the membrane in your experiment.

   Compare the observations you made from your iodine solution with the observations made by your classmates. Be sure to record which iodine solution (A, B, or C) produced which changes.

Conclude

1. **INTERPRET** Did starch diffuse through the membrane into the iodine solution? How do you know? Did iodine diffuse through the membrane into the cornstarch solution? How do you know?

2. **INTERPRET** What factors affect the diffusion of different substances through a membrane?

3. **INFER** From what you've observed, which solution contains larger molecules, cornstarch or iodine? Why weren't the larger molecules able to diffuse through the membrane?

4. **INTERPRET** Which iodine solution (A, B, or C) produced the largest color change?

5. **INTERPRET** Which solution had the highest concentration of iodine, and how do you know?

6. **IDENTIFY LIMITS** Describe any errors that you made in your procedure, or places where errors might have occurred.

7. **APPLY** Identify two real-life situations in which diffusion occurs.

INVESTIGATE Further

CHALLENGE Investigate the role of temperature in diffusion. Predict how changes in the temperature of the iodine solution will affect the speed of diffusion through the plastic membrane. Why do you think temperature would affect the diffusion process?

Diffusion

Table 1. Color Changes

Solution	Color at 0 min		Color at 20 min	
	cornstarch solution	iodine solution	cornstarch solution	iodine solution
A				
B				
C				

CONTENT REVIEW
CLASSZONE.COM

the BIG idea

All cells need energy and materials for life processes.

KEY CONCEPTS SUMMARY

2.1 Chemical reactions take place inside cells.

All cells are made of the same elements. Cells contain four types of large molecules—**carbohydrates, lipids, proteins,** and **nucleic acids**—that support cell function.

About two thirds of every cell is water. The properties of water are important to cell function.

carbohydrates

lipids

proteins

nucleic acids

VOCABULARY
chemical reaction p. 42
carbohydrate p. 42
lipid p. 43
protein p. 43
nucleic acid p. 43

2.2 Cells capture and release energy.

All cells need energy. Some cells capture light energy through **photosynthesis.** All cells release chemical energy from glucose.

Cellular respiration and **fermentation** are two ways that cells release energy from glucose.

Light Energy

Cellular Respiration

glucose

water

oxygen

Photosynthesis

carbon dioxide

Chemical Energy

VOCABULARY
chemical energy p. 47
glucose p. 47
photosynthesis p. 48
chlorophyll p. 48
cellular respiration p. 50
fermentation p. 52

2.3 Materials move across the cell's membranes.

Passive transport is the movement of materials from an area of higher concentration to an area of lower concentration. **Diffusion** and **osmosis** are examples of passive transport.

Active transport is the movement of materials from an area of lower concentration to an area of higher concentration. Cells need energy to perform active transport.

passive transport

active transport

VOCABULARY
diffusion p. 56
passive transport p. 58
osmosis p. 59
active transport p. 60

Reviewing Vocabulary

Use words from the vocabulary lists on page 66 to answer these questions.

1. Which molecule stores information?

2. Which word describes the process when two or more atoms bond together?

3. What kind of energy do cells use?

4. Which term describes the process in which cells release energy without using oxygen?

5. Which process occurs in chloroplasts?

6. From what sugar molecule do many living things release energy?

7. Which chemical that aids in photosynthesis do you find in a chloroplast?

8. Which word means "diffusion of water across cell membranes"?

9. Choose two pairs of opposite processes.

10. Use a Venn diagram to compare and contrast passive transport and active transport.

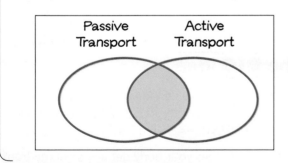

Passive Transport | Active Transport

Reviewing Key Concepts

Multiple Choice *Choose the letter of the best answer.*

11. The fats, oils, and waxes found in living things are known as
- **a.** lipids
- **b.** proteins
- **c.** carbohydrates
- **d.** glucose

12. What do cells use as a source of energy and for energy storage?
- **a.** proteins
- **b.** water
- **c.** cytoplasm
- **d.** carbohydrates

13. Leaf cells use chlorophyll to absorb
- **a.** oxygen
- **b.** light energy
- **c.** carbon dioxide
- **d.** glucose

14. The cells of a redwood tree require oxygen for the process of
- **a.** photosynthesis
- **b.** cellular respiration
- **c.** fermentation
- **d.** endocytosis

15. In fermentation, cells release energy without
- **a.** alcohol
- **b.** water
- **c.** glucose
- **d.** oxygen

16. Both a whale and a seaweed use which of the following to change glucose into energy?
- **a.** water
- **b.** photosynthesis
- **c.** cellular respiration
- **d.** bonding

17. The movement of materials across a cell membrane, requiring energy, is called
- **a.** diffusion
- **b.** osmosis
- **c.** passive transport
- **d.** active transport

Short Answer *Write a short answer to each question.*

18. Why is water needed by cells?

19. Describe the main function of nucleic acids.

20. What is the role of chlorophyll in a plant's leaves?

21. Explain why a carrot feels spongy after being soaked in salt water.

22. Explain how the ways in which plants and animals get their energy differ.

Thinking Critically

23. RECOGNIZE CAUSE AND EFFECT Explain why chemical reactions are essential to living creatures.

24. MODEL How does a glass filled with oil and water illustrate the properties of a cell membrane? What properties does it not illustrate?

The illustration below summarizes the relationship between photosynthesis and cellular respiration. Use it to answer the next three questions.

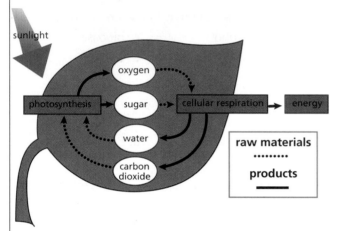

sunlight

raw materials
·········

products
—

25. OBSERVE What are the starting materials of photosynthesis? What are the starting materials of cellular respiration?

26. OBSERVE What are the products of photosynthesis? What are the products of cellular respiration?

27. DRAW CONCLUSIONS What does the diagram above reveal about the connections between photosynthesis and cellular respiration?

Process	Requires Energy?	Moves from Higher to Lower Concentration?
Diffusion	no	yes
Osmosis		
Active transport		
Passive transport		

28. CHART INFORMATION Copy and complete this chart. The first line is done for you.

29. INFER The French scientist Louis Pasteur mixed yeast and grape juice in a sealed container. When he opened the container, the grape juice contained alcohol. Explain what happened.

30. DRAW CONCLUSIONS Why would it be harmful to your health to drink seawater?

31. PREDICT Look at the diagram at the right. The bag has pores that are bigger than the sugar molecules. What will be true of the concentration of the sugar water after a few hours?

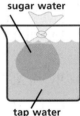

sugar water

tap water

the BIG idea

32. COMPARE AND CONTRAST Look again at the picture on pages 38–39. Why do you think the sunflowers are facing the Sun?

33. INFER Does your body get all its energy from the Sun? Explain.

34. WRITE Imagine that your community has a high level of carbon dioxide emission from cars and factories. A developer wants to build a shopping center on the remaining forest land. Would this action increase or decrease carbon dioxide levels? Why? Write a paragraph explaining your answer.

UNIT PROJECTS

Check your schedule for your unit project. How are you doing? Be sure that you have placed data or notes from your research in your project folder.

Analyzing Data

Elodea plants in beakers of water were placed at different distances from a
light source. The number of bubbles that formed on the plants was counted
and recorded. The data table shows the results.

Beaker	Distance from light	Bubbles per minute
1	200 cm	2
2	100 cm	10
3	50 cm	45
4	20 cm	83

Study the data and answer the questions below.

1. What gas do the bubbles consist of?

   a. carbon dioxide   **c.** water vapor

   b. hydrogen   **d.** oxygen

2. What is the relationship between the distance
from the light source and the rate of bubble for-
mation?

   a. The rate increases as the distance increases.

   b. The rate decreases as the distance increases.

   c. The rate stays the same as the distance
increases.

   d. The rate changes in a way unrelated to
distance.

3. If another beaker with *elodea* were placed 150 cm
from the light, about how many bubbles would
form each minute?

   a. 1   **c.** 11

   b. 7   **d.** 24

4. What is the independent variable in this
experiment?

   a. type of plant   **c.** distance from light

   b. number of bubbles   **d.** amount of time

5. Which graph best represents the data shown in
the table?

   a.

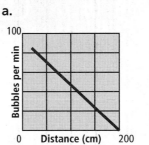

   c.

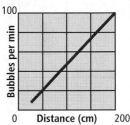

   b.

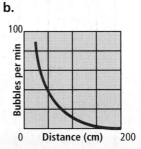

   d.

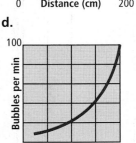

Extended Response

Answer each question. Include some of the terms
shown in the word box. In your answers underline
each term you use.

chemical energy	cellular respiration
osmosis	chloroplasts
fermentation	glucose
photosynthesis	diffusion

6. A person rides his bicycle several miles. What process is used by the cells in his legs to release energy at the beginning of the ride? At the end of the
ride? Explain.

7. A student places a plant in a sealed container and
puts the container on a window sill. She leaves the
plant there for a week. Will the plant have the
starting materials it needs to carry out photosynthesis during the entire week? Explain.

CHAPTER
3 Cell Division

the BIG idea

Organisms grow, reproduce, and maintain themselves through cell division.

Some of these bacterial cells are dividing. How are the cells formed in cell division like the other cells in the photograph?

Key Concepts

SECTION
3.1 Cell division occurs in all organisms.
Learn about the functions of cell division.

SECTION
3.2 Cell division is part of the cell cycle.
Learn about the cell cycle and the process of mitosis.

SECTION
3.3 Both sexual and asexual reproduction involve cell division.
Learn how sexual reproduction compares with asexual reproduction.

Internet Preview

CLASSZONE.COM
Chapter 3 online resources: Content Review, Simulation, Visualization, three Resource Centers, Math Tutorial, Test Practice

Dividing to Multiply

Carefully observe a maple tree samara like the ones shown here. Notice the different parts of a samara. Break a samara into two pieces. Peel back the end of each half, where you broke it.

Observe and Think
What did you find when you peeled back the ends? How does something as small as a seed produce something as large as a tree?

Division Math

Take a piece of clay and divide it in half. Now you have two pieces of clay, each half the size of the original piece. Divide each of the two new pieces in half, producing 4 pieces, each a quarter the size of the original piece.

Observe and Think What will happen if you keep dividing the pieces in half? How might the division of the cells in living things be different?

Internet Activity: Cell Division

Go to **ClassZone.com** to match images of cells dividing with the different stages of cell division.

Observe and Think Are the stages the same for plant and animal cells?

NSTA
scilinks.org
SciLINKS

Cellular Mitosis **Code: MDL033**

Getting Ready to Learn

CONCEPT REVIEW

- The cell is the basic unit of structure and function in living things.
- All cells come from other cells.
- DNA provides the instructions a cell needs to function and reproduce.

VOCABULARY REVIEW

cell membrane p. 20

nucleus p. 20

cycle *See Glossary.*

CONTENT REVIEW
CLASSZONE.COM
Review concepts and vocabulary.

TAKING NOTES

COMBINATION NOTES

To take notes about a new concept, first make an informal outline of the information. Then make a sketch of the concept and label it so you can study it later.

VOCABULARY STRATEGY

Write each new vocabulary term in the center of a **frame game** diagram. Decide what information to frame it with. Use examples, description, parts, sentences that use the term in context, or pictures. You can change the frame to fit each term.

See the Note-Taking Handbook on pages R45–R51.

SCIENCE NOTEBOOK

NOTES

Mitosis has four phases

- prophase: chromosomes become visible

- metaphase: chromosomes line up in middle

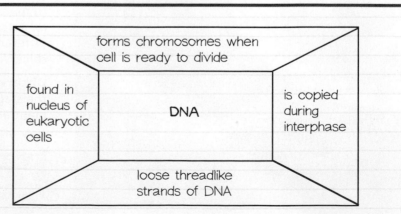

	forms chromosomes when cell is ready to divide	
found in nucleus of eukaryotic cells	**DNA**	is copied during interphase
	loose threadlike strands of DNA	

KEY CONCEPT

Cell division occurs in all organisms.

BEFORE, you learned

- Cells come from other cells
- Cells take in and release energy and materials
- In a multicellular organism, some cells specialize

NOW, you will learn

- How genetic material is organized in cells
- About the functions of cell division in multicellular organisms

VOCABULARY

DNA p. 74
chromosome p. 75

EXPLORE Cell Division

How is organization helpful?

PROCEDURE

1. Work with two other students. Obtain paired and unpaired groups of socks.

2. Two of the students put on blindfolds. One takes the paired group of socks and the other takes the unpaired group.

3. Each blindfolded student tries to separate his or her group of socks into two piles of single socks, one from each pair. The third student keeps track of time and stops the activity after 2 min.

MATERIALS
- 2 blindfolds
- socks
- stopwatch

WHAT DO YOU THINK?
Which group of socks was more accurately separated into two identical sets? Why?

Cell division is involved in many functions.

REMINDER

Most multicellular organisms are made up of eukaryotic cells. Most genetic material in eukaryotic cells is contained in the nucleus.

Cell division occurs in all organisms, but performs different functions. Unicellular organisms reproduce through cell division. In multicellular organisms, cell division is involved in growth, development, and repair, as well as in reproduction.

You are probably bigger this year than you were last year. One characteristic of all living things is that they grow. Your body is made up of cells. Although cells themselves grow, most growth in multicellular organisms occurs when cells dividing produce new cells. In this chapter you will read about cell division in eukaryotic cells.

The genetic material of eukaryotic cells is organized in chromosomes.

The genetic material of a cell contains information needed for the cell's growth and other activities. When a cell divides into two new cells, each new cell receives a full set of genetic material. The genetic material in cells is contained in DNA molecules.

DNA

The genetic material in cells is DNA—deoxyribonucleic acid (dee-AHK-see-RY-boh-noo-KLEE-ihk). **DNA** is a chemical that contains information for an organism's growth and functions. You read in chapter 1 that James Watson and Francis Crick worked with other scientists to build a model of DNA in 1953. They showed that DNA is made of two strands of molecules joined in a structure that resembles a twisted ladder or a double helix. You will learn more about DNA later in the unit.

CHECK YOUR READING   What is DNA?

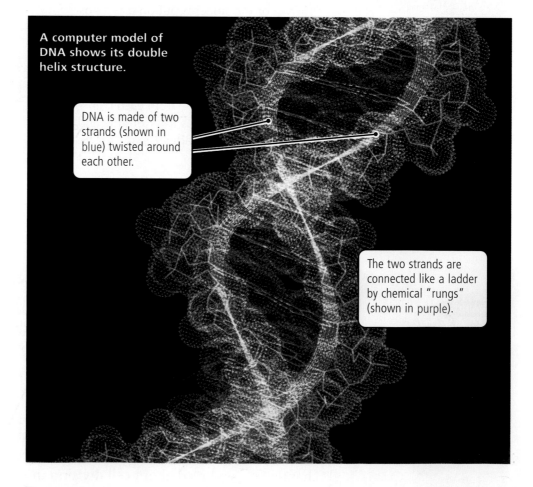

A computer model of DNA shows its double helix structure.

DNA is made of two strands (shown in blue) twisted around each other.

The two strands are connected like a ladder by chemical "rungs" (shown in purple).

Chromosomes

In a eukaryotic cell, most of the cell's DNA is in the nucleus. During most of a cell's life cycle, DNA exists as a mass of loose strands. While the DNA is spread throughout the nucleus, the cell performs the functions needed for survival. During this time, the DNA is duplicated, or copied.

DNA is wrapped around proteins like thread around a spool and compacted into structures called **chromosomes** (KROH-muh-SOHMZ). Before division, the chromosomes compact more and become visible under a light microscope. During division, a duplicated chromosome can be seen as two identical structures called chromatids that are held together by a centromere.

Within each species of organism, the number of chromosomes is constant. For example, humans have 46 chromosomes. Fruit flies, however, have 8 chromosomes, and corn plants have 20.

READING **TiP**

Compare the diagram of DNA with the computer model on page 74.

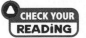 Describe the relationship between DNA and chromosomes.

Organization of Genetic Material

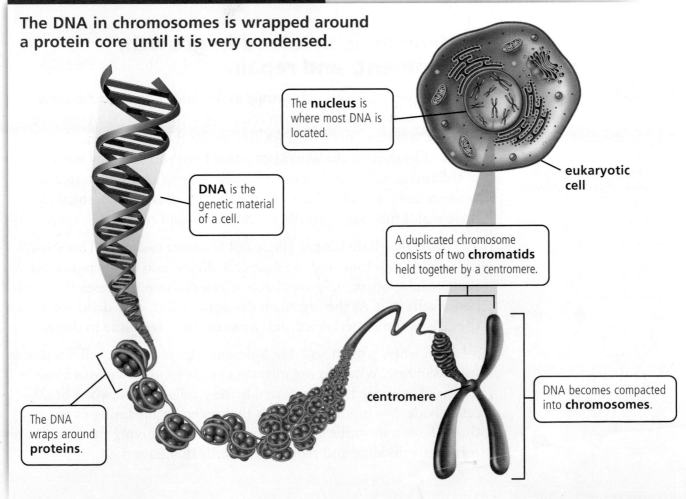

The DNA in chromosomes is wrapped around a protein core until it is very condensed.

The **nucleus** is where most DNA is located.

eukaryotic cell

DNA is the genetic material of a cell.

A duplicated chromosome consists of two **chromatids** held together by a centromere.

centromere

DNA becomes compacted into **chromosomes**.

The DNA wraps around **proteins**.

How does DNA fit inside the nucleus?

PROCEDURE

① Select four pieces of yarn of different colors and four craft sticks. Push the yarn together into a loose ball. Observe how much space it takes up and how the individual pieces are organized.

② Wrap each piece of yarn around a craft stick. Wrap the yarn so that the coils are tightly packed but do not overlap.

MATERIALS
• yarn
• craft sticks

TIME
20 minutes

WHAT DO YOU THINK?

• What did you observe about the loosely balled yarn?
• What does the loosely balled yarn represent?
• What does the yarn on the craft sticks represent?
• Why does the yarn on the craft sticks take up less space than the ball of yarn?

CHALLENGE How does the yarn's being wrapped on the craft sticks make it easier to separate the different colors?

Cell division is involved in growth, development, and repair.

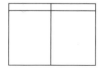

COMBINATION NOTES
Remember to take notes and draw sketches to help you understand the main idea: *Cell division is involved in growth, development, and repair.* Be sure to include the red heads in your notes.

Multicellular organisms vary greatly in size and complexity. You may not think that you have much in common with an ant or an oak tree. Actually, you share many characteristics with these organisms. One of the most important characteristics is that both you and they are made of trillions of cells. But, like most organisms, you and they started out as single cells. In multicellular organisms, cell division is essential for three major functions: growth, development, and repair.

Through cell division, a single cell becomes two cells. Those two cells divide into four, and the four cells divide into eight, and so on. A multicellular organism grows because cell division increases the number of cells in it. As the organism develops and its cells divide, many of the cells become specialized, and most of them continue to divide.

Even when growth and development appear to stop, cell division is still occurring. When an organism ages or is injured, the worn-out or damaged cells need to be replaced by new cells formed when healthy cells divide. For example, the cells that make up the lining of your throat have a short life span—two to three days. Living throat cells are constantly dividing and replacing the cells that have died.

Growth

In general, a large organism does not have larger cells than a small organism; it simply has many more cells than the small organism. When you were small, your body contained fewer cells than it has now. By the time you reach adulthood, your body will be made up of about 100 trillion cells.

Individual cells grow in size, but there are limits to the size that cells can reach. As you learned in Chapter 2, cells need a high ratio of surface area to volume in order to function. As a cell grows, that ratio decreases. When the cell divides into two smaller cells, the ratio of surface area to volume for each cell increases.

Scientists are still searching for answers about how cell size is related to the control of cell division. Some scientists think that there is no single factor that controls cell division. Instead, they think that many cell processes added together control when a cell divides.

 CHECK YOUR READING Describe how the number of cells in a multicellular organism changes as the organism grows.

Growth and Development

Organisms, like this sea turtle, grow and develop through cell division.

① The embryo growing inside this egg started as a single cell.

② When it hatches, the baby turtle has trillions of cells.

③ The adult turtle has more than a hundred times the cells of the baby turtle.

READING TiP

Connect what you have read about growth and development with the series of sea turtle photographs above.

Development

Although multicellular organisms begin as single cells, they grow into larger organisms through cell division. However, cell division alone does not allow organisms to develop. If cell division were the only process occurring in cells, all multicellular organisms would end up as spheres of identical cells. But during development, cells become specialized to perform particular functions.

These cells may take on shapes or structures that help them to perform their functions. Some cells might become layered skin cells, while others might become long, thin nerve cells. These cells still have the same set of genetic material as all the other cells in an organism's body, but as the organism develops they specialize.

CHECK YOUR READING Give two examples of specialized cells from the paragraph above.

Repair

You may have cut yourself at one time or another. Perhaps you have even broken a bone in your arm or leg. The body repairs injuries like these by means of cell division. For example, when your skin is cut, skin cells on either side of the cut make new cells to heal the wound. You can see the process of healing in the diagram below.

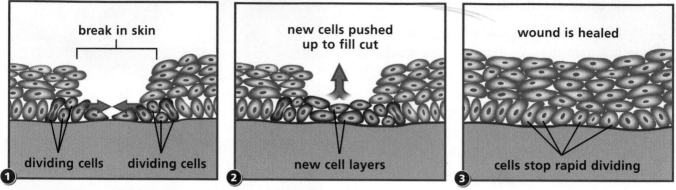

1 **break in skin**

dividing cells   dividing cells

Cells in the lower layer begin to divide quickly and move into the break.

2 **new cells pushed up to fill cut**

new cell layers

New cells begin to fill the area as cells continue to divide.

3 **wound is healed**

cells stop rapid dividing

Cells stop their rapid dividing once the break is filled.

As cells age and die, they need to be replaced. In the human body—which is made up of about 200 different types of cells—cells are replaced at different rates. Your skin cells wear out quickly, so they need to be replaced often. Every minute or so, your skin loses about 40,000 cells, which are replaced with new ones. In contrast, most of the cells in your brain live a long time and do not divide very often.

CHECK YOUR READING What role does cell division play in healing the body?

3.1 Review

KEY CONCEPTS

1. Why is cell division important?
2. How is genetic material organized in eukaryotic cells?
3. Explain how cell division is involved in the growth, development, and repair of an organism.

CRITICAL THINKING

4. **Summarize** Explain how DNA compacts before a eukaryotic cell divides.
5. **Infer** Why do you think that injuries to the skin generally heal faster than injuries to the brain?

○ CHALLENGE

6. **Apply** Describe the stages of development in a multicellular organism that is familiar to you.

Chemical Dyes Show Nerve Growth

For years, the medical community has agreed that nerve tissue, once damaged, does not repair itself. In fact, the opinion was that new nerve cells didn't grow in adults at all. However, a surprising discovery has shown that new nerve cells do grow in the mature brains of both monkeys and people!

Elizabeth Gould noticed that new nerve cells can grow in adult brains

The Discovery

The discovery involves a chemical known as bromodeoxyuridine (BrdU), which can be used to detect new cancer cells.

1 BrdU highlights the DNA of cells that are reproducing, such as cancer cells.

2 BrdU also makes it possible to count the new cells that are being created, because they stand out as well.

3 The cells that have been highlighted with BrdU can be seen under a microscope when they are illuminated with a special light.

When scientists used this technique to examine certain areas in the brains of monkeys and of adult humans who had died of cancer, they found that new nerve cells had grown in the brains of each. Thus, the chemical properties of BrdU allowed scientists to discover new nerve cells growing in places where scientists had previously never expected to see them.

Hope for the Future

If new nerve cells grow in these tissues, it may be possible to stimulate growth in damaged nerve tissue such as that in the spinal cord. If researchers discover how new growth in nerve cells is stimulated, there may be new hope for people who have nervous systems damaged by accidents or by diseases such as Parkinson's disease.

EXPLORE

1. **SYNTHESIZE** How could you use chemicals, such as small dots with a pen, in an experiment to show how your fingernails grow?

2. **CHALLENGE** What are some possible effects of being able to grow new nerve cells?

RESOURCE CENTER
CLASSZONE.COM
Find out more about new nerve cell growth.

3.2

Cell division is part of the cell cycle.

BEFORE, you learned

- Cells come from other cells through cell division
- A cell must have a full set of genetic material to function
- Cell division enables multi-cellular organisms to develop, grow, and repair themselves

NOW, you will learn

- About two main stages in the cell cycle
- About the changes that occur in cells before mitosis
- About the events that take place during mitosis

VOCABULARY

cell cycle p. 80
interphase p. 81
mitosis p. 81
cytokinesis p. 81

THINK ABOUT

What is a cycle?

Many things in your everyday life are cycles. A cycle is any activity or set of events that regularly repeats. Cycles can be short, like the sequence of events that make your heart beat, or they can be very long, like the turning of our galaxy. One example of a cycle is shown at the right. The photographs show a tree during four seasons in a northern climate. How are these seasons a cycle?

The cell cycle includes interphase and cell division.

All living things live, grow, reproduce, and die in a process called a life cycle. The life cycle of a tree, for example, begins with a seed. Under the right conditions, the seed begins to grow. It produces a very small plant, which may grow over many years into a towering tree. When it is mature, the tree makes its own seeds, and the cycle begins again.

Cells have a life cycle too, called the cell cycle. The **cell cycle** is the normal sequence of development and division of a cell. The cell cycle consists of two main phases: one in which the cell carries out its functions, called interphase, and one in which the cell divides, which can include mitosis and cytokinesis. All cells divide, but only eukaryotes undergo mitosis. Each phase in the cell cycle requires a certain period of time—from hours to days or years, depending on the type of cell.

RESOURCE CENTER
CLASSZONE.COM

Learn about the cell cycle.

A 80 Unit: Cells and Heredity

Interphase

Interphase is the part of the cell cycle during which a cell is not dividing. Much activity takes place in this phase of the cell's life. During interphase, the cell grows to about twice the size it was when it was first produced. The cell also engages in normal life activities, such as transporting materials in and transporting wastes out. Also, cellular respiration occurs, which provides the energy the cell needs.

Changes that occur during interphase prepare a cell for division. Before a cell can divide, it duplicates its DNA exactly. Correct copying of the DNA is very important. It ensures that, after cell division, each new cell gets a complete set of DNA.

CHECK YOUR READING What cell processes occur during interphase?

VOCABULARY
Make a frame game diagram for *interphase*.

Cell Division Phase

Mitosis is the part of the cell cycle during which the nucleus divides. Prokaryotes do not undergo mitosis because they have no nucleus. In most cells, mitosis is the shortest period in the life cycle. The function of mitosis is to move the DNA and other material in the parent cell into position for cell division. When the cell divides, each new cell gets a full set of DNA and other cell structures. **Cytokinesis** (SY-toh-kuh-NEE-sihs) is the division of the parent cell's cytoplasm. Cytokinesis occurs immediately after mitosis.

Cell Cycle

The events that happen during the life of a cell are called the cell cycle.

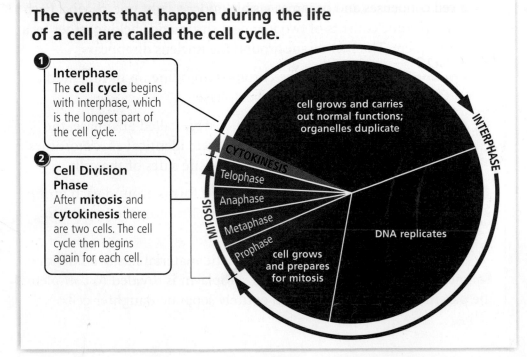

1 Interphase
The **cell cycle** begins with interphase, which is the longest part of the cell cycle.

2 Cell Division Phase
After **mitosis** and **cytokinesis** there are two cells. The cell cycle then begins again for each cell.

cell grows and carries out normal functions; organelles duplicate

INTERPHASE

CYTOKINESIS

Telophase

Anaphase

Metaphase

Prophase

MITOSIS

DNA replicates

cell grows and prepares for mitosis

READING TIP

The arrows in the Cell Cycle diagram represent the passage of time. Interphase is in red, mitosis is in purple, and cytokinesis is in yellow.

As a result of mitosis and cytokinesis, the original—or parent—cell splits into two genetically identical daughter cells. In this case, the term *daughter cell* does not imply gender. It is a term scientists use to refer to these new cells. Each daughter cell receives a complete set of DNA from the parent cell.

Cell division produces two genetically identical cells.

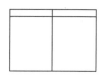
Recall that many cells in your body are continually dividing into new cells. The new cells help your body grow, develop, repair itself, and replace worn-out parts. Though your body cells divide at different rates, the same process—mitosis—divides their genetic material.

Cell division produces daughter cells that are genetically identical to each other, as well as to their parent cell, which no longer exists. Being genetically identical to their parent cell helps the new cells function properly. A skin cell, for example, divides and produces skin cells genetically identical to it.

CHECK YOUR READING How are daughter cells like the parent cell?

VISUALIZATION
CLASSZONE.COM

Watch the process of mitosis in action.

Steps of Mitosis

The process of mitosis is essential in evenly dividing the genetic material between the daughter cells. Although mitosis is a continuous process, scientists divide the events of mitosis into four phases.

1 **Chromosomes form.** During prophase, the DNA in the nucleus of a cell condenses and becomes visible under a light microscope. Each chromosome consists of two identical chromatids held together by a centromere. The membrane around the nucleus disappears.

2 **Chromosomes line up.** The chromosomes line up in the middle of the cell. This stage is called metaphase.

3 **Chromosomes separate.** During the stage called anaphase, the chromatids split, resulting in two separate identical chromosomes. These chromosomes are pulled to opposite sides of the cell.

4 **Nuclei form.** A new nuclear membrane forms around each group of chromosomes during telophase. The chromosomes return to their threadlike form.

Mitosis is finished, and the cell's genetic material has been divided. Following telophase the parent cell's cytoplasm is divided to complete the parent cell's division into two entirely separate daughter cells.

Cell Division

Before mitosis, the cell's DNA is copied during interphase.

Interphase

The cell has grown and is ready to divide.

The nucleus contains two complete copies of DNA.

Mitosis produces two new cells with identical copies of DNA.

Chromosome

chromatids

centromere

1 Chromosomes condense.
Prophase

The nuclear membrane disappears.

Long strands of DNA condense to distinct chromosomes, each with two chromatids that are exact copies of each other.

2 Chromosomes line up.
Metaphase

Chromosomes line up in the middle of the cell.

3 Chromosomes separate.
Anaphase

Chromatids of each chromosome split into two separate chromosomes.

Separated chromosomes pull to the opposite ends of the cell.

4 Nuclei form.
Telophase, Cytokinesis

New nuclear membranes form.

Cell pinches and divides

Division of the Cytoplasm

READING TiP

As you read about cytokinesis refer to the images of plant and animal cells on page 85.

Cytokinesis, or the division of the parent cell's cytoplasm, immediately follows mitosis in eukaryotic cells. Cytokinesis differs slightly in animal cells and plant cells.

During cytokinesis in an animal cell, a fiber ring forms in the center of the dividing cell. The fiber ring contracts, pulling the cell membrane inward. Eventually, the cell is pinched into two daughter cells.

In a plant cell, the cell wall prevents the cell membrane from being pulled inward. A structure called a cell plate grows between the two new nuclei. The cell plate develops into a membrane and eventually becomes part of the cell wall of each of the new cells.

CHECK YOUR READING How does cytokinesis differ in plant cells and animal cells?

INVESTIGATE Cell Division

How can you model mitosis?

PROCEDURE

1. Divide the poster board into six spaces, and draw arrows from one space to the next to indicate a cycle. Label the spaces, in order, "Interphase," "Prophase," "Metaphase," "Anaphase," "Telophase," and "Cytokinesis."

2. In each space, make a model of a cell and its DNA in the indicated phase. Make sure you represent the cell membrane, the nuclear membrane—when it is present—and the DNA.

WHAT DO YOU THINK?

- In which phases is the nuclear membrane present?
- In which phases are the chromosomes condensed?
- What do the arrows in your model show?

CHALLENGE How do you think cell division would differ in prokaryotic cells? Do you think cell division in prokaryotic cells would be more or less complex than in eukaryotic cells? Make drawings to show how you think a prokaryotic cell might divide.

SKILL FOCUS
Making models

MATERIALS
- poster board
- markers
- pipe cleaners
- packing peanuts
- glue
- scissors
- yarn

TIME
30 minutes

Cytokinesis

Cytokinesis happens in both plant and animal cells.

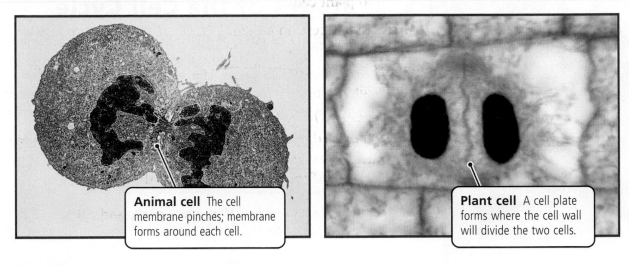

Animal cell The cell membrane pinches; membrane forms around each cell.

Plant cell A cell plate forms where the cell wall will divide the two cells.

READING VISUALS COMPARE AND CONTRAST How does the process of cytokinesis in the animal cell on the left differ from that of the plant cell on the right?

The two daughter cells are now completely separated. Each is surrounded by a cell membrane. Each daughter cell has some of its parent cell's cytoplasm. Though daughter cells are genetically identical to their parent cell, they are smaller. After division, cells may enter a period of growth, during which they take in the resources they need to increase the amount of their cytoplasm and to grow to full size. When cells are fully grown, they are about the same size as the parent cell was before division.

CHECK YOUR READING What happens to cells after cytokinesis?

3.2 Review

KEY CONCEPTS

1. What are the two main parts of the cell cycle?

2. Describe the state of a cell about to start mitosis.

3. How is the genetic material in two daughter cells similar to the genetic material in a parent cell?

CRITICAL THINKING

4. **Sequence** Describe in order the steps that occur during mitosis.

5. **Compare and Contrast** How is cytokinesis in plant cells similar to cytokinesis in animal cells? How is it different?

⬥ CHALLENGE

6. **Infer** You know that mitosis does not happen in prokaryotes. Do you think cytokinesis happens in prokaryotes? Explain your answer.

CHAPTER INVESTIGATION

MATERIALS
• prepared slides of onion root tip cells
• light microscope

Stages of the Cell Cycle

OVERVIEW AND PURPOSE In this activity you will observe cells from an onion root tip that are undergoing mitosis. You will identify and draw cells in different stages of mitosis and the cell cycle. Then you will count the number of cells in each stage. Remember to record this information in your **Science Notebook.**

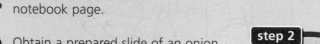
▶ Procedure

1 Make a data table like the one shown on the sample notebook page.

2 Obtain a prepared slide of an onion root tip. Place the slide on the microscope stage. Using the low-power objective, adjust the focus until the root tip is clear.

step 2

3 Move the slide until you are looking at the region just above the root tip. The cells in this area were in the process of mitosis when the slide was made.

4 Look at the boxlike cells arranged in rows. The DNA in these cells has been stained to make it more visible. Select a cell in interphase. Switch to high power and sketch this cell in your notebook.

step 4

5 Repeat step 3 for cells in the various stages of mitosis: prophase, metaphase, anaphase, and telophase. Refer to the diagram on page 83 to identify cells in each stage.

 6 Arrange your sketches to represent the order of the process of mitosis.

7 Under low-power magnification, choose 25 cells at random. Decide which stage of the cell cycle each cell is in. Record the number of cells in each stage in your data table.

▶ Observe and Analyze

1. **OBSERVE** Look at your sketches of the stages of mitosis. Describe the events in each stage.

2. **ANALYZING DATA** Was there any one stage of the cell cycle that was occurring in the majority of cells you observed? If so, which was it?

▶ Conclude

1. **INFER** What might the differences in the number of cells in each stage of the cell cycle mean?

2. **IDENTIFY LIMITS** Were there any cells that were difficult to classify as being in one particular phase of the cell cycle? What do these cells suggest to you about the process of mitosis?

3. **APPLY** Where does new root growth take place? Explain your answer.

▶ INVESTIGATE Further

CHALLENGE From your data table, calculate the percent of cells in each stage of the cell cycle. Use those numbers to predict how much time a cell spends in each stage. You can base your calculation on a total cell cycle of 24 hours.

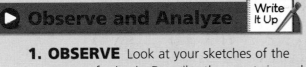

Stages of the Cell Cycle

Table 1. Number of Cells in Each Stage of the Cell Cycle

Stage	Number of Cells Observed
Interphase	
Prophase	
Metaphase	
Anaphase	
Telophase	

Both sexual and asexual reproduction involve cell division.

◀ **BEFORE, you learned**

- Cells go through a cycle of growth and division
- Mitosis produces two genetically identical cells

▶ **NOW, you will learn**

- About cell division and asexual reproduction
- How sexual reproduction and asexual reproduction compare

VOCABULARY

asexual reproduction p. 88
binary fission p. 89
regeneration p. 90

> **THINK ABOUT**
>
> ## How does cell division affect single-celled organisms?
>
>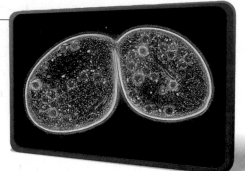
>
> In multicellular organisms, cell division functions in growth, repair, and development. But in unicellular organisms, each cell is itself an organism. Unicellular organisms, like this paramecium, also undergo cell division. What are some possible results of cell division in unicellular organisms? How might they compare with the results of cell division in multicellular organisms?

COMBINATION NOTES
Begin taking notes on the main idea: *Asexual reproduction involves one parent.* Be sure to include sketches of each method of reproducing.

Asexual reproduction involves one parent.

Mitosis and cytokinesis are the processes by which eukaryotic cells divide. In multicellular organisms, the daughter cells that result are separate cells but do not live independent lives. For example, new skin cells are part of skin tissue and cannot live independently. In multicellular organisms, mitosis and cytokinesis are not considered methods by which an organism reproduces.

Most unicellular organisms, and a few multicellular organisms, use cell division to reproduce, in a process called asexual reproduction. In **asexual reproduction,** one organism produces one or more new organisms that are identical to itself and that live independently of it. The organism that produces the new organism or organisms is the parent. Each new organism is an offspring. The offspring produced by asexual reproduction are genetically identical to the parent.

Cell Division in Unicellular Organisms

Cell division and reproduction are the same thing in all single-celled organisms. However, the process of cell division in prokaryotes and in single-celled eukaryotes differs.

Binary fission is the form of asexual reproduction occurring in prokaryotes. Binary fission occurs when the parent organism splits in two, producing two completely independent daughter cells. Genetically, the daughter cells are exactly like the parent cell. Since all prokaryotic organisms are single-celled, cell division and reproduction by binary fission are the same process for them.

In single-celled eukaryotic organisms, however, reproduction by cell division involves mitosis and cytokinesis. The unicellular organism undergoes mitosis, duplicating and separating its chromosomes. Then its cytoplasm is divided through cytokinesis. The result is two separate, independent, and genetically identical offspring. Examples of single-celled eukaryotic organisms that reproduce by cell division include algae, some yeasts, and protozoans, such as paramecium.

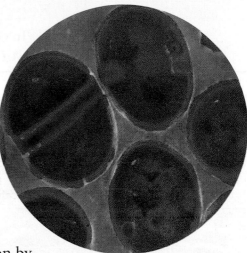

Binary fission results in two nearly equal, independent cells, as shown in these bacteria.

Budding

Both unicellular and multicellular organisms can reproduce by budding. Budding is a process in which an organism develops tiny buds on its body. Each bud forms from the parent's cells, so the bud's genetic material is the same as the parent's. The bud grows until it forms a complete or nearly complete new organism that is genetically identical to the parent.

In some budding organisms, buds can form from any part of the body. In other organisms, buds can be produced only by specialized cells in particular parts of the body. A new organism produced by budding may remain attached to its parent. Most often, when a bud reaches a certain size, it breaks free of the parent and becomes a separate, independent organism.

Some yeast and single-celled organisms reproduce asexually by budding. But budding is most notable in multicellular organisms. Hydras are freshwater animals that are famous for reproducing by budding. Among plants, the kalanchoe (KAL-uhn-KOH-ee) produces tiny buds from the tips of its leaves. Each kalanchoe bud that lands on a suitable growing surface will develop into a mature kalanchoe plant that is genetically identical to the parent plant.

Budding Hydras reproduce by pinching off small buds.

CHECK YOUR READING How is budding different in unicellular and multicellular organisms?

Regeneration

In certain multicellular organisms, specialized cells at the site of a wound or lost limb are able to become different types of tissues. The process of new tissue growth at these sites is called **regeneration.** Although one function of regeneration is the regrowth of damaged or missing body parts, in some organisms asexual reproduction is another function of regeneration.

Regeneration
This starfish is regenerating its legs that were lost.

Regeneration can be observed in many animals called starfish. If a starfish is cut in half, each half can regenerate its missing body parts from its own cells. The result is two complete, independent, and genetically identical starfish. Sometimes a starfish will drop off one of its limbs. The animal will eventually form a new limb. In these cases, regeneration is considered a form of asexual reproduction.

The growth of plants from cuttings is also a kind of asexual reproduction through regeneration. Cells near a cut made in a plant's stem begin to produce the missing part of the plant. Once the missing part is grown, the cutting can be planted in soil. The cutting will grow into a new, independent plant that is genetically identical to the plant from which the cutting was taken.

CHECK YOUR READING Describe the process of regeneration in starfish.

Asexual Reproduction and Health

RESOURCE CENTER
CLASSZONE.COM

Learn more about asexual reproduction.

You have probably had the following experience. In the morning you feel fine. By afternoon, you have a strange feeling that something is not quite right, but you are well enough to function normally. You may even continue to feel well at dinner, and you eat heartily. Then, later that evening, it hits you. You're sick. That tickle in your throat has become a sore throat requiring a visit to the doctor and antibiotics. How did you get so sick so fast?

You could have picked up bacteria in school that morning. Perhaps another student coughed, spreading the bacteria that cause strep throat. A population of bacteria, like populations of other organisms that reproduce asexually through binary fission, increases in number geometrically. Two cells become 4, which become 8, which become 16, and so on.

The reason you get sick so fast is that for many bacteria the generation time is very short. Generation time is the time it takes for one generation to produce offspring—the next generation. In fact, some types of bacteria can produce a new generation of cells in less than 30 minutes. In about an hour the number of bacteria can increase to four times the starting number.

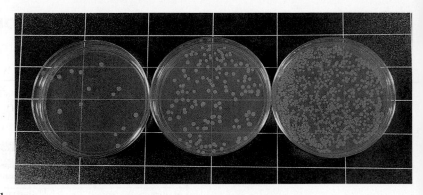

Asexual reproduction
These bacteria are quickly multiplying through asexual reproduction.

Although all offspring are genetically identical, the rare genetic random change does occasionally occur during cell division. The rapid reproduction rate makes it more likely that some offspring will have a random genetic change, which may be beneficial.

INVESTIGATE Asexual Reproduction

Which parts of plants can reproduce?

Some organisms can regenerate offspring from any part of their body. Others can regenerate offspring from only one specialized body part. In this activity, you will discover if a houseplant regenerates from various parts.

PROCEDURE

1. Obtain a plant part (leaf, stem, stem with leaf, or root) from your teacher. Also get one flowerpot filled with potting soil.

2. Dip the plant part in water and set it into the soil, about 1 in. deep, but make sure that most of the plant part is above the level of the soil. Water the soil lightly.

3. Place all the class's pots on the same window sill. Observe your plant part every day for two to three weeks. Record your observations.

WHAT DO YOU THINK?

- Which plant parts, if any, were able to regenerate a new plant?
- What can you conclude about the ability of different plant parts to grow into new plants?

CHALLENGE How does the plant in the experiment compare with the kalanchoe plant you read about in the text? What accounts for plants' different abilities to produce viable offspring?

SKILL FOCUS
Drawing conclusions

MATERIALS
- houseplant
- flowerpot
- soil
- water

TIME
15 minutes

Sexual reproduction involves two parent organisms.

Reproduction of multicellular organisms often involves sexual reproduction as well as asexual cell division. The table shows some differences between asexual and sexual reproduction.

Comparing Asexual and Sexual Reproduction

Asexual Reproduction	Sexual Reproduction
Cell Division	Cell division and other processes
One parent organism	Two parent organisms
Rate of reproduction is rapid	Rate of reproduction is slower than rate for asexual reproduction
Offspring identical to parent	Offspring have genetic information from two parents

If you grow a plant from a cutting, the new plant will be identical to the parent. However, plants that grow from seeds contain genetic material from two parents. Plants growing from seeds and animals growing from eggs are examples of organisms that reproduce through sexual reproduction.

Cell division is part of both sexual and asexual reproduction. The process of mitosis produces cells identical to the parent cells. The diversity of life on Earth is in part possible because of the combining of genetic materials from two parents in sexual reproduction. In the next chapter, you will read about cell processes involved in sexual reproduction.

CHECK YOUR READING List two major differences between asexual and sexual reproduction.

3.3 Review

KEY CONCEPTS

1. How does binary fission relate to cell division?
2. What is a bud, and where does it form on an organism that reproduces asexually?
3. Compare sexual and asexual reproduction.

CRITICAL THINKING

4. **Predict** Do you think prokaryotes undergo regeneration? Why or why not?
5. **Compare and Contrast** How is binary fission in prokaryotic organisms similar to and different from mitosis and cytokinesis in single-celled eukaryotic organisms?

CHALLENGE

6. **Synthesize** Some bacteria can exchange pieces of genetic material with one another through a process called conjugation. What effect might this exchange have on the offspring of the bacteria that underwent conjugation?

MATH in SCIENCE

MATH TUTORIAL
CLASSZONE.COM

Click on Math Tutorial for more help with exponents.

SKILL: USING EXPONENTS

Divide and Multiply

Each time a parent cell divides, the result is two new cells. The new cells are a new generation that in turn divides again. The increase in the number of cells can be shown using exponents. Each cell of each new generation produces two cells. This type of increase in the number of objects is often called exponential growth.

Example

What is the numerical sequence when cells divide to form new cells? You can model this type of progression by using a plain piece of paper.

(1) To represent the first division, fold the piece of paper in half.

(2) Fold it in half again, and it will show the second division. Fold it again and again to represent succeeding divisions.

(3) Write the sequence that shows the number of boxes on the paper after each fold.

2, 4, 8, 16, . . .

(4) Notice that after one division (fold), there are 2 cells (boxes), or 2^1. Two divisions yield $2 \cdot 2$ cells, or 2^2. And after three divisions, there are $2 \cdot 2 \cdot 2$ cells, or 2^3.

ANSWER The sequence can be written with exponents:
$2^1, 2^2, 2^3, 2^4, . . .$

Answer the following questions.

1. Suppose the cells divide for one more generation after the 4 described above. How can this be written as an exponent of 2? How many cells will there be?

2. How many cells would exist in the tenth generation? Write the number using an exponent.

3. Suppose you took the paper in the example and folded it in thirds each time, rather than in half. Make a table showing the number of boxes after each folding. Use numbers with exponents to write the sequence.

4. Write the following number sequence as a sequence of numbers with exponents: 5, 25, 125, 625, . . .

5. Write the following number sequence as a sequence of numbers with NO exponents: $10^1, 10^2, 10^3, 10^4, . . .$

CHALLENGE Before you begin folding, you have a single sheet of paper, or 1 box. The parent cell is also a single unit. Use this information to explain why $2^0 = 3^0$.

the BIG idea

Organisms grow, reproduce, and maintain themselves through cell division.

CONTENT REVIEW
CLASSZONE.COM

◀ KEY CONCEPTS SUMMARY

3.1 Cell division occurs in all organisms.

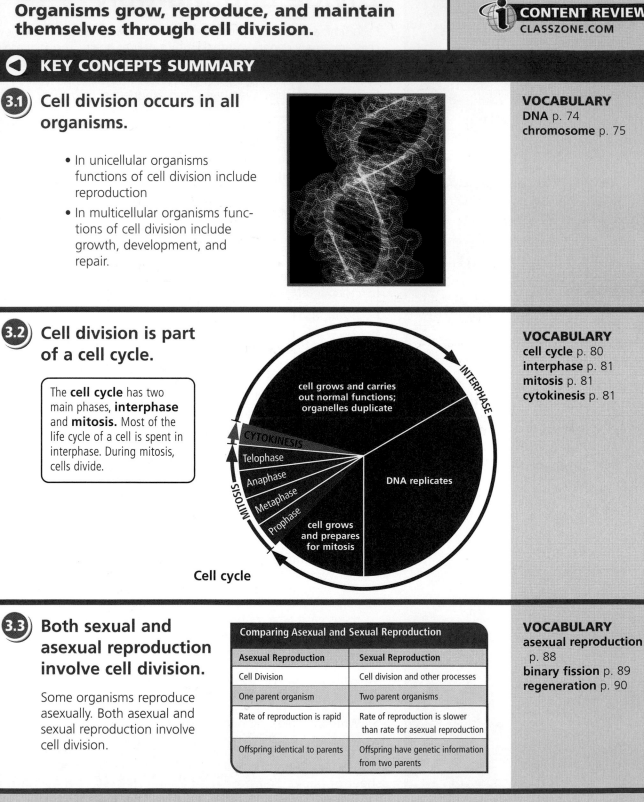

- In unicellular organisms functions of cell division include reproduction
- In multicellular organisms functions of cell division include growth, development, and repair.

VOCABULARY
DNA p. 74
chromosome p. 75

3.2 Cell division is part of a cell cycle.

The **cell cycle** has two main phases, **interphase** and **mitosis.** Most of the life cycle of a cell is spent in interphase. During mitosis, cells divide.

INTERPHASE

cell grows and carries out normal functions; organelles duplicate

DNA replicates

CYTOKINESIS

Telophase

Anaphase

Metaphase

Prophase

MITOSIS

cell grows and prepares for mitosis

Cell cycle

VOCABULARY
cell cycle p. 80
interphase p. 81
mitosis p. 81
cytokinesis p. 81

3.3 Both sexual and asexual reproduction involve cell division.

Some organisms reproduce asexually. Both asexual and sexual reproduction involve cell division.

Comparing Asexual and Sexual Reproduction

Asexual Reproduction	Sexual Reproduction
Cell Division	Cell division and other processes
One parent organism	Two parent organisms
Rate of reproduction is rapid	Rate of reproduction is slower than rate for asexual reproduction
Offspring identical to parents	Offspring have genetic information from two parents

VOCABULARY
asexual reproduction p. 88
binary fission p. 89
regeneration p. 90

Reviewing Vocabulary

On a separate sheet of paper, write a sentence describing the relationship between the two vocabulary words in each pair.

1. cell cycle, interphase

2. mitosis, cytokinesis

3. chromosome, DNA

4. parent, offspring

Reviewing Key Concepts

Multiple Choice *Choose the letter of the best answer.*

5. Most of the growth in your body occurs because your cells
  a. grow larger   **c.** make proteins
  b. take in oxygen   **d.** divide

6. The stage in a cell's life when it is not in the process of dividing is called
  a. interphase   **c.** mitosis
  b. the cell cycle   **d.** cell division

7. What material in the cell makes up chromosomes?
  a. carbohydrates   **c.** the nucleus
  b. chromatids   **d.** nucleic acids

8. What ratio increases when a cell divides into two smaller cells?
  a. volume to length
  b. length to width
  c. surface area to volume
  d. width to surface area

9. The process of cytokinesis results in
  a. two daughter cells that are different from one another
  b. two genetically identical daughter cells
  c. identical pairs of chromosomes
  d. identical pairs of chromatids

10. What is the step that follows mitosis, in which the cytoplasm divides?
  a. prophase   **c.** anaphase
  b. synthesis   **d.** cytokinesis

11. A cell's chromosomes must be duplicated before mitosis occurs so that
  a. they can form chromatids
  b. they can attach to the spindle
  c. each daughter cell gets a full number of chromosomes
  d. each daughter cell does not have to duplicate its own chromosomes

12. Binary fission differs from mitosis because the new cells
  a. cannot function without the parent
  b. grow from missing limbs
  c. have half the normal number of chromosomes
  d. live independently of the parent cell

13. If a starfish is cut in half, it can regrow its missing body through
  a. binary fission   **c.** healing
  b. budding   **d.** regeneration

14. Which is an example of reproduction?
  a. binary fission in unicellular organisms
  b. cell division in a multicellular organism
  c. cell division around a broken bone
  d. division of cytoplasm

15. Which sequence is correct for mitosis?
  a. chromosomes form, chromosomes separate, chromosomes line up, nuclei form
  b. chromosomes form, chromosomes line up, chromosomes separate, nuclei form
  c. chromosomes line up, nuclei form, chromosomes separate, chromosomes form
  d. chromosomes separate, chromosomes form, nuclei form, chromosomes line up

Short Answer *Write a short answer to each question.*

16. What is the difference between cytokinesis in plant and animal cells?

17. Describe what happens in a cell during interphase. Your answer should mention DNA.

18. Describe the functions of cell division in both unicellular and multicellular organisms.

19. IDENTIFY CAUSE Describe some of the reasons that cells divide.

This illustration shows a plant and the cutting that was taken from it, which is growing in a container of water. Use the illustration to answer the next six questions.

20. OBSERVE From which part of the plant was the cutting taken?

21. INFER Where did the cutting get the genetic information that controls its development?

22. INFER What is the genetic relationship between the original plant and the cutting?

23. SYNTHESIZE What process causes both the cutting and the original plant to grow?

24. SUMMARIZE Write a brief summary of the process that causes growth in both plants.

25. PREDICT These plants can also reproduce from fertilized seeds. How is the cutting the same as the plant that would grow from a seed? How is the cutting different?

26. CALCULATE A single bacterium enters your body at 10:00 A.M. These bacteria reproduce at a rate of one generation every 30 minutes. How many bacteria of this type will be in your body by 8:00 P.M. that evening?

The diagrams below show 4 parts of a process. Use them to answer the following three questions.

a. c.

b. d.

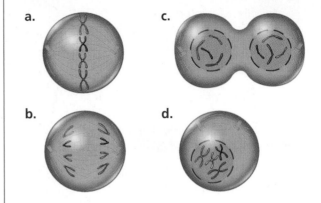

27. SEQUENCE What is the correct order of the four diagrams above?

28. SYNTHESIZE Draw two diagrams, one showing what you would see before the process shown above begins, and one showing what you would see after the conclusion of the process.

29. MODEL On a separate sheet of paper, draw your own simple model of the process of mitosis.

the BIG idea

30. SUMMARIZE Look again at the question on the photograph on pages 70–71. Now that you have studied this chapter, how would you change your answer to the question?

31. SYNTHESIZE How do the concepts in this chapter relate to the concepts in the cell theory?

UNIT PROJECTS

If you need to do an experiment for your unit project, gather the materials. Be sure to allow enough time to observe results before the project is due.

Analyzing Data

This diagram shows the length of the cell cycle for a typical skin cell in the human body.

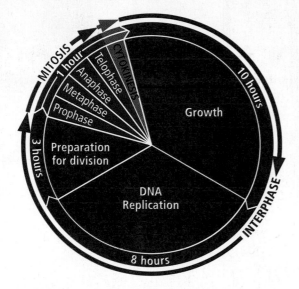

Use the diagram to answer the questions below.

1. How long does the growth phase of the cell cycle take?

a. 1 hour   **c.** 8 hours
b. 3 hours   **d.** 10 hours

2. How much time does the cell cycle spend in interphase?

a. 1 hour   **c.** 21 hours
b. 10 hours   **d.** 22 hours

3. What is the total length of time it takes for the skin cell to complete one full cell cycle?

a. 10 hours   **c.** 21 hours
b. 18 hours   **d.** 22 hours

4. What phase of the cell cycle takes about 8 hours?

a. DNA replication
b. mitosis
c. growth
d. preparation for cell division

5. Suppose another type of skin cell takes 44 hours to complete one cell cycle. If all of the phases are proportional to the length of time shown in the diagram, how long will the preparation for cell division phase last?

a. 3 hours   **c.** 10 hours
b. 6 hours   **d.** 20 hours

6. According to the diagram, what is the second stage in mitosis?

a. prophase   **c.** telophase
b. metaphase   **d.** cytokinesis

Extended Response

Answer the two questions. Include some of the terms shown in the word box. Underline each term you use in your answers.

cell cycle	metaphase	mitosis
anaphase	prophase	telophase

7. A scientist is studying the stages of cell division in the cells of an onion root. The scientist counts 100 cells and identifies which stage of cell division each cell is in at a given moment. He counts a total of 85 cells in interphase, 8 cells in prophase, 3 cells in metaphase, and 2 cells each in anaphase and telophase. A typical onion cell takes about 12 hours to complete the cell cycle. Using the information in the diagram and the data given here, how can you account for these numbers?

8. Your science class is investigating the effect of temperature on the rate of mitosis in onion plants. You hypothesize that the higher the temperature, the faster cells undergo mitosis. How could you set up an experiment to support your hypothesis? Describe the materials you would use and the steps you would take in your procedure.

Patterns of Heredity

In sexual reproduction, genes are passed from parents to offspring in predictable patterns.

Key Concepts

SECTION

4.1 Living things inherit traits in patterns.
Learn about traits and how living things inherit traits from their parents.

SECTION

4.2 Patterns of heredity can be predicted.
Learn how math can be used to predict patterns of heredity.

SECTION

4.3 Meiosis is a special form of cell division.
Learn about the process of meiosis.

Internet Preview

CLASSZONE.COM

Chapter 4 online resources: Content Review, two Simulations, two Resource Centers, Math Tutorial, Test Practice

> *What similarities can you see between this mother wolf and her two offspring?*

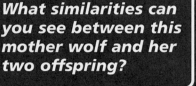

How Are Traits Distributed?

Ask 10 people you know if they are left-handed or right-handed, if they have dimples, and if they can roll their tongue. For each trait, write down how many people have that trait.

Observe and Think Were any of the traits evenly distributed? Why do you think that is?

Combinations

Take one bag with 4 blue slips of paper and one bag with 4 red slips of paper. Consider different ways to mix or combine the materials in the bags.

Observe and Think How many ways could you think of mixing the materials? How were the combinations similar and different?

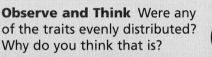

Internet Activity: Mendel's Experiment

Go to **ClassZone.com** to try a virtual version of Mendel's experiments with peas. Learn about heredity as you breed plants with different traits.

Observe and Think What does Mendel's experiment teach us about heredity?

NSTA
scilinks.org
SCiLINKS

Heredity Code: MDL034

Getting Ready to Learn

CONCEPT REVIEW

- Life comes from life.
- Mitosis produces identical cells.
- Some organisms reproduce with asexual reproduction.

VOCABULARY REVIEW

chromosome p. 75

mitosis p. 81

asexual reproduction p. 88

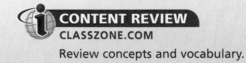

CONTENT REVIEW
CLASSZONE.COM
Review concepts and vocabulary.

TAKING NOTES

CHOOSE YOUR OWN STRATEGY

Take notes using one or more of the strategies from earlier chapters—**main idea webs, combination notes,** or **mind maps.** Feel free to mix and match the strategies, or use an entirely different note-taking strategy.

VOCABULARY STRATEGY

Think about a vocabulary term as a **magnet word** diagram. Write the other terms or ideas related to that term around it.

See the Note-Taking Handbook on pages R45–R51.

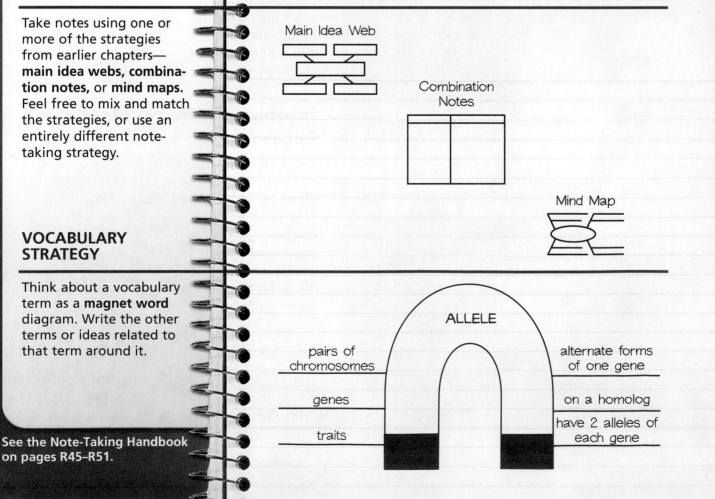

SCIENCE NOTEBOOK

Main Idea Web

Combination Notes

Mind Map

ALLELE

pairs of chromosomes

genes

traits

alternate forms of one gene

on a homolog

have 2 alleles of each gene

4.1

Living things inherit traits in patterns.

> ## BEFORE, you learned
>
> - Life comes from life
> - Cells contain chromosomes
> - Some organisms reproduce with asexual reproduction

> ## NOW, you will learn
>
> - How genes for traits are passed from parent to offspring
> - About discoveries made by Gregor Mendel
> - About dominant and recessive alleles

VOCABULARY

sexual reproduction p. 102
gene p. 102
heredity p. 102
allele p. 103
phenotype p. 106
genotype p. 106
dominant p. 107
recessive p. 107

THINK ABOUT

What characteristics might be inherited?

Make a list of characteristics you can observe about the girl in the photograph to the right. Perhaps your list includes the fact that she has pale skin, or that she can read. Some of these characteristics are qualities or abilities learned or acquired from the environment around her. However, some of the characteristics were probably inherited from her parents. Of the characteristics on your list, which do you think were inherited and which do you think were acquired?

NOTETAKING STRATEGY
Take notes on the idea that parents and off-spring are similar by using a strategy from an earlier chapter or one of your own.

Parents and offspring are similar.

You are an individual who has a unique combination of characteristics. These characteristics are also known as traits. Many of your traits may resemble those your parents have, including your hair color, eye color, and blood type. These characteristics are called inherited traits.

Some traits are acquired, not inherited. An acquired trait is developed during your life. Learned behaviors are one type of acquired trait. For example, your ability to read and write is an acquired trait—a skill you learned. You were not born knowing how to ride a bike, and if you have children, they will not be born knowing how to do it either. They will have to learn the skill just as you did.

A

Some acquired traits are not learned but result from interaction with the environment. Skin color, for example, has both an inherited component and an environmental one. The skin color of many light-skinned people darkens when they are exposed to the Sun.

 CHECK YOUR READING How are inherited traits and acquired traits different? Give one example of each.

RESOURCE CENTER
CLASSZONE.COM

Find out more about sexual reproduction.

In this chapter, you will learn about inheritance that happens through sexual reproduction. During **sexual reproduction** a cell containing genetic information from the mother and a cell containing genetic information from the father combine into a completely new cell, which becomes the offspring. You will learn more about the mechanics of sexual reproduction in Section 4.3.

Genes are on chromosome pairs.

Inherited traits are controlled by the structures, materials, and processes you learned about in Chapters 1 and 2. In turn, these structures, materials, and processes are coded for by genes. A **gene** is a unit of heredity that occupies a specific location on a chromosome and codes for a particular product. **Heredity** is the passing of genes from parents to offspring.

Individuals inherit their genes from their parents. The genes code for the expression of traits. It is important to understand that an organism does not inherit the traits themselves from its parents. It inherits the genes that code for the traits it has. Most traits are not coded for by just one gene. Some characteristics are affected by many genes in complicated ways. We have much to learn about which genes might affect which characteristics.

In most eukaryotes, cells contain pairs of chromosomes, with one chromosome of each pair coming from each of two parents. The chromosomes in a pair are called homologs. They resemble each other, having the same size and shape, and carrying genetic information for particular traits.

On each homolog are sites where specific genes are located. Let us say, for example, that the gene that determines

Chromosomes and Genes

The letters on the pair of chromosomes below represent alleles.

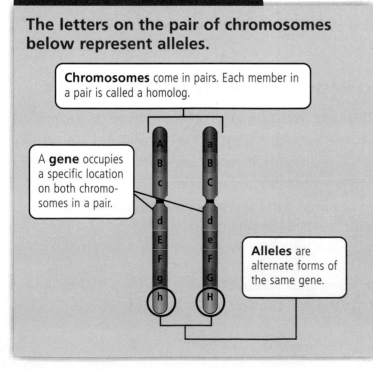

Chromosomes come in pairs. Each member in a pair is called a homolog.

A **gene** occupies a specific location on both chromosomes in a pair.

Alleles are alternate forms of the same gene.

whether or not a plant is tall is located at place A on a pair of homologs. Though both homologs have the gene for height at site A, the genes may not be identical. They may be variations instead. The various forms of the same gene are called **alleles** (uh-LEELZ).

Thus, the homolog from one parent might have an allele for regular height at site A, while the gene from the other parent might have an allele for short height at site A. The alleles on a pair of homologs may or may not be different. Though any one plant can have only two alleles of a gene, there can be many alleles for a particular gene within a population.

CHECK YOUR READING What are alleles?

READING TiP
The word *homolog* comes from the Greek words *homos,* which means "same," and *logos,* which means "proportion."

Each species has a characteristic number of chromosomes. Chimpanzees have 24 pairs of chromosomes, for a total of 48 chromosomes. Fruit flies have 4 pairs of chromosomes, or 8 in all. Humans have 23 pairs, for a total of 46 chromosomes. Scientists refer to chromosomes by their number. Human chromosomes are numbered 1 through 22; the 23rd pair are the sex chromosomes.

In humans, the sex chromosomes are called the X-chromosome and the Y-chromosome. A human female has two X-chromosomes, while a human male has one X-chromosome and one Y-chromosome. In addition to determining the sex of an offspring, the X- and Y-chromosomes contain important genes, just as the other, numbered chromosomes do.

Human Chromosomes

Humans have 23 pairs of chromosomes, for a total of 46. One of these pairs, shown below, determines the sex of the offspring.

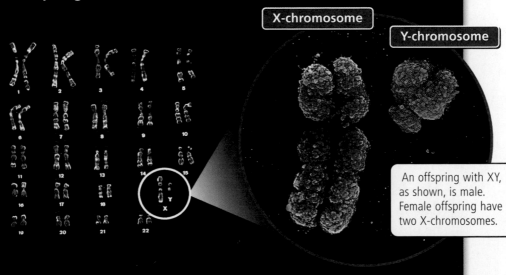

X-chromosome

Y-chromosome

An offspring with XY, as shown, is male. Female offspring have two X-chromosomes.

Gregor Mendel made some important discoveries about heredity.

The first major experiments investigating heredity were performed by a monk named Gregor Mendel, who lived in Austria during the mid-1800s. Before Mendel became a monk, he attended university and received training in science and mathematics. This training served him well when he began investigating the inheritance of traits among the pea plants in the monastery's garden.

Mendel took very detailed notes, carefully recording all the data from his many experiments. He worked with seven different traits: plant height, flower and pod position, seed shape, seed color, pod shape, pod color, and flower color. He studied each trait separately, always starting with plants that were true-breeding for that one particular trait. A true-breeding plant is one that will always produce offspring with a particular trait when allowed to self-pollinate.

READING TiP

The root of the word *trait* means to "draw out." It was originally used in the sense of drawing out a line. This same idea works in heredity if you think of drawing a connection between parents and offspring.

One Example

In his experiments with plant height, Mendel took two sets of plants, one true-breeding for plants of regular height and the other true-breeding for plants of short or dwarf height.

❶ Instead of letting the plants self-pollinate as they do naturally, he deliberately paired as parents one plant from each set. Mendel called the plants that resulted from this cross the first generation. All of the plants from this first generation were of regular height. The dwarf-height trait seemed to have disappeared entirely.

❷ Mendel then let the first-generation plants self-pollinate. He called the offspring that resulted from this self-pollination the second generation. About three fourths of the second-generation plants were of regular height, but about one fourth were of dwarf height. So the trait that seemed to disappear in the first generation reappeared in the second generation.

Mendel's experiments with other traits showed similar patterns.

 CHECK YOUR READING Summarize the pattern shown in Mendel's experiments with plant height.

Mendel's Conclusions

Mendel drew upon his knowledge of mathematics while analyzing his data in order to suggest a hypothesis that would explain the patterns he observed. Mendel realized that each plant must have two "factors" for each possible trait, one factor from each parent. Some traits, such as dwarf height, could be masked—dwarf height could be seen in the

Mendel's Pea Plants

Mendel observed variation in the height of pea plants (regular or dwarf height). By crossing plants with specific traits, he deduced that offspring get factors for each trait from both parents.

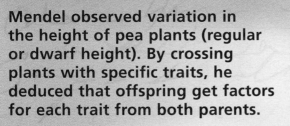

Parent Plants

X

regular   dwarf

1 First generation Crossing a true-breeding regular pea plant with a true-breeding dwarf pea plant produces all regular pea plants in the first generation.

regular   regular   regular   regular

X

2 Second generation Allowing the first generation pea plants to self-pollinate resulted in about three-fourths regular pea plants and one-fourth dwarf pea plants.

regular   regular   regular   dwarf

plant only if both of the plant's factors were for dwarf height. All of the plants in the first generation had one dwarf factor and one regular factor. A plant with one dwarf-height factor and one regular-height factor would be of regular height, because the regular-height factor masks the dwarf-height factor.

Later experiments allowed Mendel to draw a number of other conclusions about how these factors are distributed. Since the mid-1800s, Mendel's experiments and conclusions have been the basis for most of the scientific thought about heredity. Those things he called "factors" are what we now call genes and alleles.

CHECK YOUR READING How many factors or genes does each plant have for each possible trait?

Alleles interact to produce traits.

The pea-plant traits Gregor Mendel chose to study were all controlled by single genes, and each of the genes was on a different chromosome. As you learned earlier, most traits are not controlled by only one gene. However, simple examples such as Mendel's peas do help us better understand heredity.

Phenotype and Genotype

What color eyes do you have? The eye color you see when you look in the mirror is your phenotype. An organism's **phenotype** describes the actual characteristics that can be observed. Your height, the size of your feet, the presence or absence of a fold in your eyelids—all are observable traits and are part of your phenotype.

By contrast, the genes that control the development of eyefolds are part of your genotype. **Genotype** is the name for the genes an organism has. Your genotype is not always obvious from your phenotype. If you have eyefolds, your genotype definitely contains at least one eyefold-producing allele. But it may also have one allele for no eyefolds. Sometimes your genes contain information that is not expressed in your phenotype.

CHECK YOUR READING Which term describes characteristics that can be observed?

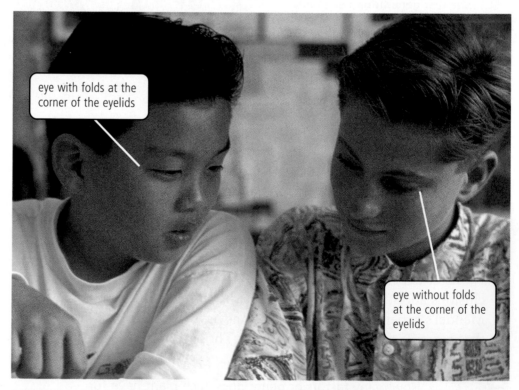

eye with folds at the corner of the eyelids

eye without folds at the corner of the eyelids

COMPARE The photograph above shows **phenotypes** of the eyefold gene. A person with eyefolds is shown to the left, a person without eyefolds to the right.

Dominant and Recessive Alleles

The eyefold gene, which controls the development of folds in the eyelids, has two alleles: eyefolds and no-eyefolds. If you have even one copy of the allele for eyefolds, you will have eyefolds. This happens because the allele that codes for eyefolds is dominant. A **dominant** allele is one that is expressed in the phenotype even if only one copy is present in the genotype—that is, even if the other allele is an alternative form.

Suppose your genotype contains a no-eyefolds allele. The no-eyefolds allele is recessive. A **recessive** allele is one that is expressed in the phenotype only when two copies of it are present on the homologs. If one chromosome in the pair contains a dominant allele and the other contains a recessive allele, the dominant allele will be expressed in your phenotype. If you do not have eyefolds, it is because you got two no-eyefolds genes—one from each parent.

CHECK YOUR READING — Under what conditions is a recessive allele expressed in an offspring's phenotype?

The interaction of dominant and recessive alleles means that it is possible for two brown-haired parents to have a blond child.

Hair color is determined by multiple genes, can be affected by the environment, and sometimes changes over time. However, in some cases it has a dominant-recessive pattern similar to that of the eyefold gene. As in the family shown at right, parents who both have brown hair can have a blond child. The allele for brown hair is dominant, so if both parents have alleles for both brown hair and blond hair, the brown-hair allele is more likely to be expressed. Their child, however, could have two blond-hair alleles (one from each parent) and therefore have blond hair instead of brown.

4.1 Review

KEY CONCEPTS

1. Explain the difference between acquired and inherited traits.

2. Describe the conclusions that Mendel drew from his experiments with pea plants.

3. What type of alleles are expressed only if two identical copies exist on the homologs of the offspring?

CRITICAL THINKING

4. **Compare and Contrast** What is the difference between a genotype and a phenotype?

5. **Analyze** Explain why a person with an allele for a particular trait may not have a phenotype that shows the trait.

○ CHALLENGE

6. **Apply** In guinea pigs, the allele for black fur is dominant over the allele for brown fur. If you had two parent guinea pigs, each with brown fur, what color fur might the offspring have, and why?

CHAPTER INVESTIGATION

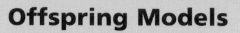

Offspring Models

OVERVIEW AND PURPOSE Sexual reproduction combines genes from two parent organisms and results in diversity among offspring. In this activity, you will
- design a model of an offspring
- determine how the offspring exhibits portions of both genotype and phenotype from its parents

▶ Problem

Write It Up

How are traits passed from parent to offspring?

▶ Procedure

1 Make data tables like those shown on the sample notebook page.

2 Your teacher will supply bags containing alleles written on slips. Capital letters represent dominant alleles, and lower-case letters represent recessive alleles. Each bag will have two alleles for one trait. Six of the bags, one for each of 6 traits, will represent the female parent's alleles. Another set of 6 bags will represent the male parent's alleles. From each bag, choose one allele.

3 In Table 1, record the alleles for both parents, and the allele pairs for the offspring. Then place the slips back into the bags. You will use the alleles to build a model offspring.

4 Use the information in the table below to determine the phenotype of the offspring. Write the phenotype in the fourth column in Table 1.

MATERIALS
- foam balls (body segments)
- colored toothpicks (antennae)
- small paperclips (wings)
- colored pipe cleaners (legs)
- colored pushpins (eyes)

Genotypes and Phenotypes	
BB or Bb = 3 body segments	bb = 2 body segments
WW or Ww = 2 pairs of wings	ww = 1 pair of wings
AA or Aa = green antennae	aa = red antennae
PP or Pp = 3 pairs of legs	pp = 2 pairs of legs
CC or Cc = yellow legs	cc = orange legs
EE or Ee = blue eyes	ee = green eyes

5 Choose the materials you need to assemble the offspring. You can use toothpicks to attach the body segments. Push the pipe cleaners, toothpicks, and wings into the foam balls. **CAUTION:** Take care when handling the pushpins.

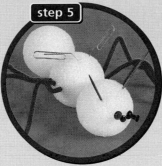

step 5

▶ Observe and Analyze

Write It Up

1. **OBSERVE** Does your offspring look the way you would expect either parent to look? Explain.

2. **ANALYZE** How many different genotypes are possible for each trait? Explain.

▶ Conclude

Write It Up

1. **INFER** What are the possible genotypes of the parents? Fill in Table 2.

2. **INTERPRET** Can you tell how the genotypes of the parents differ from that of the offspring? Explain.

3. **INTERPRET** How does your offspring model illustrate what you have learned about heredity?

4. **IDENTIFY LIMITS** What sources of error might you have experienced?

5. **APPLY** In humans, blue eyes are the phenotype for two recessive alleles. Can parents with blue eyes have a brown-eyed offspring? Explain.

▶ INVESTIGATE Further

CHALLENGE Repeat the procedure, but this time use alleles taken from your model offspring and those of a model offspring made by one of your classmates. Record the genotype and determine the phenotype of this second-generation offspring.

Offspring Models

Table 1. Parent and Offspring Family Traits

	Female Allele	Male Allele	Offspring Genotype	Offspring Phenotype
Body segments				
Pairs of wings				
Antennae color				
Pairs of legs				
Color of legs				
Color of eyes				

Table 2. Possible Parent Genotypes

Trait	Female Parent	Male Parent
Body segments		
Pairs of wings		
Antennae color		
Pairs of legs		
Color of legs		
Color of eyes		

Patterns of heredity can be predicted.

◀ BEFORE, you learned

- Genes are passed from parents to offspring
- Offspring inherit genes in predictable patterns

▶ NOW, you will learn

- How Punnett squares can be used to predict patterns of heredity
- How ratios and probability can be used to predict patterns of heredity

VOCABULARY

Punnett square p. 110
ratio p. 112
probability p. 112
percentage p. 112

EXPLORE Probability

How can probability help predict results?

PROCEDURE

1. Toss both coins 10 times. For each toss, record the combination of heads and/or tails.

2. For each combination (two heads, two tails, or a head and a tail), add up the number of tosses.

MATERIALS

- two coins
- pencil and paper

WHAT DO YOU THINK?

- Which combination happened most often?
- If you tossed both coins one more time, which combination would be the most likely result? Can you know for sure? Why or why not?

Punnett squares show possible outcomes for inheritance.

NOTETAKING STRATEGY
Use a strategy from an earlier chapter or design one of your own to take notes on how Punnett squares show possible patterns of heredity.

Mendel noticed that traits are inherited in patterns. One tool for understanding the patterns of heredity is a graphic called a Punnett square. A **Punnett square** illustrates how the parents' alleles might combine in offspring.

Each parent has two alleles for a particular gene. An offspring receives one allele from each parent. A Punnett square shows how the parents' alleles may be passed on to potential offspring.

The Punnett square on page 111 shows how alleles for pea-plant height would be distributed among offspring in Mendel's first-generation cross. The dominant allele (D) is regular height, and the recessive allele (d) is dwarf height.

The top of the Punnett square shows one parent's alleles for this trait—two dominant regular alleles (DD). The side of the Punnett square shows the other parent's alleles for this trait—two recessive dwarf alleles (dd).

Each box in the Punnett square shows a way the alleles from each parent would combine in potential offspring. You can see that each potential offspring would have the same genotype: one dominant and one recessive allele (Dd). The phenotype of each offspring would show the dominant allele, in this case regular height.

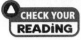
CHECK YOUR READING What is a Punnett square?

Using Punnett Squares

The Punnett square below shows the possible allele combinations for an offspring of one parent with two dominant (D) regular-height alleles and one parent with two recessive (d) dwarf-height alleles.

SIMULATION
CLASSZONE.COM
Predict offspring traits with virtual Punnett squares.

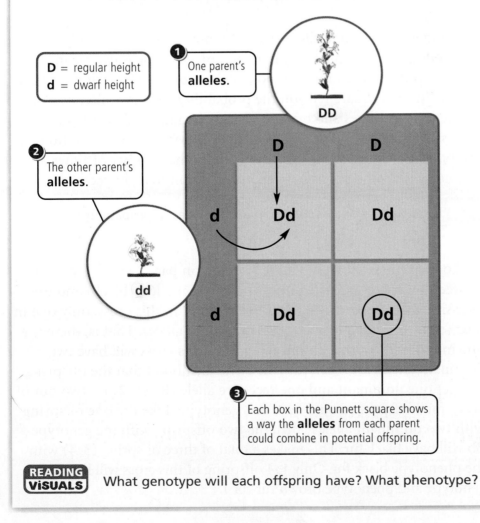

D = regular height
d = dwarf height

1 One parent's **alleles**.

DD

2 The other parent's **alleles**.

dd

	D	D
d	Dd	Dd
d	Dd	Dd

3 Each box in the Punnett square shows a way the **alleles** from each parent could combine in potential offspring.

READING VISUALS What genotype will each offspring have? What phenotype?

Ratios and percentages can express the probability of outcomes.

VOCABULARY
Remember to create a word magnet diagram for the term *ratio*.

The Punnett square on page 111 for the first generation of pea plants shows that all potential offspring will be of regular height, because they all have one dominant allele. You can say that 100 percent of the offspring will be of regular height. Or you could say that the ratio of regular-height offspring to total offspring is four to four. A **ratio** compares, or shows the relationship between, two quantities. A ratio is usually written 4:4 and read as "four to four." This can be interpreted as "four out of four." The Punnett square shows that four out of four offspring will express the dominant gene for regular height.

4:4
ratio of blue squares to total squares

1:4 red
3:4 blue

Punnett squares and the ratios they show express probability. **Probability** is the likelihood, or chance, of a specific outcome in relation to the total number of possible outcomes. The ratios derived from a Punnett square tell you the probability that any one offspring will get certain genes and express a certain trait. Another way of expressing probability is as a percentage. A **percentage** is a ratio that compares a number to 100. That is, it states the number of times a particular outcome might happen out of a hundred chances.

CHECK YOUR READING What are two ways that you can express a probability?

Look at the guinea-pig Punnett square on page 113. This cross is between two parents, each with one dominant allele (black) and one recessive allele (brown) for the trait fur color. In this cross, only one in four (ratio 1:4) offspring gets two dominant alleles. That is, there is a one in four chance that an offspring from this cross will have two dominant alleles for black fur (BB). The likelihood that the offspring will get one dominant and one recessive allele (Bb) is 2:4—two out of every four offspring would have this genotype. Like the one offspring with two dominant alleles (BB), the two offspring with the genotype Bb will have black fur. This makes a total of three offspring (3:4) with the phenotype black fur. Only 1:4 offspring of this cross will have the genotype and phenotype brown fur (bb).

Punnett Square and Probability

The Punnett square below shows the possible ways alleles could combine in the offspring of two parent guinea pigs. Each parent has one dominant allele for black fur (B) and one recessive allele for brown fur (b).

B = black fur
b = brown fur

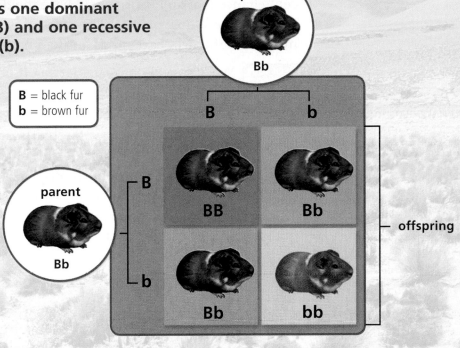

parent
Bb

parent
Bb

B   b

B

| BB | Bb |

b

| Bb | bb |

offspring

The table below shows the probability of the various genotypes and phenotypes from the Punnett square above. Each probability is shown as both a ratio and a percentage.

bb

The genes the guinea pig has are its **genotype.**

Phenotype refers to the guinea pig's actual characteristics.

Genotype	Ratio	Percentage	Phenotype	Ratio	Percentage
BB	1:4	25%	Black fur	3:4	75%
Bb	2:4	50%			
bb	1:4	25%	Brown fur	1:4	25%

READING VISUALS Connect the four shaded sections of the Punnett square to the matching genotypes in the chart.

When one parent has two dominant alleles and the other has two recessive alleles, there is a 100 percent chance that an offspring will have the dominant phenotype. The pea-plant example on page 111 shows this pattern. All the offspring are of regular height. When both parents have one dominant and one recessive allele, there is a 75 percent chance that an offspring will have the dominant phenotype. The guinea-pig example on page 113 shows this pattern. Chances are that more offspring will have black fur than brown fur.

CHECK YOUR READING What is the probability that an offspring from the pea plant cross on page 111 will be of dwarf height?

In humans, females have two X-chromosomes (XX), and males have an X- and a Y-chromosome (XY). The Punnett square on page 115 shows the possible sexes of human offspring. Unlike the guinea-pig Punnett square, this one shows only two possible outcomes, XX and XY. The diagram also shows how to find the percentage chance that a potential offspring will be female.

INVESTIGATE Multiple Probabilities

Do probabilities affect each other?
PROCEDURE

1. Put a square of masking tape on each side of all four coins. On both large coins, write the letter *Y* for yellow peas on one side and the letter *y* on the other, for green peas. On both small coins, write the letter *R* for round peas on one side and the letter *r* on the other, for wrinkled peas.

2. Toss all four coins together 40 times and record the letter combinations of each toss.

3. For each of the three small-coin letter combinations, add up the number of tosses, and calculate the ratio and percentage chance of each. Do the same for the three large-coin letter combinations.

WHAT DO YOU THINK?
- What letter combinations happened most often?
- Do the results of the small-coin letter combinations affect the results of the large-coin letter combinations? How might this observation apply to heredity?

CHALLENGE Design a version of this experiment to model Mendel's first-generation cross. Explain why it would be a boring experiment to perform.

SKILL FOCUS
Analyzing data

MATERIALS
- two large coins
- two small coins
- masking tape
- marker

TIME
30 minutes

Calculating Probability

Two humans, a female (XX) and a male (XY), have an offspring. The Punnett square below can be used to calculate the probability that an offspring will be female or male.

To find the percentage chance of a female offspring, first find the ratio by counting the number of XX offspring out of the four possible outcomes.

2 Two out of 4 (ratio 2:4, or 2/4) offspring will be female.

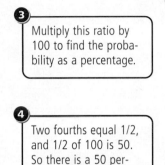
Multiply this ratio by 100 to find the probability as a percentage.

4 Two fourths equal 1/2, and 1/2 of 100 is 50. So there is a 50 percent chance that an offspring will be female.

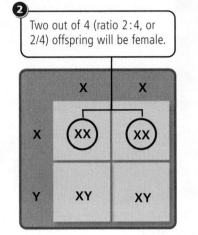

	X	X
X	(XX)	(XX)
Y	XY	XY

READING VISUALS Compare this Punnett square with the pea-plant Punnett square on page 111 and the guinea-pig Punnett square on page 113. How is it similar? How is it different?

It is important to realize that Punnett squares and probability do not guarantee the outcome of a genetic cross. They indicate the probability of different outcomes. While there is a 75 percent chance that an offspring will have black fur according to the Punnett square on page 113, you cannot know with any certainty what color fur a particular offspring will actually have. Actual experimental results may not match predicted outcomes.

CHECK YOUR READING Can a Punnett square tell you the specific outcome of a genetic cross? Why or why not?

4.2 Review

KEY CONCEPTS

1. Explain how Punnett squares predict the outcomes of a genetic cross.

2. How are ratios and percentages related?

3. How can you find a percentage chance from a Punnett square?

CRITICAL THINKING

4. **Predict** Mendel studied the colors of flowers in his experiments with pea plants. Let P stand for purple and p stand for white. Purple is dominant. Make a Punnett square for a cross between two Pp plants. Find the percentage chance for each outcome.

○ CHALLENGE

5. **Apply** In pea plants, the allele for smooth peas is dominant over the allele for wrinkled peas. Create a Punnett square and calculate the probability that two smooth-pea plants will have an offspring with wrinkled peas if each parent has one smooth and one wrinkled allele.

MATH TUTORIAL

Click on Math Tutorial for more help with probability.

SKILL: USING PUNNETT SQUARES

Coat Coloring

The Shetland sheepdog, or Sheltie, has patches of color on its silky coat. A gene controls marbling of the colors, or merling. The merle gene comes in two forms: M for merle, or m for no merle.

A Sheltie with Mm has a merle coat.

A Sheltie with MM is mostly white.

A Sheltie with mm has solid patches, no merling.

Example

One Sheltie parent has a merle coat (Mm), and one has no merling (mm). With these two parents, what is the probability of a puppy with a merle coat?

(1) Make a Punnett square. Put the alleles from one parent on top. Put those of the other on the side.

(2) Fill in the blocks by combining the alleles.

(3) The total number of blocks is the second part of a ratio. ___ : 4

(4) To find the probability of an outcome, count the blocks of that outcome.

ANSWER: There is a 2 : 4, or 2 out of 4 probability.

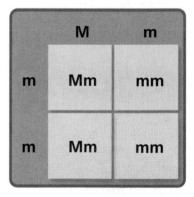

	M	m
m	Mm	mm
m	Mm	mm

Now, make your own Punnett square for Shelties.

1. Make a Punnett square to show two Sheltie parents, both with merle coats (Mm).

2. What is the probability of a merle puppy?

3. What are the chances of a puppy with no merling?

CHALLENGE Write each of the probabilities in questions 2 and 3 and the example as a percentage.

4.3 Meiosis is a special form of cell division.

◀ BEFORE, you learned

- Mitosis produces two genetically identical cells
- In sexual reproduction, offspring inherit traits from both parents
- Genetic traits are inherited in predictable patterns

▶ NOW, you will learn

- Why meiosis is necessary for sexual reproduction
- How cells and chromosomes divide during meiosis
- How meiosis differs from mitosis

VOCABULARY

gamete p. 118
egg p. 118
sperm p. 118
fertilization p. 118
meiosis p. 119

EXPLORE Meiosis

Why does sexual reproduction need a special form of cell division?

PROCEDURE

1. Suppose the cells that combine during sexual reproduction are produced by mitosis, with the same pairs of chromosomes as most cells. Model this combination with the pipe cleaners; both red pipe cleaners and both blue pipe cleaners end up in the new cell.

2. Now model a way for the new cell to end up with the same number of chromosomes as most other cells.

MATERIALS
- 2 blue pipe cleaners
- 2 red pipe cleaners

WHAT DO YOU THINK?
- What was wrong with the new cell produced at the end of step 1?
- Describe your model of the way a new cell could end up with the correct number of chromosomes.

Meiosis is necessary for sexual reproduction.

In Section 4.1 you learned that two cells combine during the process of sexual reproduction. One of the cells contains genetic information from the mother. The other contains genetic information from the father. The two cells combine into a completely new cell, which becomes the offspring.

CHECK YOUR READING How does the genetic material of offspring produced by sexual reproduction compare with the genetic material of the parents?

Most human cells, which can be referred to as body cells, contain 46 chromosomes—the full number of chromosomes that is normal for a human being. Any cell that contains the full number of chromosomes (two sets) for a species is a $2n$ cell, also called a diploid cell. The $2n$ cells for a fruit fly, for example, contain 8 chromosomes.

Think about what would happen if two body cells were to combine. The resulting cell would have twice the normal number of chromosomes. Reproductive cells, called gametes, differ from body cells.

Gametes are cells that contain half the usual number of chromosomes—one chromosome from each pair. Gametes are $1n$ cells, also called haploid cells. Human gametes contain 23 unpaired chromosomes. The gametes of a fruit fly contain 4 unpaired chromosomes. Gametes are found only in the reproductive organs of plants and animals. An **egg** is a gamete that forms in the reproductive organs of a female. A gamete that forms in the reproductive organs of a male is a **sperm**.

VOCABULARY
Be sure to make a word magnet for the term *gamete*.

CHECK YOUR READING What is a gamete?

During sexual reproduction two gametes combine to become a $2n$ cell that can grow into a new offspring. **Fertilization** is the process that takes place when a sperm and an egg combine to form one new cell. The diagram below shows what happens to the chromosomes in gametes during fertilization. In humans, an egg cell with 23 chromosomes joins a sperm cell with 23 chromosomes to form a new $2n$ cell with 46 chromosomes.

Fertilization

During fertilization, a $1n$ egg cell from a female combines with a $1n$ sperm cell from a male, producing a $2n$ fertilized egg cell, which develops into an offspring.

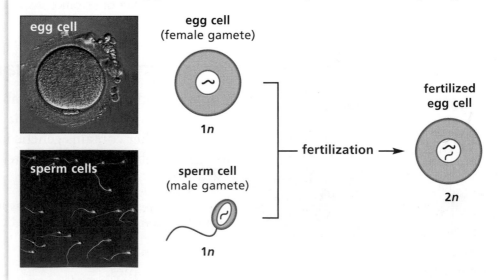

egg cell

egg cell
(female gamete)

$1n$

sperm cells

sperm cell
(male gamete)

$1n$

fertilization →

fertilized
egg cell

$2n$

You know that body cells divide by the process called mitosis. Mitosis produces two daughter cells, each containing exact copies of the chromosomes in the parent cell. Each daughter cell formed by mitosis is a standard diploid ($2n$) cell.

But to produce gametes, which are haploid, a different kind of cell division is necessary. **Meiosis** is a special kind of cell division that produces haploid ($1n$) cells. During meiosis, a single cell goes through two cell divisions—meiosis I and meiosis II. Meiosis takes place only in the reproductive tissues of an organism.

Cells divide twice during meiosis.

Before meiosis begins, the chromosomes of the parent cell are copied. A cell that is ready to divide contains two copies of each chromosome pair—twice as many chromosomes as usual. So to end up with cells that have half the usual number of chromosomes, there must be two divisions.

Remember that the two chromosomes in a pair are called homologs. At the beginning of meiosis I, the cell has two copies of each homolog, attached together. During meiosis I the homologs separate. The starting cell divides into two cells. One cell contains the two copies of one homolog of each pair, while the other cell contains the two copies of the other homolog of each pair. Then, during meiosis II, each of the two cells is divided, producing four haploid cells. Each haploid cell has one unpaired set of chromosomes.

NOTETAKING STRATEGY
Use an earlier strategy or one that you think works well to take notes on the division of cells during meiosis.

Meiosis I

As you can see in the diagram on page 121, there are four steps in meiosis I: prophase I, metaphase I, anaphase I, and telophase I. Included in telophase I is a cytokinesis, the division of the cytoplasm. The diagram shows what would happen during meiosis I in a species that has four chromosomes in its 2n body cells.

READING TiP

As you read about meiosis I and meiosis II, match the numbers in the text to the numbers in the diagram on page 121.

1 Prophase I The duplicated chromosomes pair up with their partners. There are two sets of each of the chromosome pairs in the parent cell. The chromatids are attached together. There are pairs of doubled homologs.

2 Metaphase I The chromosome pairs line up along the center of the cell.

3 Anaphase I The two copies of one homolog are pulled apart from the two copies of the other homolog. This separating of the homologs is the most significant step of meiosis I.

4 Telophase I and Cytokinesis A new cell membrane forms at the center of the cell, dividing the parent cell into two daughter cells.

CHECK YOUR READING What happens to the parent cell during telophase I?

Meiosis II

RESOURCE CENTER
CLASSZONE.COM

Learn more about meiosis.

During meiosis I, two daughter cells are formed. The chromosomes of these two cells are not copied before meiosis II begins. Both of these cells divide during meiosis II, to produce a total of four daughter cells. The four steps in meiosis II, shown on page 121, are prophase II, metaphase II, anaphase II, and telophase II (with cytokinesis).

5 Prophase II In each daughter cell, there are two copies of each of n chromosomes. The copies are attached together.

6 Metaphase II Each duplicated chromosome lines up separately along each cell's center.

7 Anaphase II The two attached copies of each chromosome separate and are pulled to opposite poles in each cell.

8 Telophase II and Cytokinesis A new cell membrane forms in the center of each cell, as each cell divides into two 1n daughter cells, producing a total of four 1n cells.

During meiosis, one cell in an organism's reproductive system divides twice to form four 1n cells. In male organisms, these gametes become sperm. In female organisms, at least one of these cells becomes an egg. In some species, including humans, only one of the four daughter cells produced by a female during meiosis becomes an egg. The rest dissolve back into the organism or, in some cases, are never produced.

Meiosis

Meiosis reduces the number of chromosomes by half, producing four 1n cells.

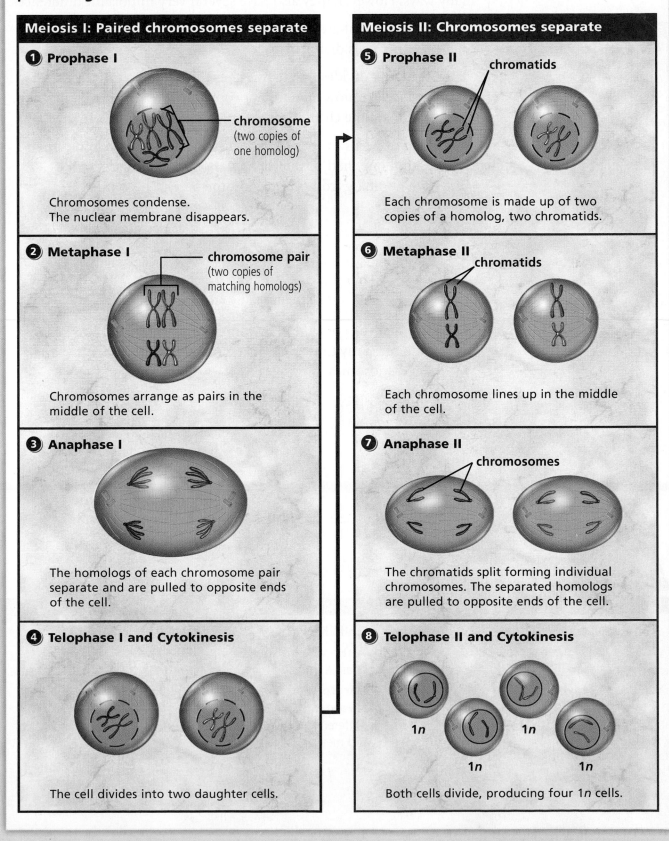

Meiosis I: Paired chromosomes separate

1 Prophase I

chromosome
(two copies of one homolog)

Chromosomes condense.
The nuclear membrane disappears.

2 Metaphase I

chromosome pair
(two copies of matching homologs)

Chromosomes arrange as pairs in the middle of the cell.

3 Anaphase I

The homologs of each chromosome pair separate and are pulled to opposite ends of the cell.

4 Telophase I and Cytokinesis

The cell divides into two daughter cells.

Meiosis II: Chromosomes separate

5 Prophase II

chromatids

Each chromosome is made up of two copies of a homolog, two chromatids.

6 Metaphase II

chromatids

Each chromosome lines up in the middle of the cell.

7 Anaphase II

chromosomes

The chromatids split forming individual chromosomes. The separated homologs are pulled to opposite ends of the cell.

8 Telophase II and Cytokinesis

1n   1n

1n   1n

Both cells divide, producing four 1n cells.

Meiosis and mitosis differ in some important ways.

You can see that the processes of meiosis and mitosis are similar in many ways. However, they also have several very important differences.

READING **TiP**

As you read about how meiosis and mitosis are different, refer to the diagrams on pages 83 and 121.

- Only cells that are to become gametes go through meiosis. All other cells divide by mitosis.

- A cell that divides by meiosis goes through two cell divisions, but the chromosomes are not copied before the second division. In mitosis, the chromosomes are always copied before division.

- Daughter cells produced by meiosis, which are haploid ($1n$), contain only half of the genetic material of the parent cell (one homolog from a chromosome pair).

single chromosome

Cell produced by meiosis

- Daughter cells produced by mitosis, which are diploid ($2n$), contain exactly the same genetic material as the parent (pairs of chromosomes).

chromosome pair

Cell produced by mitosis

CHECK YOUR READING — What are four ways in which meiosis differs from mitosis?

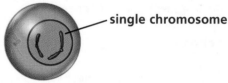

4.3 Review

KEY CONCEPTS

1. What kind of cell is produced by meiosis?
2. What is fertilization?
3. In your own words, describe the differences between meiosis and mitosis.

CRITICAL THINKING

4. **Compare** How do prophase I and prophase II differ?
5. **Communicate** Make a Venn diagram to show the similarities and differences between mitosis and meiosis.

⬤ CHALLENGE

6. **Synthesize** Why does meiosis II result in four $1n$ cells rather than four $2n$ cells?

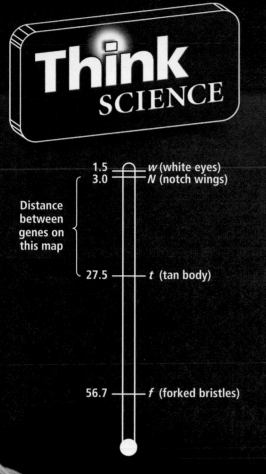

1.5 ——— *w* (white eyes)
3.0 ——— *N* (notch wings)

Distance between genes on this map

27.5 ——— *t* (tan body)

56.7 ——— *f* (forked bristles)

Genes have a particular location on a chromosome. A gene map shows the location.

Are Traits Linked?

Fruit flies are easy to breed in a laboratory and have an assortment of easily recognized genetic traits—different eye colors, body patterns, limb characteristics, and wing shapes. For these reasons, early geneticists used fruit flies to study patterns of inheritance. Some of the experiments produced puzzling results. Here is an example from the laboratory of Thomas Hunt Morgan.

◗ Observations

- In a batch of fruit flies, most red-eyed individuals were born with short wings.
- In the same batch, at least one fruit fly was born with red eyes and normal-sized wings.

◗ Hypotheses

Morgan and his coworkers made these hypotheses about the inherited traits:

- The gene for red eyes and the gene for short wings are linked together on a fruit fly's chromosomes. These linked genes are usually inherited together.
- Sometimes during meiosis, one of the linked genes will "cross over" from one chromosome to a homologous one. When this happens, a fruit fly will be born with one but not both of the linked genes—red eyes without short wings.
- Genes that are farthest from each other on a chromosome are most likely to become separated and cross over during meiosis. Genes that are closest (linked) to each other are least likely to.

◗ Further Discoveries

By studying the results of many breeding experiments, Morgan and his student, Alfred Sturtevant, could determine which genes were closest and farthest from each other on the same chromosome. From this information, they drew a simple map showing the location of each of the fruit fly's linked genes.

◗ Determine Relevance

On Your Own Look at the map of a chromosome on this page. Which of the traits are most likely to be inherited together? Which might be most easily separated and cross over during meiosis?

As a Group Is it reasonable to think that information about a fruit fly's genes could apply to the genes of a human being? Discuss this topic in a small group and see if the group can agree.

Chapter Review

the BIG idea

In sexual reproduction, genes are passed from parents to offspring in predictable patterns.

CONTENT REVIEW
CLASSZONE.COM

◀ KEY CONCEPTS SUMMARY

4.1) Living things inherit traits in patterns.

Offspring inherit **alleles**, which are forms of **genes**, from their parents. Alleles can be **dominant** or **recessive**. The alleles you have are your **genotype**; the observable characteristics that come from your genotype are your **phenotype**.

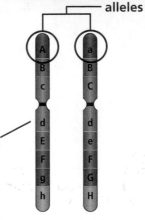

alleles

a gene

VOCABULARY
sexual reproduction
p. 102
gene p. 102
heredity p. 102
allele p. 103
phenotype p. 106
genotype p. 106
dominant p. 107
recessive p. 107

4.2) Patterns of heredity can be predicted.

Punnett squares show possible outcomes of heredity. **Ratios** and **percentages** can be used with Punnett squares to express the **probability** of particular outcomes.

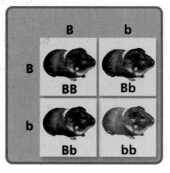

B = black fur
b = brown fur

	B	b
B	BB	Bb
b	Bb	bb

VOCABULARY
Punnett square p. 110
ratio p. 112
probability p. 112
percentage p. 112

4.3) Meiosis is a special form of cell division.

- At the beginning of meiosis I, the parent cell has two copies of each chromosome pair.
- During meiosis I, the homologs of the chromosome pair separate; there are two cells, each with two copies of one homolog from each pair.
- During meiosis II, the two copies of each homolog separate; each daughter cell has one homolog.

Meiosis I

Meiosis II

1n   1n

1n   1n

VOCABULARY
gamete p. 118
egg p. 118
sperm p. 118
fertilization p. 118
meiosis p. 119

Reviewing Vocabulary

Make a frame for each of the vocabulary terms listed below. Write the term in the center. Think about how each term is related to the Big Idea of the chapter. Decide what information to frame it with. Use definitions, examples, descriptions, parts, or pictures.

1. allele   **3.** ratio

2. heredity   **4.** probability

Describe how the vocabulary terms in the following pairs of words are related to each other. Explain the relationship in a one- or two-sentence answer. Underline each vocabulary word or term in your answers.

5. phenotype, genotype

6. dominant, recessive

Reviewing Key Concepts

Multiple Choice *Choose the letter of the best answer.*

7. Which is an example of an acquired trait?
   a. eye color   **c.** blood type
   b. hair color   **d.** ability to read

8. The unit of heredity that determines a particular trait is known as
   a. a chromosome   **c.** a gene
   b. a gamete   **d.** a phenotype

9. A human female would have which set of sex chromosomes?
   a. XX   **c.** XY
   b. YY   **d.** XxYy

10. If one copy of a dominant allele is present in a genotype, then the trait the allele codes for is
   a. expressed in the phenotype
   b. not expressed in the phenotype
   c. partially expressed in the phenotype
   d. not expressed in an offspring's phenotype

11. In guinea pigs, the allele for black fur (B) is dominant, and the allele for brown fur (b) is recessive. If a BB male mates with a Bb female, what percentage of offspring are likely to have black fur?
   a. 100 percent   **c.** 50 percent
   b. 75 percent   **d.** 25 percent

12. If one parent has two dominant alleles and another parent has two recessive alleles, the offspring will have
   a. the recessive phenotype
   b. the dominant phenotype
   c. two dominant alleles
   d. two recessive alleles

13. Cells that contain half the usual number of chromosomes are
   a. fertilized egg cells   **c.** alleles
   b. gametes   **d.** diploid cells

14. The process that produces haploid ($1n$) cells is known as
   a. mitosis   **c.** meiosis
   b. reproduction   **d.** fertilization

15. What happens when fertilization occurs?
   a. Two $2n$ cells combine in a new cell.
   b. Two $1n$ cells combine into a new cell.
   c. Two $2n$ daughter cells are produced.
   d. Two $1n$ daughter cells are produced.

16. Which does not occur during meiosis?
   a. Four haploid daughter cells are produced.
   b. Two diploid daughter cells are produced.
   c. Only cells that are gametes are produced.
   d. Daughter cells are produced that contain half the chromosomes of the parent cell.

Short Answer *Write a short answer to each question.*

17. In what case would a recessive allele be expressed in the phenotype of an offspring?

18. Describe the purpose of a Punnett square.

19. How does the number of chromosomes in a person's sex cells compare with the number of chromosomes in the body cells?

Thinking Critically

20. INFER How was Mendel able to infer that each offspring of two parent pea plants had a pair of "factors" for a particular trait?

21. COMMUNICATE Briefly describe how heredity works. Use the terms *gene* and *chromosome* in your explanation.

22. APPLY Can a dwarf pea plant ever have a dominant allele? Explain.

23. ANALYZE How is a Punnett Square used to show both the genotype and phenotype of both parents and offspring?

24. APPLY In rabbits, the allele for black fur is dominant over the allele for white fur. Two black rabbits have a litter of eight offspring. Six of the offspring have black hair and two have white hair. What are the genotypes of the parents? Explain.

Use the Punnett square below to answer the next two questions.

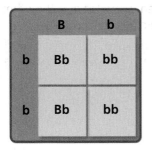

25. CALCULATE A parent has one dominant allele for black fur (B) and one recessive allele for white fur (b). The other parent has two recessive alleles for white fur. In this cross what is the chance that an offspring will be born with black fur? With white fur?

26. CALCULATE What is the percentage chance that an offspring will have the recessive phenotype?

27. ANALYZE This diagram shows the process of fertilization. Which of the cells shown are haploid? Explain.

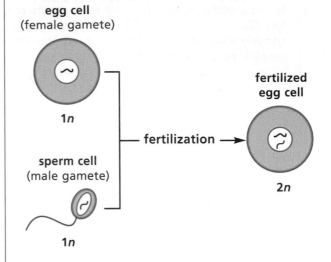

28. SUMMARIZE Briefly describe what happens during meiosis I and meiosis II. What is the function of meiosis?

the BIG idea

29. INFER Look again at the picture on pages 98–99. Now that you have finished the chapter, how would you change or add details to your answer to the question on the photograph?

30. SYNTHESIZE Write one or more paragraphs explaining how Mendel's observations of pea plants contributed to the study of modern genetics. Use these terms in your explanation.

gene	phenotype
allele	dominant
trait	recessive
genotype	

UNIT PROJECTS

If you need to create graphs or other visuals for your project, be sure you have grid paper, poster board, markers, or other supplies.

Analyzing data

The chart below shows the phenotypes of pea-plant offspring.

Phenotypes of Pea Plants	
Phenotype	Number of Offspring
Regular (D)	12
Dwarf (d)	4

Use the chart to answer the questions below.

1. What percentage of pea plants showed the dominant phenotype?

  a. 100 percent

  b. 75 percent

  c. 50 percent

  d. 25 percent

2. What percentage of pea plants showed the recessive phenotype?

  a. 100 percent

  b. 75 percent

  c. 50 percent

  d. 25 percent

3. What is the genotype of the dwarf pea plants?

  a. DD

  b. Dd

  c. dd

  d. cannot tell

4. What are the possible genotypes of the regular pea plants?

  a. DD and dd

  b. DD and Dd

  c. Dd and dd

  d. cannot tell

5. What are the genotypes of the parents?

  a. Dd and dd

  b. DD and Dd

  c. Dd and Dd

  d. dd and dd

6. Which statement is true, based on the data in the chart?

  a. If both parents were Dd, then none of the offspring would be dwarf.

  b. If both parents were DD, then none of the offspring would be dwarf.

  c. If one parent were Dd and the other were dd, then none of the offspring would be regular.

  d. If one parent were DD and the other parent were dd, then none of the offspring would be regular.

Extended Response

7. Traits for a widow's peak hairline (W) and curly hair (C) are controlled by dominant alleles. A family of eight has three children with widow's peaks. All six children have curly hair. Use your knowledge of heredity to write one or two paragraphs explaining the possible genotypes of the parents.

8. A student proposes a hypothesis that traits that are dominant are more common in the general population than traits with recessive alleles. Describe a procedure you might use to test this hypothesis.

THE STORY OF Genetics

The human genome project, DNA evidence in criminal cases, cloning—news about genetics is everywhere. Some of the most exciting research in science today involves genes. The timeline shows that some important concepts that underline the study of genetics were discovered relatively early. You will notice the influence of two major advances in technology—the development of the microscope during the 1600s, and the development of computer technology during the later half of the 1900s. The boxes below the timeline show how technology has led to new understanding and to applications of those understandings.

1674
Cells Are Everywhere
Anton van Leeuwenhoek uses a microscope to study pond water and discovers the water is full of microscopic organisms, some made of single cells. These drawings show some of what he saw.

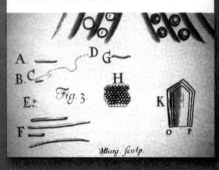

1665
Cells Discovered
Robert Hooke uses a microscope to study living matter. What he sees and then records in this drawing are tiny repeating units, which he calls cells.

EVENTS

1650   1660   1670   1680

APPLICATIONS AND TECHNOLOGY

APPLICATION

Corn in Every Shape and Size
Native Americans grew 700 different kinds of popcorn. Their popcorn plants were a kind of grass with big, hard seeds that exploded when they were heated. People who didn't want to have to explode their corn to eat it chose plants with softer seeds and grew them, and then chose the softest of those seeds to plant. Over hundreds of years, by choosing which plants to grow, people produced what we now eat as corn on the cob.

TECHNOLOGY

Seeing into the Cell
Single-glass lenses, such as the one van Leeuwenhoek used, were available as long ago as 1267. The compound microscope was first made in 1595, but it was over 200 years before it provided clear images. Until the 1930s, all microscopes focused light on objects. Eventually, light microscopes could magnify objects up to 2000 times.

1831
Cells Have Structure
As the power of microscopes improves, scientists start to describe the inner structure of cells. Robert Brown describes a central structure found in many cells, a structure that he calls the nucleus.

1882
Cells Divide, Chromosomes Split!
Scientists observe how cells divide. Walther Flemming describes how structures within the cell separate. These structures are the chromosomes. Chromosomes determine the traits of living things.

1866
Austrian Monk Describes Patterns of Heredity
Gregor Mendel's experiments with garden peas show that traits are passed on from parents to offspring in predictable patterns.

1928
Researchers Study the Chromosomes of Fruit Flies and Find Genes
Working with fruit flies, Thomas Hunt Morgan discovers that genes are found in specific locations on chromosomes.

1830   1840   1850   1860   1870   1880   1930

Cells have a highly organized structure. Color dyes are used to help us see the different parts of a cell.

1944
DNA—Genetic Material
Researchers studying *Streptococcus* transformation find that bacterial cells get their characteristics from DNA.

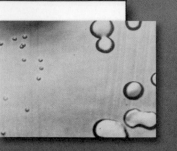

1973
DNA Recombined
In an amazing breakthrough, scientists have cut DNA from two different sources and recombined the DNA. The new DNA molecule reproduces when placed inside a bacterium. Such bacteria can be used to make proteins useful to humans.

1951
Scientists Capture Image of DNA
Scientists searching for the secret of DNA structure get an enormous clue when Rosalind Franklin uses x-ray crystallography to create an image of DNA. Maurice Wilkins, James Watson, and Francis Crick are awarded the Nobel Prize in 1962 for building a model of the DNA double helix molecule.

1984
Chinese Scientists Alter Fish!
In an effort to produce fast-growing fish for food, a team working with Zuoyan Zhu has made the first genetically modified (GM) fish.

1950   1960   1970   1980

TECHNOLOGY
Seeing Molecules
In the 1930s, a microscope came into use that focuses a beam of electrons, instead of a beam of light, on an object. Now we can see things as small as the molecules inside cells.

The image of the chromosome at left was made using an electron microscope.

APPLICATION
DNA Frees Innocent Prisoner
Kevin Green was convicted of murder and spent 16 years in prison. While he was in jail, the California Department of Justice created a DNA database that contained the DNA fingerprints of many other convicted felons. When Green's defenders compared the DNA found at the murder scene with DNA fingerprints in the database, they found that it matched someone else's fingerprint. The real murderer confessed, and Green is now a free man, thanks to genetics.

1984

Living Things Have Genetic Fingerprints

Human fingers have their own unique fingerprints. In a similar way, the DNA of different people has its own unique patterns. These DNA fingerprints are compared here.

2000

Scientists Sequence Human Genome

Two groups of researchers, Celera and the Human Genome Project, succeed in publishing the first draft of the sequence of DNA for all the chromosomes in the human body.

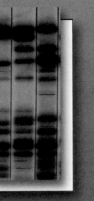

RESOURCE CENTER
CLASSZONE.COM
Find recent genetics updates.

1990   2000   Today

APPLICATION

Saved by a Gene Donor

In 1986 a baby girl named Ashanti DeSilva was born. One single mistake in her DNA meant that Ashanti's body could not make an important disease-fighting protein.

In 1981, researchers had figured out how to move a working gene from one mammal to another. Ashanti became the first person ever to receive a gene from someone else. Ashanti's doctors injected some of her white blood cells with healthy copies of the sick gene. Now her white blood cells worked. Researchers and doctors are trying to apply the same techniques to other genetic disorders. There is still much work to be done.

INTO THE FUTURE

Genetics is a young science. The timeline spans 350 years, but the real study of genetics began in 1900 with the rediscovery of the work of Gregor Mendel. Since then, scientists have determined the structure and function of DNA—and ways to use this knowledge.

In medicine, genetics is used to identify genes that play a role in inherited diseases. Questions remain about how this knowledge can be used to treat or even prevent disease.

In agriculture, genetics is used to modify the genes of plant and animal stocks to give them desirable traits, such as resistance to disease. Questions remain about what effect modified genes might have once they enter a population of plants or animals.

In biology, genetics is used to determine how different types of organisms have changed over time and how one species relates to another. Questions remain about whether similar genes found in different organisms behave in the same way.

In society, genetic profiles are used to help solve crimes or make identifications. Questions remain about how to protect individuals and their personal information.

ACTIVITIES

Reliving History

Use a hand lens or microscope to study water from a pond or puddle. See if your sample contains structures similar to those drawn by van Leeuwenhoek in 1674.

Writing About Science: Biography

Sharing information is important to scientific discovery. Learn more about individuals or groups involved in the discovery of DNA structure or sequencing the human genome. How important was cooperation in their work?

DNA and Modern Genetics

the BIG idea

DNA is a set of instructions for making cell parts.

What can a model of DNA show you about its structure?

Key Concepts

SECTION
5.1 DNA and RNA are required to make proteins.
Learn about DNA, RNA, and protein synthesis.

SECTION
5.2 Changes in DNA can produce variation.
Learn about the effects of changes in DNA and how some changes can cause genetic disorders.

SECTION
5.3 Modern genetics uses DNA technology.
Learn about some applications of DNA technology and the Human Genome Project.

Internet Preview

CLASSZONE.COM

Chapter 5 online resources: Content Review, Visualization, four Resource Centers, Math Tutorial, Test Practice

EXPLORE (the BIG idea)

What Is the Pattern?

Sometimes by looking at the parts of a whole you can guess how the pieces fit together. Some evidence for the structure of DNA came when people noticed that certain types of chemical subunits came in pairs. Try this activity with a friend. Take 9 index cards and write 2 letters, A T or C G, on each card. Now cut the pairs in half and give your friend the individual pieces. See if he or she can find the pattern.

Observe and Think How long did it take your friend to see the pattern? Were there any other clues that he or she used?

What Vegetable Is That?

Buy a broccoflower from your local supermarket. Describe what it looks like, what it tastes like, and how it smells.

Observe and Think What properties of each vegetable does the broccoflower have? What gives an organism its traits?

Internet Activity: Human Genome

Go to **ClassZone.com** to find out how scientists put together a sequence of the DNA in the human genome.

Observe and Think What are the benefits of having a map of the human genome?

NSTA
scilinks.org
SCiLINKS

Genetics Code: MDL035

Getting Ready to Learn

◀ **CONCEPT REVIEW**

- Traits are controlled by genes on chromosomes.
- Genes can be dominant or recessive.
- Cells have DNA, RNA, and proteins.

◀ **VOCABULARY REVIEW**

organelle p. 20

protein p. 43

gene p. 102

technology *See Glossary.*

 **CONTENT REVIEW**
CLASSZONE.COM
Review concepts and vocabulary.

▶ **TAKING NOTES**

SUPPORTING MAIN IDEAS

Make a chart to show main ideas and the information that supports them. Copy each blue heading; then add supporting information, such as reasons, explanations, and examples.

CHOOSE YOUR OWN STRATEGY

Take notes about new vocabulary terms using one or more of the strategies from earlier chapters —**four square, word triangle, frame game,** or **magnet word.** Feel free to mix and match the strategies, or use an entirely different vocabulary strategy.

See the Note-Taking Handbook on pages R45–R51.

SCIENCE NOTEBOOK

DNA sequences can change.

Variations in DNA make one organism different from another.

Human DNA has 6 billion base pairs; yeast DNA has 12 million base pairs.

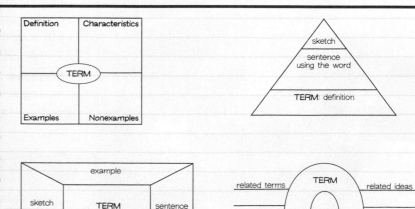

DNA and RNA are required to make proteins.

BEFORE, you learned	NOW, you will learn
• Traits pass from parents to off-spring in predictable patterns • Traits are passed on through genes • In sexual reproduction, off-spring get half their genes from each parent	• How the structure of DNA stores information the cell needs • How DNA is copied • How RNA uses the information from DNA to make proteins

VOCABULARY

replication p. 137
RNA p. 138

EXPLORE Templates

How does a template work?

PROCEDURE

MATERIALS
• paper
• pencil

1. Write a set of rules to describe how the characters in line A relate to the characters in line B.

A ☐ ◉ ○ △ △ ☐
B △ ○ ◉ ☐ ☐ △

2. Place a piece of paper just under line C below. Use the rules from step 1 to produce a template—the corresponding pattern that goes with line C.

C ◉ △ △ ☐ ○ ○

3. Give the rules and the template to a classmate to produce a copy of line C.

WHAT DO YOU THINK?
What is a template and how does it differ from a copy?

DNA is the information molecule.

SUPPORTING MAIN IDEAS
Make a chart of information supporting the main idea: *DNA is the information molecule.*

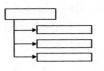

DNA is a molecule that stores information—that's all it does. You could compare the information in DNA to the books in your local library. You might find a book describing how to bake a cake, make a model sailboat, or beat your favorite computer game. The books, however, don't actually do any of those things—you do. The "books" in the DNA "library" carry all the information that a cell needs to function, to grow, and to divide. However, DNA doesn't do any of those things. Proteins do most of the work of a cell and also make up much of the structure of a cell.

Proteins and Amino Acids

Proteins are large molecules that are made up of chains of amino acids. Twenty different amino acids come together in enough combinations to make up the thousands of different proteins found in the human body. Some proteins are small. For example, lysozyme is a digestive protein that is made up of a sequence of 129 amino acids. Some proteins are large. For example, dystrophin is a huge structural protein that is made up of 3685 amino acids.

RESOURCE CENTER
CLASSZONE.COM
Learn more about DNA.

CHECK YOUR READING What is the relationship between proteins and amino acids?

DNA stores the information that enables a cell to put together the right sequences of amino acids needed to produce specific proteins. Scientists describe DNA as containing a code. A code is a set of rules and symbols used to carry information. For example, your computer uses a code of ones and zeroes to store data and then translates the code into the numbers, letters, and graphics you see on a computer screen. To understand how DNA functions as a code, you first need to learn about the structure of the DNA molecule.

DNA molecule

DNA and the Genetic Code

The DNA molecule takes the shape of a double-stranded spiral, which, as you can see from the diagram, looks something like a twisted ladder. In Chapter 2, you read about different subunits that make up the molecules found in cells. Nucleotide subunits make up each of the two strands of the DNA molecule. One part of the nucleotide forms the side rail of the DNA "ladder." The other part, the nucleotide base, forms the rung. Actually, two bases come together to form the rung, as one nucleotide base attaches to another from the opposite strand. You can see how the parts fit together in the diagram to the left.

strand

strand

nucleotide bases

eukaryotic cell

nucleus

There are four different nucleotides in DNA, identified by their bases: adenine (A), thymine (T), cytosine (C), and guanine (G). Because of differences in size and shape, adenine always pairs with thymine (A-T) and cytosine always pairs with guanine (C-G). The bases fit together like two pieces of a jigsaw puzzle. These bases are often referred to simply by their initials—A, T, C, and G. The phrase "all tigers can growl" may help you remember them.

DNA Base Pairs

C   G
Cytosine pairs with guanine.

A   T
Adenine pairs with thymine.

It is the sequence—the order—of bases in a strand of DNA that forms the code for making proteins. Like a list of ingredients in a recipe book, a set of bases specifies the amino acids needed to form a particular protein. The cookbook uses just 4 bases—A, T, G, and C— to code for 20 amino acids. A code of 2 bases to 1 amino acid gives only 16 possible combinations. However, a code of 3 bases to 1 amino acid gives 64 possible combinations.

The genetic code is, in fact, a triplet code. A specific sequence of 3 nucleotide bases codes for 1 amino acid. For example, the triplet T-C-T on a strand of DNA codes for the amino acid arginine. Some amino acids have two different codes. Others have three, and some have four. A gene is the entire sequence of the bases that codes for all the amino acids in a protein. Each gene is made up of a sequence of bases at a particular location on the DNA.

T – C – T
(DNA triplet)

codes for

arginine
(amino acid)

Replication

When a cell divides into two cells, each daughter cell receives an identical copy of the DNA. Before a cell divides, all of its DNA is copied, a process referred to as **replication.** Let's follow the process through for one DNA molecule. First, the two strands of DNA separate, almost like two threads in a string being unwound. Nucleotides in the area around the DNA match up, base by base, with the nucleotides on each DNA strand. C matches up with G, and A matches up with T. When replication is complete, there are two identical DNA molecules. Each molecule has one strand of old DNA and one strand of new DNA.

READING TiP

Replicate includes the root word meaning "to repeat."

Replication

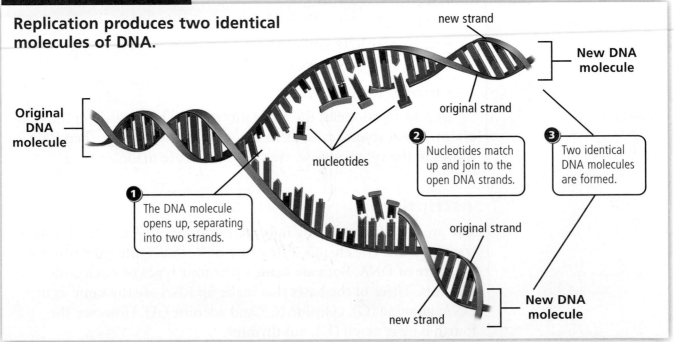

Replication produces two identical molecules of DNA.

new strand

New DNA molecule

Original DNA molecule

original strand

nucleotides

2 Nucleotides match up and join to the open DNA strands.

3 Two identical DNA molecules are formed.

1 The DNA molecule opens up, separating into two strands.

original strand

new strand

New DNA molecule

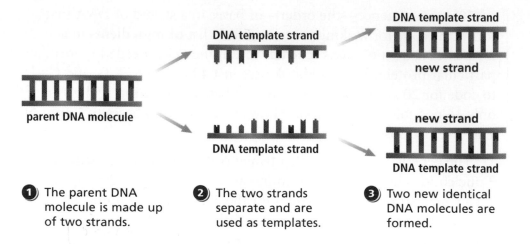

1 The parent DNA molecule is made up of two strands.

2 The two strands separate and are used as templates.

3 Two new identical DNA molecules are formed.

READING TiP

Complementary has a root that means "to complete."

During replication, each strand of DNA is used as a template to produce a copy of the other strand. A template is a pattern or shape that produces a matching, or complementary, product. If you've ever made a plaster model of your hand, you've worked with a template. You press your hand into a soft material that leaves a mold of your hand. You then pour liquid plaster into the mold to produce a copy of your hand. The mold is a template. Its shape allows you to make a complementary shape that matches your hand.

RNA is needed to make proteins.

VOCABULARY

Remember to choose strategies from an earlier chapter or some of your own to take notes on the term *RNA*.

DNA is not used to make proteins directly. Translating the genetic code of DNA involves another type of molecule, RNA. **RNA,** or ribonucleic acid, carries the information from DNA to a ribosome, where the amino acids are brought together to form a protein. DNA actually codes for RNA. Three different types of RNA are involved in making proteins. They are named for their functions:

- messenger RNA (mRNA)
- ribosomal RNA (rRNA)
- transfer RNA (tRNA)

In prokaryotic cells, RNA and proteins are both made in the cytoplasm. In eukaryotic cells, DNA is copied in the nucleus, then RNA moves to the cytoplasm, where the proteins are made.

Transcription

The process of transferring information from DNA to RNA is called transcription. The chemical structure of RNA is quite similar to the structure of DNA. Both are made up of four types of nucleotide subunits. Three of the bases that make up RNA are the same as in DNA: guanine (G), cytosine (C), and adenine (A). However, the fourth base is uracil (U), not thymine.

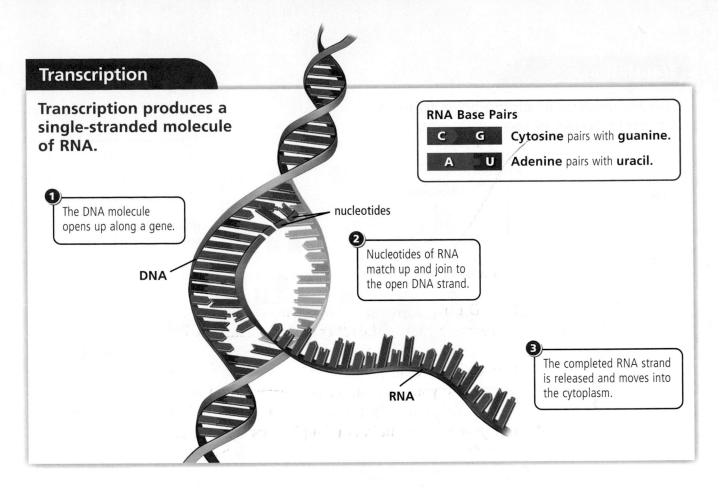

Transcription

Transcription produces a single-stranded molecule of RNA.

RNA Base Pairs

| C | G | Cytosine pairs with **guanine**. |
| A | U | Adenine pairs with **uracil**. |

1 The DNA molecule opens up along a gene.

nucleotides

2 Nucleotides of RNA match up and join to the open DNA strand.

DNA

3 The completed RNA strand is released and moves into the cytoplasm.

RNA

During transcription, DNA is again used as a template, this time to make a complementary strand of RNA. Only individual genes are transcribed, not a whole DNA molecule. The DNA again opens up, just where the gene is located. As shown in the diagram above, RNA bases match up to complementary bases on the DNA template. Adenine pairs with uracil (A-U) and cytosine pairs with guanine (C-G).

Transcription is different from replication in some important ways. Only one strand of DNA is transcribed, which means just a single strand of RNA is produced. When transcription is complete, the RNA is released, it does not stay attached to DNA. This means that many copies of RNA can be made from the same gene in a short period of time. At the end of transcription, the DNA molecule closes.

▼ **REMINDER**

DNA base pairs:
C-G, A-T
RNA base pairs:
C-G, A-U

Translation

Replication and transcription involve passing along information that is coded in the language of nucleotide bases. To make proteins, cells have to translate this language of nucleotide bases into the language of amino acids. Three specific bases equal one amino acid. The actual assembly of the amino acids in their proper sequence is the translation. Translation takes place in the cytoplasm of a cell. It involves all three types of RNA.

DNA

Transcription

↓

RNA

Translation

↓

Protein

Translation

The assembling of amino acids to form a protein occurs in the cytoplasm.

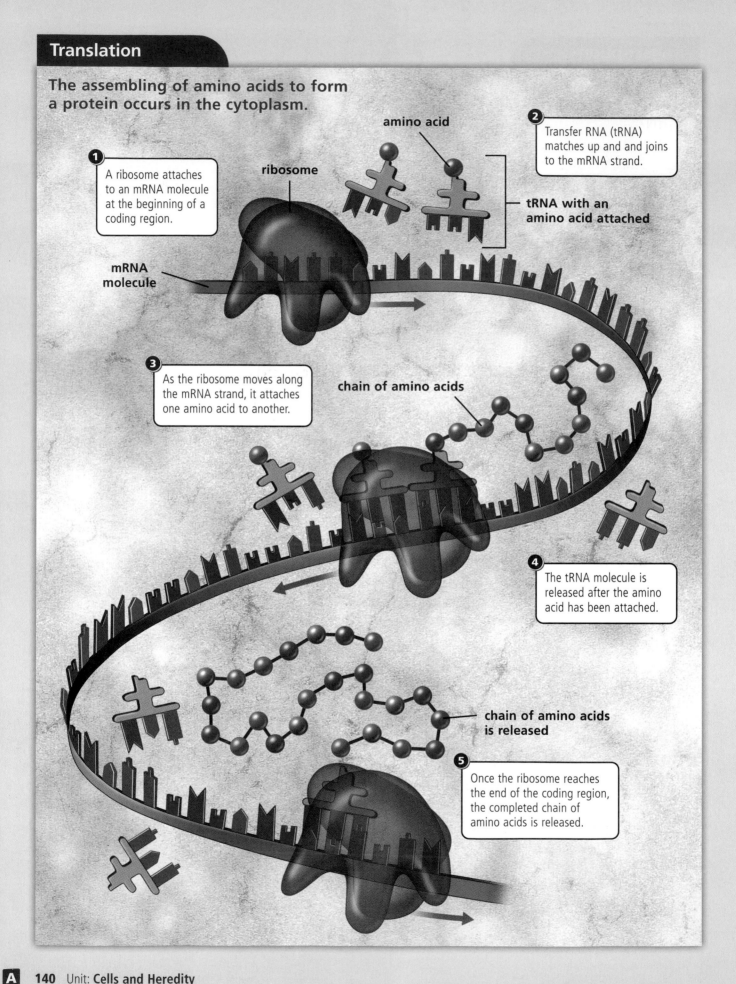

1 A ribosome attaches to an mRNA molecule at the beginning of a coding region.

amino acid

ribosome

2 Transfer RNA (tRNA) matches up and and joins to the mRNA strand.

tRNA with an amino acid attached

mRNA molecule

3 As the ribosome moves along the mRNA strand, it attaches one amino acid to another.

chain of amino acids

4 The tRNA molecule is released after the amino acid has been attached.

chain of amino acids is released

5 Once the ribosome reaches the end of the coding region, the completed chain of amino acids is released.

Proteins are made on ribosomes, structures that are made up of ribosomal RNA and proteins. If you think of DNA as a cookbook for making different proteins, and mRNA as a recipe for making a protein, then the ribosome is the place where the cooking gets done. In this analogy, tRNA gathers the ingredients, which are amino acids.

A tRNA molecule is shaped in such a way that one end of it can attach to a specific amino acid. The other end of tRNA has a triplet of bases that is complementary to a triplet of bases on mRNA. Transfer RNA does the actual translation of bases to amino acid when it matches up with mRNA. The diagram on page 140 shows the whole process.

READING TiP

Refer to the diagram on page 140 as you read the text. The numbers in the text match the numbers in the diagram.

1 Translation begins when a ribosome attaches to the beginning end of an mRNA molecule.

2 A tRNA molecule carrying an amino acid matches up to a complementary triplet on mRNA on the ribosome.

3 The ribosome attaches one amino acid to another as it moves along the mRNA molecule.

4 The tRNA molecules are released after the amino acids they carry are attached to the growing chain of amino acids.

5 The ribosome completes the translation when it reaches the end of the mRNA strand. The newly made protein molecule, in the form of a chain of amino acids, is released.

CHECK YOUR READING Describe how the three different types of RNA work together in protein synthesis.

The process of making proteins is basically the same in all cells. The flow of information in a cell goes from DNA to RNA to protein.

VISUALIZATION
CLASSZONE.COM

Watch an animation of how proteins are made.

5.1 Review

KEY CONCEPTS

1. Describe the shape of the DNA molecule and how nucleotide bases fit into that structure.

2. What is a protein and what is it made up of?

3. Identify three types of RNA involved in protein synthesis and briefly describe what they do.

CRITICAL THINKING

4. **Infer** What might happen if the wrong amino acid is put on a tRNA molecule?

5. **Apply** Copy the following sequence of DNA bases: A-T-C-A-G-G. Write the complementary mRNA and tRNA sequences for this.

⚠ CHALLENGE

6. **Synthesize** Study the sequences you wrote for question 5. How does the tRNA sequence compare to the original DNA sequence?

CHAPTER INVESTIGATION

Extract and Observe DNA

OVERVIEW AND PURPOSE In this activity, you will work with several simple chemicals that can break down the membranes of a cell. You will extract DNA from raw wheat germ. Then you will examine the properties of the extracted DNA.

▶ Procedure

1 Make a table in your **Science Notebook** like the one shown on page 143.

2 Place a small scoop of wheat germ in a test tube. The wheat germ should be about 1 cm high in the test tube.

3 Add enough distilled water to wet and cover all of the wheat germ in the test tube.

4 Add 25–30 drops of detergent solution to the test tube.

5 For 3 minutes, gently swirl the test tube contents by rotating your wrist while holding the tube. Try not to make bubbles.

6 Add 25–30 drops of the salt solution to the test tube, and swirl for 1 more minute.

7 Hold the test tube tilted at an angle. Slowly add alcohol so that it runs down the inside of the test tube and forms a separate layer on top of the the material already in the tube. Add enough alcohol to double the total volume you started with. Let the test tube stand for 2 minutes.

MATERIALS
- raw wheat germ
- scoop
- test tube
- warm distilled water
- detergent solution
- salt solution
- cold ethyl or isopropyl alcohol
- bent paper clip

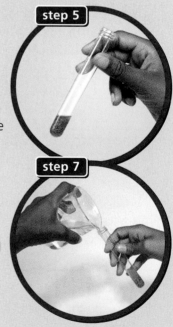

step 5

step 7

8 Watch for stringy, cloudy material to rise up from the bottom layer into the alcohol layer. This is the DNA.

9 Use the bent paper clip to remove some DNA. Be careful to probe only the alcohol layer and not disturb the material at the bottom of the test tube.

step 9

10 Wash your hands after working with the chemicals.

▶ Observe and Analyze
Write It Up

1. **OBSERVE** How do your observations of the DNA you just extracted compare with what you know about DNA. Record these comparisons in your notebook in a table similar to the one shown.

2. **INFER** What type of organism is wheat? Where is the DNA located in a wheat germ cell?

3. **INFER** What do you think was the purpose of using detergent in this experiment? Hint: How does soap work on greasy dishes?

4. **IDENTIFY LIMITS** What might happen if the wheat germ were not mixed properly with the detergent solution?

▶ Conclude
Write It Up

1. **INFER** If you had used cooked or toasted wheat germ in this experiment, you would not have gotten good results. Why do you think this is the case?

2. **INFER** Would this experiment work with cells from other organisms, such as bananas, onions, or cells from your own cheek? Why or why not?

3. **INFER** Would DNA from a single cell be visible to the naked eye?

4. **APPLY** The procedure that you performed today is used by many people to obtain DNA for further study. Give some examples of how DNA information is used in the world today.

▶ INVESTIGATE Further

CHALLENGE Repeat the experiment replacing the alcohol with water in step 7. Compare the results with the results you obtained using alcohol.

Extract and Observe DNA

Table 1. Properties and Observations

Properties of DNA	Observations

5.2 Changes in DNA can produce variation.

BEFORE, you learned	NOW, you will learn
• DNA contains information in the form of a sequence of bases	• About mutations, any changes in DNA
• Genes code for RNA and proteins	• About the possible effects of mutations
• DNA is transcribed into RNA, which is used to make proteins	• About pedigrees and how they are used

VOCABULARY

mutation p. 145
pedigree p. 147

EXPLORE Codes

What happens to a code if small changes occur?

PROCEDURE

MATERIALS
• pencil
• paper

1 Language is a type of code. Look at the English sentence below.

One day the cat ate the rat.

2 Insert an extra *a* into the word *cat* in the sentence above, but keep the spacing the same. That is, keep a space after every third letter.

WHAT DO YOU THINK?

• Does the sentence still make sense? How were the rest of the words affected?
• How would other small changes affect the meaning of the sentence? Try substituting, removing, and switching letters.

DNA sequences can change.

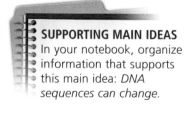

SUPPORTING MAIN IDEAS
In your notebook, organize information that supports this main idea: *DNA sequences can change.*

Differences, or variations, in DNA are what make one organism different from another. The number of differences in the DNA sequences between two species is large. Each human cell, with its 46 chromosomes, contains an astounding 3 billion base pairs in its DNA. A yeast cell, by comparison, has 12 million base pairs in its DNA.

The number of differences between any two individuals of the same species is small. For example, about 99.9 percent of the DNA in the cells of two different humans is the same. Just 0.1 percent variation in DNA makes you the unique person you are. That averages out to one base in a thousand.

How can there be such great variety among people if their DNA is so similar? The reason is that of the 6 billion base pairs in human DNA, only 5 percent are in the genes that code for RNA and proteins. As you learned in Chapter 4, genes and their interaction with the environment are what determine the traits of a person.

Differences in genes affect the height of people or the color of their eyes, hair, or skin. Genes produce variation because the type or amount of the proteins they code for can vary from person to person. For example, skin color comes from a protein called melanin. The amount of melanin an individual produces affects the color of their skin.

Many traits, including skin tones, are affected by genes.

Given the huge number of base pairs in the DNA of any organism, it is not surprising that errors occur when DNA is copied. DNA is also affected by the environment. For example, exposure to ultraviolet radiation or x-rays can damage DNA. Both natural and human-made toxins, which are harmful chemicals, can also damage DNA.

Any change in DNA is called a **mutation.** Cells have different ways to repair mistakes in a DNA sequence. Certain enzymes actually proofread DNA, for example correcting mismatched base pairs. Other enzymes enable damaged DNA to be fixed.

CHECK YOUR READING What is a mutation?

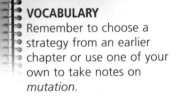

VOCABULARY
Remember to choose a strategy from an earlier chapter or use one of your own to take notes on *mutation*.

When a mutation occurs in a gene, the coding region of DNA, the wrong amino acid might be placed in the amino-acid chain. If this happens, there are three possible outcomes.

❶ **The mutation causes no effect.** Since some amino acids have more than one code, a mutation may not change the resulting protein. Also, since each cell has two sets of DNA, even if one gene is not working, enough protein may be produced.

❷ **The effect of a mutation is minor.** A change in the genes that control the amount of melanin produced could affect not only how light or dark a person's skin is, it could also affect eye or hair color. The change, in this case, is a change in appearance.

❸ **The effect of a mutation is great.** The effect can be good, such as a plant having an increased resistance to disease. Or the effect can be bad, causing a genetic disorder or disease.

Remember, only 5 percent of human DNA is in genes. If a mutation occurs in a noncoding region of DNA, then chances are that the mutation will have no effect. Such a mutation is neutral.

RESOURCE CENTER
CLASSZONE.COM

Find out more about mutations.

How does a large number of noncoding sequences affect mutations?

PROCEDURE

1. Circle ten words on the page of a newspaper to represent genes. Place the newspaper on your desk.

2. Use a handful of paper-punch circles to represent mutations and scatter them onto the newspaper.

3. Count the number of paper-punch "mutations" that landed on "genes" and those that did not.

WHAT DO YOU THINK?

- What percentage of "mutations" affected gene sequences?
- What does this model suggest about the probability of mutations affecting genes that are only a small part of a DNA sequence?

CHALLENGE Most of the sequences in bacterial DNA are genes. How could you use the same model to evaluate the effect of mutations on bacterial DNA?

SKILL FOCUS
Making models

MATERIALS
- newspaper
- pen
- paper-punch circles

TIME
15 minutes

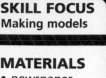

Mutations can cause genetic disorders.

A genetic disorder is a disease or condition that results from mutations that affect the normal functioning of a cell. Sometimes these disorders are inherited, passed on from parent to offspring. Examples of inherited disorders include Tay-Sachs disease, cystic fibrosis, sickle cell disease, and albinism. Other genetic disorders result from mutations that occur during a person's lifetime. Most cancers fall into this category.

CHECK YOUR READING What is a genetic disorder?

Sometimes a person carries a tendency for a disease, such as diabetes, glaucoma, Alzheimer's disease, or emphysema. In some cases, a person's behavior can help prevent the disease. Cigarette smoke is a leading cause of lung cancer. Smoke also greatly increases the risk of people with a genetic tendency for emphysema to develop that disease.

Sickle cell disease is an interesting example of how a mutation can have more than one effect. The mutation occurs in one of the genes that code for hemoglobin. Hemoglobin is a protein that carries oxygen in red blood cells. The mutation causes one amino acid to be replaced with another.

normal hemoglobin
(protein)

glutamate
(amino acid)

sickle cell hemoglobin
(protein)

valine
(amino acid)

Sickle cell disease is a recessive disorder. Only people who carry two recessive alleles are affected. Recall that an allele is one form of a gene. Because of the amino acid change, some red blood cells can take on a sickle shape. See the photograph at the right. The pedigree below shows the pattern of inheritance of the sickle cell allele through three generations of a family. A **pedigree** is a diagram of family relationships that includes two or more generations.

Sickle cell disease is a severe disease. Sickled red blood cells tend to break more easily than normal red blood cells. People with sickle cell disease do not get enough oxygen delivered to their body tissues, and the tissues become damaged. The disease is common in Africa and parts of India and the Middle East.

What is interesting about the sickle cell allele is that it provides protection against dying of malaria. Malaria is a severe disease, also common in Africa, India, and the Middle East. It is caused by microscopic organisms that reproduce in red blood cells. Scientists do not yet completely understand why people with the sickle cell allele are better able to survive malaria. However the effect of this protection is that the sickle allele remains common in populations that live in regions where malaria is common.

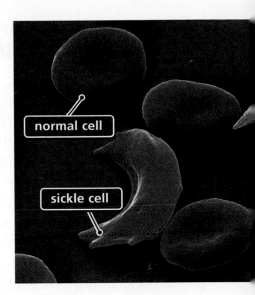

normal cell

sickle cell

Pedigree for Sickle Cell Disease

Sickle cell disease is a recessive disorder.

□ ○ person does not carry sickle cell allele (*SS*)

■ ◐ person has one sickle cell allele but does not have sickle cell disease (*Ss*)

■ ● person has two sickle cell alleles and sickle cell disease (*ss*)

chromosome 11

sickle cell allele

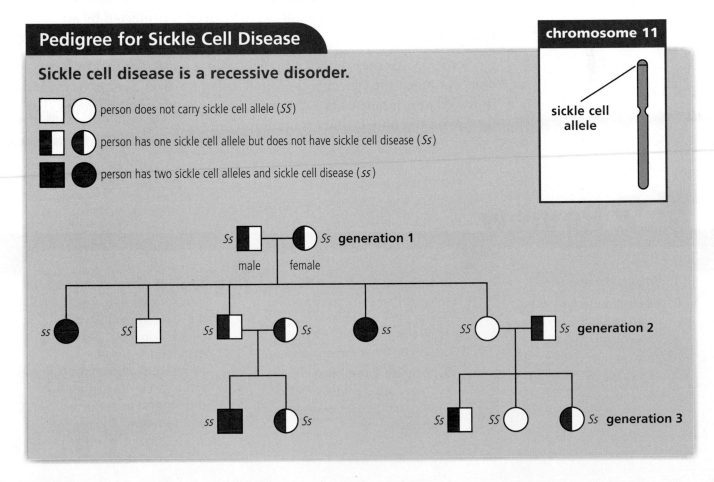

Cancer is a genetic disorder that affects the cell cycle.

Cancer cells, such as the ones shown here, have abnormal shapes. Cancer cells reproduce uncontrollably and crowd out normal cells.

Cancer is not a single genetic disorder; but rather it is a group of disorders. All cancers are characterized by the uncontrolled division of cells. Normally, cells in a multicellular organism function to maintain the health of an organism. Cell division is controlled so that an organism has the number of cells it needs to function. Cancer cells are, in a way, "selfish" cells. Where normal cells stay within the same tissue, cancer cells spread quickly and can invade other tissues. A normal cell has a definite life span. Cancerous cells become "immortal"—they divide indefinitely.

CHECK YOUR READING What is a characteristic of all cancers?

Most cancers are caused by mutations to DNA that happen during a person's lifetime. Some mutations come from mistakes made during replication. But many are caused by harmful chemicals often referred to as *carcinogens* (kahr-SIHN-uh-juhnz). Many plants naturally produce carcinogens in their tissues. Nicotine is a carcinogen naturally found in tobacco leaves. There are other carcinogens in tobacco.

Ultraviolet and nuclear radiation as well as x-rays can also cause cancer. That is why, if you get an x-ray at the doctor's or dentist's office, the part of your body not being x-rayed is protected by a lead apron.

Some people may inherit a tendency for a particular cancer. That does not mean the cancer will occur. Cancer involves a series of mutations. What is inherited is a mutation that is one step in the series. The disease occurs only if other mutations come into play.

5.2 Review

KEY CONCEPTS

1. What is a mutation?
2. How do mutations affect an organism?
3. What effect does cancer have on the cell cycle of a cancerous cell?

CRITICAL THINKING

4. **Infer** A mutation in a triplet code that ends up coding for the same amino acid is referred to as a silent mutation. In what sense is it silent?
5. **Provide Examples** Identify three causes of genetic disorders and give an example of each.

⚫ CHALLENGE

6. **Analyze** Why are genetic diseases carried by genes on the X chromosome more common in male offspring than female offspring? Hint: Think about how X and Y chromosomes are distributed in males and females.

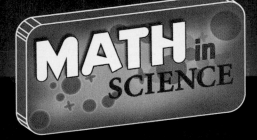

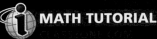

MATH TUTORIAL

Click on Math Tutorial for more help with the percent equation.

protein fiber

Protein fibers form around red blood cells forming a blood clot.

Source: ©Dennis Kunkel/Dennis Kunkel Microscopy, Inc.

Percents and Populations

Hemophilia is a genetic disorder in which blood does not clot properly. In any group of people who have hemophilia, approximately 80 percent have type A, which is caused by a mutation in one gene. Usually about 12 percent have type B, a different gene mutation.

To express what part of a population carries a gene mutation, scientists can use percentages. Once you know the percentage of a population, you can find out how many individuals that percent represents.

Example

Suppose a doctor is treating a group of people who have the disease hemophilia. The group has 400 people. About how many individuals would you expect to have hemophilia A?

(1) Write the percent as a decimal.

$$80\% = 0.80$$

(2) Multiply the decimal number by the total population.

$$0.80 \cdot 400 = 320.00$$

(3) Be sure the answer has the same number of decimal places as the total number of decimal places in the original factors.

$$0.80 \cdot 400 = 320.00$$
2 decimal places

ANSWER There are probably about 320 people with hemophilia A.

Answer the following questions for a group of 400 hemophilia patients.

1. How many patients are likely to have hemophilia B?

2. Suppose a new doctor begins treatment of 20 percent of the hemophilia A patients. How many individuals is that?

3. In as many as 30 percent of cases of hemophilia, there is no family history of the disorder. In the group of 400, how many individuals probably did not have a family history of hemophilia?

CHALLENGE Write a fraction in simplest terms equal to each percentage: 80 percent, 30 percent, 12 percent, 3 percent. When you multiply these fractions by 400, do you get the same or different results as when you multiply 400 by the percentages? Explain why the results may be different.

KEY CONCEPT

Modern genetics uses DNA technology.

BEFORE, you learned	NOW, you will learn
• Mutations are changes to DNA	• How scientists can change organisms by changing DNA
• Not all mutations have an effect on an organism	• About some applications of DNA technology
• Mutations can lead to genetic disorders	• About some issues surrounding the use of DNA technology

VOCABULARY

selective breeding p. 151
genetic engineering
  p. 151
genome p. 154
cloning p. 154

THINK ABOUT

What type of animal is this?

Look at the photograph of the animal to the right. The cells in this animal contain DNA from two different species. For a long time humans have been able to mix genes by breeding together animals of different but similar species. Now scientists have the technology to mix together genes from two very different species by inserting genes from one organism into the cells of another. What do the characteristics of this animal suggest about the source of its genes?

Changes in DNA can change an organism.

SUPPORTING MAIN IDEAS
Begin a chart of information to support this main idea: *Changes in DNA can change an organism.*

Organisms change over time. Changes come about because of mutations in DNA. Random changes in DNA may introduce new traits into an organism. Over time, certain traits may become more common in one group of organisms as they interact with the environment and each other.

Are all changes in a group of organisms random? There are dogs, such as bloodhounds, that are particularly well suited to tracking. There are cows that give large quantities of milk and crops that produce large quantities of grain. Changes such as these are not random, but result from careful breeding directed by humans.

Selective Breeding

For thousands of years, humans have been carefully selecting and breeding certain plants and animals that have desirable traits. As the years have passed, horses have gotten faster, pigs have gotten leaner, and corn has become sweeter. **Selective breeding** is the process of selecting and breeding parent organisms to pass on particular traits to the offspring.

Selective breeding can be successful as long as the desirable traits are controlled by genes. In fact, what these early farmers were actually selecting were alleles, particular versions of a gene. The alleles were already present in some members of the population. People were not changing DNA, but they were causing certain alleles to become more common in a particular breed. The different dog breeds are a good example of this. All dogs share a common ancestor, the wolf. However, thousands of years of selective breeding have produced dogs with a variety of characteristics.

Bloodhounds, with their strong sense of smell, are used in police work for tracking.

CHECK YOUR READING How does selective breeding affect DNA?

Genetic Engineering

Within the last fifty years it has become possible to directly change the DNA of an organism. **Genetic engineering** is the process in which a sequence of DNA from an organism is first isolated, then inserted into the DNA of another organism, changing that organism's DNA. The DNA that is engineered often codes for some particular trait of interest. Using technology, scientists can take a gene from one species and transfer it into the DNA of an organism from another species. The resulting organisms are referred to as genetically modified (GM), or transgenic.

READING TiP
The root *trans-* means "across." *Transgenic* refers to the movement of genes across species.

CHECK YOUR READING What are three steps involved in genetic engineering?

One application of genetic engineering across species involves making plants more insect-resistant. Genetic engineers have isolated genes in microorganisms that produce natural insect-killing chemicals, or pesticides. They have succeeded in transferring these genes into the DNA of crop plants, such as corn and soybeans. The cells of the genetically modified plants then produce their own pesticide, reducing the amount of chemical pesticide farmers need to use on their fields.

These tomatoes have been genetically modified to grow in conditions that would not support naturally occurring tomatoes.

genetically modified tomatoes

Genetic engineering can address very specific needs. For example, in many parts of the world, soils are poor in nutrients. Or the soil may contain salts. Such soil is not good for growing food crops. Genetic engineers have inserted a gene from a salt-tolerant cabbage into tomatoes. The salt-tolerant tomatoes can grow in soil that natural tomatoes cannot grow in. These tomatoes can also be grown using brackish water, which is water with a higher salt content than fresh water.

There are risks and benefits associated with genetic engineering.

Genetic engineering offers potential benefits to society, but also carries potential risks. Probably most people in the United States have eaten foods made from genetically modified corn or soybeans. The plants have bacterial genes that make them more resistant to plant-eating insects. This increases food production and reduces the amount of chemical pesticides needed. Less chemical pesticide on the ground reduces the risk of environmental pollution.

However, many people worry that the natural pesticides produced by a genetically modified plant might have some effect on humans. What if genetically modified plants cross-breed with other plants, and give protection to plants that are considered weeds? There is also the question of how to let people know if the food they eat is genetically modified. Many people think that such food should be labeled.

CHECK YOUR READING What are some risks and benefits associated with using genetic engineering in food crops?

There is uncertainty about how the DNA of genetically modified organisms might affect natural populations. For example, scientists are working with salmon that are genetically modified to grow more quickly. Fish are an important food source, and natural fish populations are decreasing. However, the salmon are raised in pens set in rivers or the sea. If the fish escape, they may breed with fish from wild populations. Government officials have yet to decide whether the benefit of having these fast-growing fish is worth the risk to wild populations.

salmon pens

ANALYZE How would the genetic material of wild salmon change if they were to breed with genetically modified salmon?

DNA technology has many applications.

DNA technology is used in many different ways. It can be used to add nutrients to foods to make them more nutritious. It can be used to produce new and better drugs for treating disease. DNA technology can also be used to determine whether a particular drug might cause side effects in an individual. And it can be used to screen for and perhaps treat genetic disorders.

DNA Identification

You may have seen news stories about how DNA evidence is used to solve a crime. Law enforcement specialists gather as much DNA evidence as they can from a crime scene—for example, skin, hair, or blood. In a laboratory, they scan about ten regions of the DNA that are known to vary from individual to individual. They use this information to produce a DNA profile—a DNA fingerprint. This fingerprint is unique to a person, unless that person has an identical twin. If DNA analysis of tissue found at the crime scene matches the DNA fingerprint of a suspect, then police know the suspect was at the scene.

The more matches found between crime-scene DNA and the suspect's DNA, the higher the probability that the suspect is guilty. Experts currently recommend that at least four to six DNA regions be matched to establish a person's guilt. The chances are very small that another person would have exactly the same DNA profile for all the DNA regions tested. Of course, the courts also take other forms of evidence into account before an individual is convicted of a crime.

RESOURCE CENTER
CLASSZONE.COM

Learn more about DNA technology.

Studying Genomes

VOCABULARY
Don't forget to choose a strategy to take notes on the term *genome*.

One of the most challenging scientific projects ever undertaken was the Human Genome Project. A **genome** is all the genetic material in an organism. The primary goal of the project was to sequence the 3 billion nucleotide pairs in a single set of human chromosomes. The initial sequence was published in 2001. Scientists are now working to identify the approximately 30,000 genes within the human genome.

Scientists have completed sequencing the genomes of many organisms. These organisms, often referred to as model organisms, enable scientists to compare DNA across species. Many of the genes found in model organisms, such as the fruit fly and mouse, are also found in the human genome.

Scientists are aware that there are many ethical, legal, and social issues that arise from the ability to change DNA. We as a society have to decide when it is acceptable to change DNA and how to use the technology we have. **Cloning** is a technique that uses technology to make copies. It can be applied to a segment of DNA or to a whole organism. Cloning has been used in bacteria to produce proteins and drugs that help fight disease. Human insulin, which is used to treat people with a certain form of diabetes, is now produced in large quantities as the result of cloning techniques.

The same technology, which is so helpful in one application, can be a cause of concern when applied in a different way. In 1996, scientists produced the first clone of a mammal, a sheep named Dolly. All of Dolly's DNA came from a single body cell of another sheep. The ability to clone such a complex animal raised many concerns about future uses of cloning. This, as well as many other possible applications of technology, makes it important that people understand the science of genetics. Only then can they make informed decisions about how and when the technology should be used.

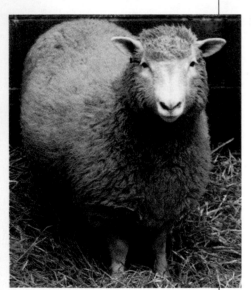

Dolly was the first successful clone of a mammal.

5.3 Review

KEY CONCEPTS

1. What is a genetically modified organism?
2. What is the Human Genome Project?
3. List three different applications of DNA technology.

CRITICAL THINKING

4. **Compare and Contrast** How is selective breeding different from genetic engineering? How is it the same?

5. **Analyze** Do you think a genetically modified trait in an organism can be undone? Why or why not?

○ CHALLENGE

6. **Analyze** Why might a genetically engineered drug, such as insulin, be better for treatment of disease than a drug that is manufactured chemically?

DNA OF EXTINCT ANIMALS

Modern Genetics Meets the Dodo and the Solitaire

Hunted to Extinction

The dodo bird was first sighted around 1600 by Portuguese sailors arriving on the shores of the island of Mauritius in the Indian Ocean. Portuguese sailors hunted the dodo, which was unable to fly, and used its meat for food. The bird, never having had contact with humans, did not run away. Only a mere 80 years later, the dodo was extinct.

DNA Evidence

Few bone specimens of the dodo bird remain today. Scientists collected and analyzed genetic material from preserved dodo specimens and specimens of another, similar extinct bird called the solitaire bird. The DNA evidence was compared with the genetic material of about 35 species of living pigeons and doves.

The model shows a solitaire bird, a close relative of the dodo.

The DNA had a story to tell. Evidence suggests that the dodo and solitaire bird were close relatives. Their nearest living relative is a species of pigeon found in nearby southeast Asia. From this evidence, scientists hypothesize that the dodo and solitaire birds species became separate almost 25 million years ago. In the geographic location of the island of Mauritius, the dodo developed its distinct characteristics, which eventually led to its extinction.

EXPLORE

1. **MAKE INFERENCES** How can scientists use what they know from analyzing dodo bones to help them form conclusions about the physical characteristics of the bird?

2. **CHALLENGE** Several factors contributed to the extinction of the dodo bird. Look online to find out more about these factors. How can learning about what happened to the dodo help save today's endangered species from extinction?

Chapter Review

the BIG idea

DNA is a set of instructions for making cell parts.

CONTENT REVIEW
CLASSZONE.COM

◀ KEY CONCEPTS SUMMARY

5.1 DNA and RNA are required to make proteins.

DNA contains a code that enables a cell to make RNA and proteins. Replication copies the code before a cell divides.

- DNA's triplet code enables a cell to code for proteins
- mRNA, tRNA, and ribosomes translate the code into a sequence of amino acids.
- The amino acids form a protein needed for cell function.

| DNA | → | RNA | → | Proteins |

VOCABULARY
replication p. 137
RNA p. 138

5.2 Changes in DNA can produce variation.

Differences in DNA produce variations. Any change to DNA is a mutation. Many mutations have little or no effect. However, some mutations can change the way a cell works—sometimes helping an organism, sometimes hurting it.

Genetic disorders are caused by mutations in DNA. Some are inherited and can be followed through different generations of a family by using a pedigree. Other genetic disorders, such as cancer, are caused by mutations that occur during a person's lifetime.

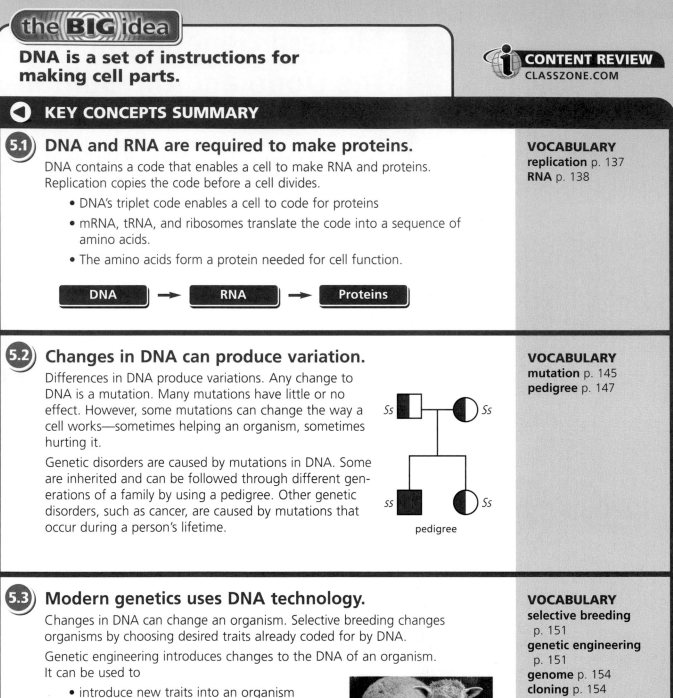

pedigree

VOCABULARY
mutation p. 145
pedigree p. 147

5.3 Modern genetics uses DNA technology.

Changes in DNA can change an organism. Selective breeding changes organisms by choosing desired traits already coded for by DNA.

Genetic engineering introduces changes to the DNA of an organism. It can be used to

- introduce new traits into an organism
- produce medicines and other products
- identify individuals
- clone genes as well as organisms
- sequence the genome of an organism

DNA technology raises important issues for society.

Dolly was the first clone of a mammal.

VOCABULARY
selective breeding p. 151
genetic engineering p. 151
genome p. 154
cloning p. 154

Reviewing Vocabulary

Copy the chart below and write the definition for each word. Use the meaning of the word's root to help you.

Term	Root Meaning	Definition
1. replication	to repeat	
2. mutation	to change	
3. genome	relating to offspring	
4. cloning	to branch off	

Reviewing Key Concepts

Multiple Choice *Choose the letter of the best answer.*

5. Genes are sequences of DNA, which are made up of
- **a.** nucleotides
- **c.** phosphates
- **b.** chromosomes
- **d.** ribosomes

6. What happens during replication?
- **a.** DNA is copied.
- **b.** RNA is copied.
- **c.** Ribosomes are made.
- **d.** Proteins are made.

7. Which base is found only in RNA?
- **a.** thymine
- **b.** guanine
- **c.** adenine
- **d.** uracil

8. The main function of mRNA in protein synthesis is to
- **a.** transfer amino acids to a ribosome
- **b.** carry proteins to the ribosome
- **c.** transcribe genes from DNA
- **d.** connect nucleotides together

9. Proteins are made up of a sequence of
- **a.** chromosomes
- **c.** nucleotides
- **b.** amino acids
- **d.** base pairs

10. Mutations are changes in
- **a.** DNA
- **c.** tRNA
- **b.** the cell cycle
- **d.** proteins

11. Which is a known cause of genetic mutations?
- **a.** poor nutrition
- **b.** malaria
- **c.** ultraviolet radiation
- **d.** cancer

12. A pedigree shows
- **a.** how proteins are synthesized
- **b.** how genes are inherited in a family
- **c.** where mutations are located in a sequence of DNA
- **d.** which triplet of bases matches up with a particular amino acid

13. The main goal of the Human Genome Project was to
- **a.** find cures for genetic diseases
- **b.** find all mutations in human DNA
- **c.** count the number of genes in human DNA
- **d.** sequence all DNA on human chromosomes

14. Genetic engineering involves
- **a.** inserting changed DNA into an organism
- **b.** cross-breeding plants
- **c.** testing new medicines for genetic diseases
- **d.** using x-rays to change DNA

Short Answer *Write a short answer to each question.*

15. DNA is described as the information molecule. What is the information that DNA carries?

16. What is the difference between selective breeding and genetic engineering?

17. List three applications of DNA technology and how these uses benefit humans.

Thinking Critically

Use the diagram to answer the next three questions.

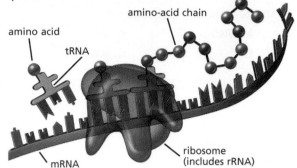

18. **ANALYZE** How does the mRNA strand above compare with the DNA template that produced it? Use the words *guanine, cytosine, thymine, adenine, and uracil* in your answer.

19. **SUMMARIZE** Three types of RNA are needed for protein synthesis. What are the three types and what is the function of each?

20. **APPLY** A protein contains 131 amino acids. How many bases will there be on the mRNA strand corresponding to these amino acids and how do you know?

21. **ANALYZE** A cell contains two sets of DNA. If the gene on one molecule of DNA has a mutation, how will that affect the gene on the other molecule of DNA?

22. **SYNTHESIZE** A mutation occurs during DNA replication. The following sequence

    A-T-T-A-C-A-G-G-G

    is copied as,

    A-T-A-C-A-G-G-G

    with one base missing. How does that affect the triplet code?

23. **SEQUENCE** List the steps in making a protein. Start with a gene on a DNA molecule. Include the chemical subunits involved in each step.

24. **EVALUATE** A person who carries a gene for a genetic disorder may not get the disorder. How can that be?

25. **INFER** How might a scientist determine if a neutral mutation has occurred in an organism?

26. **PREDICT** A mutation in an Arctic hare causes brown spots to appear on normally white fur. Explain how the mutation might affect the ability of the hare to survive.

27. **EVALUATE** Doctors can sometimes cure cancer by removing cancerous cells from a person's body. Why is it important for the doctors to remove all the cells?

28. **EVALUATE** How might selective breeding of a type of animal limit genetic diversity within the breed?

29. **EVALUATE** If a scientist compares the genome of a mouse to that of a human and discovers that the two organisms have many of the same genes, what can the scientist infer about how the cells in the two organisms function?

the BIG idea

30. **DRAWING CONCLUSIONS** Look again at the photograph on pages 132–133. How have models helped scientists understand the function of DNA?

31. **CONNECT** A local newspaper has written an editorial against the use of genetic engineering. The writer argues that humans should never change the DNA in an organism, even though they have the technology to do so. Write a response to the editorial, stating whether you think the benefits humans get from genetic engineering are worth the risks.

UNIT PROJECTS

Evaluate all the data, results, and information from your project folder. Prepare to present your project. Be ready to answer questions posed by your classmates about your results.

Standardized Test Practice

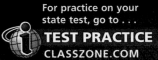

For practice on your
state test, go to . . .
TEST PRACTICE
CLASSZONE.COM

Analyzing Data

Use the following information and the pedigree chart to answer the questions.

Red-green colorblindness is one of the most common genetic conditions in the human population. About 5 percent of males are red-green colorblind. A male receives just one allele for this trait, on the X chromosome he inherits from his mother. If he receives the allele for red-green colorblindness, he will be colorblind. His genotype will be cb/Y.

Females inherit two alleles for the trait. Colorblindness (cb) is recessive and the allele for regular color vision (Cb) is dominant. A female with both the recessive allele and the dominant allele will have normal color vision. Her genotype would be Cb/cb. However, if the female has a male child, her child may be colorblind. The pedigree chart shows colorblindness in three generations.

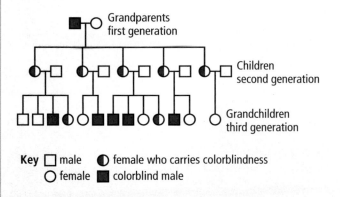

Grandparents
first generation

Children
second generation

Grandchildren
third generation

Key ☐ male ◑ female who carries colorblindness
○ female ■ colorblind male

1. How many individuals in the first generation are colorblind?
   a. two
   b. one
   c. none
   d. three

2. How many individuals in the second generation are female?
   a. none
   b. one
   c. two
   d. five

3. Which statement describes the pattern of inheritance for colorblindness?
   a. Grandmother and granddaughter are both colorblind.
   b. Grandmother and son are both colorblind.
   c. Grandfather and granddaughter are both colorblind.
   d. Grandfather and grandson are both colorblind.

4. What are the genotypes of the males in the third generation?
   a. Cb/Y, Cb/Y, Cb/Y, cb/Y, cb/Y, cb/Y, cb/Y
   b. cb/Y, cb/Y, cb/Y, cb/Y,cb/Y, cb/Y, cb/Y
   c. Cb/Y, Cb/Y, Cb/Y, Cb/Y, Cb/Y, Cb/Y, CbY
   d. Cb/Y, Cb/Y, cb/Y, cb/y, cb/y ,cb/Y, cb/Y

Extended Response

5. Write a paragraph explaining why a color-blind man who has three daughters and one son with normal color vision might have two grandsons who are color-blind. Use the terms in the vocabulary box in your answer. Underline each term.

6. The same color-blind man has four granddaughters. Would you predict the granddaughters to be colorblind? Explain why or why not. Use the terms in the vocabulary box.

genotype	phenotype	allele
recessive	dominant	generation

Student Resource Handbooks

Scientific Thinking Handbook

Making Observations

An **observation** is an act of noting and recording an event, characteristic, behavior, or anything else detected with an instrument or with the senses.

Observations allow you to make informed hypotheses and to gather data for experiments. Careful observations often lead to ideas for new experiments. There are two categories of observations:

- **Quantitative observations** can be expressed in numbers and include records of time, temperature, mass, distance, and volume.

- **Qualitative observations** include descriptions of sights, sounds, smells, and textures.

EXAMPLE

A student dissolved 30 grams of Epsom salts in water, poured the solution into a dish, and let the dish sit out uncovered overnight. The next day, she made the following observations of the Epsom salt crystals that grew in the dish.

> To determine the mass, the student found the mass of the dish before and after growing the crystals and then used subtraction to find the difference.

> The student measured several crystals and calculated the mean length. (To learn how to calculate the mean of a data set, see page R36.)

Table 1. Observations of Epsom Salt Crystals

Quantitative Observations	Qualitative Observations
• mass = 30 g • mean crystal length = 0.5 cm • longest crystal length = 2 cm	• Crystals are clear. • Crystals are long, thin, and rectangular. • White crust has formed around edge of dish.

> Photographs or sketches are useful for recording qualitative observations.

Epsom salt crystals

MORE ABOUT OBSERVING

- Make quantitative observations whenever possible. That way, others will know exactly what you observed and be able to compare their results with yours.

- It is always a good idea to make qualitative observations too. You never know when you might observe something unexpected.

Predicting and Hypothesizing

A **prediction** is an expectation of what will be observed or what will happen. A **hypothesis** is a tentative explanation for an observation or scientific problem that can be tested by further investigation.

EXAMPLE

Suppose you have made two paper airplanes and you wonder why one of them tends to glide farther than the other one.

1. Start by asking a question.

2. Make an educated guess. After examination, you notice that the wings of the airplane that flies farther are slightly larger than the wings of the other airplane.

3. Write a prediction based upon your educated guess, in the form of an "If . . . , then . . ." statement. Write the independent variable after the word *if*, and the dependent variable after the word *then*.

4. To make a hypothesis, explain why you think what you predicted will occur. Write the explanation after the word *because*.

---

1. Why does one of the paper airplanes glide farther than the other?

2. The size of an airplane's wings may affect how far the airplane will glide.

3. Prediction: If I make a paper airplane with larger wings, then the airplane will glide farther.

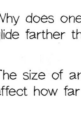

To read about independent and dependent variables, see page R30.

4. Hypothesis: If I make a paper airplane with larger wings, then the airplane will glide farther, because the additional surface area of the wing will produce more lift.

Notice that the part of the hypothesis after *because* adds an explanation of why the airplane will glide farther.

MORE ABOUT HYPOTHESES

- The results of an experiment cannot prove that a hypothesis is correct. Rather, the results either support or do not support the hypothesis.

- Valuable information is gained even when your hypothesis is not supported by your results. For example, it would be an important discovery to find that wing size is not related to how far an airplane glides.

- In science, a hypothesis is supported only after many scientists have conducted many experiments and produced consistent results.

Inferring

An **inference** is a logical conclusion drawn from the available evidence and prior knowledge. Inferences are often made from observations.

EXAMPLE

A student observing a set of acorns noticed something unexpected about one of them. He noticed a white, soft-bodied insect eating its way out of the acorn.

The student recorded these observations.

Observations

- There is a hole in the acorn, about 0.5 cm in diameter, where the insect crawled out.
- There is a second hole, which is about the size of a pinhole, on the other side of the acorn.
- The inside of the acorn is hollow.

Here are some inferences that can be made on the basis of the observations.

Inferences

- The insect formed from the material inside the acorn, grew to its present size, and ate its way out of the acorn.
- The insect crawled through the smaller hole, ate the inside of the acorn, grew to its present size, and ate its way out of the acorn.
- An egg was laid in the acorn through the smaller hole. The egg hatched into a larva that ate the inside of the acorn, grew to its present size, and ate its way out of the acorn.

When you make inferences, be sure to look at all of the evidence available and combine it with what you already know.

MORE ABOUT INFERENCES

Inferences depend both on observations and on the knowledge of the people making the inferences. Ancient people who did not know that organisms are produced only by similar organisms might have made an inference like the first one. A student today might look at the same observations and make the second inference. A third student might have knowledge about this particular insect and know that it is never small enough to fit through the smaller hole, leading her to the third inference.

Identifying Cause and Effect

In a **cause-and-effect relationship,** one event or characteristic is the result of another. Usually an effect follows its cause in time.

There are many examples of cause-and-effect relationships in everyday life.

Cause	Effect
Turn off a light.	Room gets dark.
Drop a glass.	Glass breaks.
Blow a whistle.	Sound is heard.

Scientists must be careful not to infer a cause-and-effect relationship just because one event happens after another event. When one event occurs after another, you cannot infer a cause-and-effect relationship on the basis of that information alone. You also cannot conclude that one event caused another if there are alternative ways to explain the second event. A scientist must demonstrate through experimentation or continued observation that an event was truly caused by another event.

EXAMPLE

Make an Observation

Suppose you have a few plants growing outside. When the weather starts getting colder, you bring one of the plants indoors. You notice that the plant you brought indoors is growing faster than the others are growing. You cannot conclude from your observation that the change in temperature was the cause of the increased plant growth, because there are alternative explanations for the observation. Some possible explanations are given below.

- The humidity indoors caused the plant to grow faster.

- The level of sunlight indoors caused the plant to grow faster.

- The indoor plant's being noticed more often and watered more often than the outdoor plants caused it to grow faster.

- The plant that was brought indoors was healthier than the other plants to begin with.

To determine which of these factors, if any, caused the indoor plant to grow faster than the outdoor plants, you would need to design and conduct an experiment.

See pages R28–R35 for information about designing experiments.

Recognizing Bias

Television, newspapers, and the Internet are full of experts claiming to have scientific evidence to back up their claims. How do you know whether the claims are really backed up by good science?

Bias is a slanted point of view, or personal prejudice. The goal of scientists is to be as objective as possible and to base their findings on facts instead of opinions. However, bias often affects the conclusions of researchers, and it is important to learn to recognize bias.

When scientific results are reported, you should consider the source of the information as well as the information itself. It is important to critically analyze the information that you see and read.

SOURCES OF BIAS

There are several ways in which a report of scientific information may be biased. Here are some questions that you can ask yourself:

1. **Who is sponsoring the research?**

   Sometimes, the results of an investigation are biased because an organization paying for the research is looking for a specific answer. This type of bias can affect how data are gathered and interpreted.

2. **Is the research sample large enough?**

   Sometimes research does not include enough data. The larger the sample size, the more likely that the results are accurate, assuming a truly random sample.

3. **In a survey, who is answering the questions?**

   The results of a survey or poll can be biased. The people taking part in the survey may have been specifically chosen because of how they would answer. They may have the same ideas or lifestyles. A survey or poll should make use of a random sample of people.

4. **Are the people who take part in a survey biased?**

   People who take part in surveys sometimes try to answer the questions the way they think the researcher wants them to answer. Also, in surveys or polls that ask for personal information, people may be unwilling to answer questions truthfully.

SCIENTIFIC BIAS

It is also important to realize that scientists have their own biases because of the types of research they do and because of their scientific viewpoints. Two scientists may look at the same set of data and come to completely different conclusions because of these biases. However, such disagreements are not necessarily bad. In fact, a critical analysis of disagreements is often responsible for moving science forward.

Identifying Faulty Reasoning

Faulty reasoning is wrong or incorrect thinking. It leads to mistakes and to wrong conclusions. Scientists are careful not to draw unreasonable conclusions from experimental data. Without such caution, the results of scientific investigations may be misleading.

EXAMPLE

Scientists try to make generalizations based on their data to explain as much about nature as possible. If only a small sample of data is looked at, however, a conclusion may be faulty. Suppose a scientist has studied the effects of the El Niño and La Niña weather patterns on flood damage in California from 1989 to 1995. The scientist organized the data in the bar graph below.

The scientist drew the following conclusions:

1. The La Niña weather pattern has no effect on flooding in California.
2. When neither weather pattern occurs, there is almost no flood damage.
3. A weak or moderate El Niño produces a small or moderate amount of flooding.
4. A strong El Niño produces a lot of flooding.

Flood and Storm Damage in California

Weak–moderate El Niño

Strong El Niño

Starting year of season
(July 1–June 30)

SOURCE: *Governor's Office of Emergency Services, California*

For the six-year period of the scientist's investigation, these conclusions may seem to be reasonable. However, a six-year study of weather patterns may be too small of a sample for the conclusions to be supported. Consider the following graph, which shows information that was gathered from 1949 to 1997.

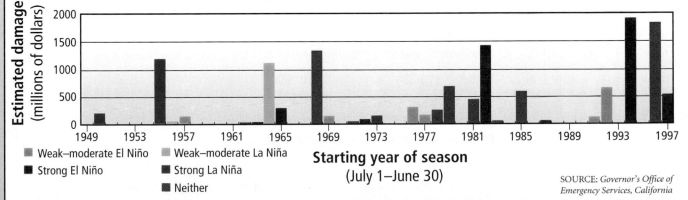

Flood and Storm Damage in California from 1949 to 1997

Weak–moderate El Niño Weak–moderate La Niña
Strong El Niño Strong La Niña
Neither

Starting year of season
(July 1–June 30)

SOURCE: *Governor's Office of Emergency Services, California*

The only one of the conclusions that all of this information supports is number 3: a weak or moderate El Niño produces a small or moderate amount of flooding. By collecting more data, scientists can be more certain of their conclusions and can avoid faulty reasoning.

Analyzing Statements

To **analyze** a statement is to examine its parts carefully. Scientific findings are often reported through media such as television or the Internet. A report that is made public often focuses on only a small part of research. As a result, it is important to question the sources of information.

Evaluate Media Claims

To **evaluate** a statement is to judge it on the basis of criteria you've established. Sometimes evaluating means deciding whether a statement is true.

Reports of scientific research and findings in the media may be misleading or incomplete. When you are exposed to this information, you should ask yourself some questions so that you can make informed judgments about the information.

1. **Does the information come from a credible source?**

   Suppose you learn about a new product and it is stated that scientific evidence proves that the product works. A report from a respected news source may be more believable than an advertisement paid for by the product's manufacturer.

2. **How much evidence supports the claim?**

   Often, it may seem that there is new evidence every day of something in the world that either causes or cures an illness. However, information that is the result of several years of work by several different scientists is more credible than an advertisement that does not even cite the subjects of the experiment.

3. **How much information is being presented?**

   Science cannot solve all questions, and scientific experiments often have flaws. A report that discusses problems in a scientific study may be more believable than a report that addresses only positive experimental findings.

4. **Is scientific evidence being presented by a specific source?**

   Sometimes scientific findings are reported by people who are called experts or leaders in a scientific field. But if their names are not given or their scientific credentials are not reported, their statements may be less credible than those of recognized experts.

Differentiate Between Fact and Opinion

Sometimes information is presented as a fact when it may be an opinion. When scientific conclusions are reported, it is important to recognize whether they are based on solid evidence. Again, you may find it helpful to ask yourself some questions.

1. **What is the difference between a fact and an opinion?**

   A **fact** is a piece of information that can be strictly defined and proved true. An **opinion** is a statement that expresses a belief, value, or feeling. An opinion cannot be proved true or false. For example, a person's age is a fact, but if someone is asked how old they feel, it is impossible to prove the person's answer to be true or false.

2. **Can opinions be measured?**

   Yes, opinions can be measured. In fact, surveys often ask for people's opinions on a topic. But there is no way to know whether or not an opinion is the truth.

HOW TO DIFFERENTIATE FACT FROM OPINION

Human Activities and the Environment

Opinions
Notice words or phrases that express beliefs or feelings. The words *unfortunately* and *careless* show that opinions are being expressed.

Unfortunately, human use of fossil fuels is one of the most significant developments of the past few centuries. Humans rely on fossil fuels, a non-renewable energy resource, for more than 90 percent of their energy needs.

This careless misuse of our planet's resources has resulted in pollution, global warming, and the destruction of fragile ecosystems. For example, oil pipelines carry more than one million barrels of oil each day across tundra regions. Transporting oil across such areas can only result in oil spills that poison the land for decades.

Facts
Statements that contain statistics tend to be facts. Writers often use facts to support their opinions.

Opinion
Look for statements that speculate about events. These statements are opinions, because they cannot be proved.

Lab Handbook

Safety Rules

Before you work in the laboratory, read these safety rules twice. Ask your teacher to explain any rules that you do not completely understand. Refer to these rules later on if you have questions about safety in the science classroom.

Directions

- Read all directions and make sure that you understand them before starting an investigation or lab activity. If you do not understand how to do a procedure or how to use a piece of equipment, ask your teacher.
- Do not begin any investigation or touch any equipment until your teacher has told you to start.
- Never experiment on your own. If you want to try a procedure that the directions do not call for, ask your teacher for permission first.
- If you are hurt or injured in any way, tell your teacher immediately.

Dress Code

goggles

apron

gloves

- Wear goggles when
  — using glassware, sharp objects, or chemicals
  — heating an object
  — working with anything that can easily fly up into the air and hurt someone's eye
- Tie back long hair or hair that hangs in front of your eyes.
- Remove any article of clothing—such as a loose sweater or a scarf—that hangs down and may touch a flame, chemical, or piece of equipment.
- Observe all safety icons calling for the wearing of eye protection, gloves, and aprons.

Heating and Fire Safety

fire
safety

heating
safety

- Keep your work area neat, clean, and free of extra materials.
- Never reach over a flame or heat source.
- Point objects being heated away from you and others.
- Never heat a substance or an object in a closed container.
- Never touch an object that has been heated. If you are unsure whether something is hot, treat it as though it is. Use oven mitts, clamps, tongs, or a test-tube holder.
- Know where the fire extinguisher and fire blanket are kept in your classroom.
- Do not throw hot substances into the trash. Wait for them to cool or use the container your teacher puts out for disposal.

Electrical Safety

electrical
safety

- Never use lamps or other electrical equipment with frayed cords.
- Make sure no cord is lying on the floor where someone can trip over it.
- Do not let a cord hang over the side of a counter or table so that the equipment can easily be pulled or knocked to the floor.
- Never let cords hang into sinks or other places where water can be found.
- Never try to fix electrical problems. Inform your teacher of any problems immediately.
- Unplug an electrical cord by pulling on the plug, not the cord.

Chemical Safety

chemical
safety

poison

fumes

- If you spill a chemical or get one on your skin or in your eyes, tell your teacher right away.
- Never touch, taste, or sniff any chemicals in the lab. If you need to determine odor, waft. Wafting consists of holding the chemical in its container 15 centimeters (6 in.) away from your nose, and using your fingers to bring fumes from the container to your nose.
- Keep lids on all chemicals you are not using.
- Never put unused chemicals back into the original containers. Throw away extra chemicals where your teacher tells you to.
- Pour chemicals over a sink or your work area, not over the floor.
- If you get a chemical in your eye, use the eyewash right away.
- Always wash your hands after handling chemicals, plants, or soil.

Wafting

Glassware and Sharp-Object Safety

sharp
objects

- If you break glassware, tell your teacher right away.
- Do not use broken or chipped glassware. Give these to your teacher.
- Use knives and other cutting instruments carefully. Always wear eye protection and cut away from you.

Animal Safety

- Never hurt an animal.
- Touch animals only when necessary. Follow your teacher's instructions for handling animals.
- Always wash your hands after working with animals.

Cleanup

disposal

- Follow your teacher's instructions for throwing away or putting away supplies.
- Clean your work area and pick up anything that has dropped to the floor.
- Wash your hands.

Using Lab Equipment

Different experiments require different types of equipment. But even though experiments differ, the ways in which the equipment is used are the same.

Beakers

- Use beakers for holding and pouring liquids.
- Do not use a beaker to measure the volume of a liquid. Use a graduated cylinder instead. (See page R16.)
- Use a beaker that holds about twice as much liquid as you need. For example, if you need 100 milliliters of water, you should use a 200- or 250-milliliter beaker.

Test Tubes

- Use test tubes to hold small amounts of substances.
- Do not use a test tube to measure the volume of a liquid.
- Use a test tube when heating a substance over a flame. Aim the mouth of the tube away from yourself and other people.
- Liquids easily spill or splash from test tubes, so it is important to use only small amounts of liquids.

Test-Tube Holder

- Use a test-tube holder when heating a substance in a test tube.
- Use a test-tube holder if the substance in a test tube is dangerous to touch.
- Make sure the test-tube holder tightly grips the test tube so that the test tube will not slide out of the holder.
- Make sure that the test-tube holder is above the surface of the substance in the test tube so that you can observe the substance.

Test-Tube Rack

- Use a test-tube rack to organize test tubes before, during, and after an experiment.

- Use a test-tube rack to keep test tubes upright so that they do not fall over and spill their contents.

- Use a test-tube rack that is the correct size for the test tubes that you are using. If the rack is too small, a test tube may become stuck. If the rack is too large, a test tube may lean over, and some of its contents may spill or splash.

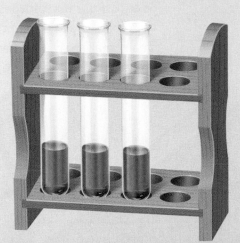

Forceps

- Use forceps when you need to pick up or hold a very small object that should not be touched with your hands.

- Do not use forceps to hold anything over a flame, because forceps are not long enough to keep your hand safely away from the flame. Plastic forceps will melt, and metal forceps will conduct heat and burn your hand.

Hot Plate

- Use a hot plate when a substance needs to be kept warmer than room temperature for a long period of time.

- Use a hot plate instead of a Bunsen burner or a candle when you need to carefully control temperature.

- Do not use a hot plate when a substance needs to be burned in an experiment.

- Always use "hot hands" safety mitts or oven mitts when handling anything that has been heated on a hot plate.

Microscope

Scientists use microscopes to see very small objects that cannot easily be seen with the eye alone. A microscope magnifies the image of an object so that small details may be observed. A microscope that you may use can magnify an object 400 times—the object will appear 400 times larger than its actual size.

Body The body separates the lens in the eyepiece from the objective lenses below.

Nosepiece The nosepiece holds the objective lenses above the stage and rotates so that all lenses may be used.

High-Power Objective Lens This is the largest lens on the nosepiece. It magnifies an image approximately 40 times.

Stage The stage supports the object being viewed.

Diaphragm The diaphragm is used to adjust the amount of light passing through the slide and into an objective lens.

Mirror or Light Source Some microscopes use light that is reflected through the stage by a mirror. Other microscopes have their own light sources.

Eyepiece Objects are viewed through the eyepiece. The eyepiece contains a lens that commonly magnifies an image 10 times.

Coarse Adjustment This knob is used to focus the image of an object when it is viewed through the low-power lens.

Fine Adjustment This knob is used to focus the image of an object when it is viewed through the high-power lens.

Low-Power Objective Lens This is the smallest lens on the nosepiece. It magnifies an image approximately 10 times.

Arm The arm supports the body above the stage. Always carry a microscope by the arm and base.

Stage Clip The stage clip holds a slide in place on the stage.

Base The base supports the microscope.

VIEWING AN OBJECT

1. Use the coarse adjustment knob to raise the body tube.

2. Adjust the diaphragm so that you can see a bright circle of light through the eyepiece.

3. Place the object or slide on the stage. Be sure that it is centered over the hole in the stage.

4. Turn the nosepiece to click the low-power lens into place.

5. Using the coarse adjustment knob, slowly lower the lens and focus on the specimen being viewed. Be sure not to touch the slide or object with the lens.

6. When switching from the low-power lens to the high-power lens, first raise the body tube with the coarse adjustment knob so that the high-power lens will not hit the slide.

7. Turn the nosepiece to click the high-power lens into place.

8. Use the fine adjustment knob to focus on the specimen being viewed. Again, be sure not to touch the slide or object with the lens.

MAKING A SLIDE, OR WET MOUNT

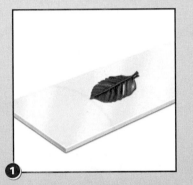

1 Place the specimen in the center of a clean slide.

2 Place a drop of water on the specimen.

3 Place a cover slip on the slide. Put one edge of the cover slip into the drop of water and slowly lower it over the specimen.

4 Remove any air bubbles from under the cover slip by gently tapping the cover slip.

5 Dry any excess water before placing the slide on the microscope stage for viewing.

Spring Scale (Force Meter)

- Use a spring scale to measure a force pulling on the scale.
- Use a spring scale to measure the force of gravity exerted on an object by Earth.
- To measure a force accurately, a spring scale must be zeroed before it is used. The scale is zeroed when no weight is attached and the indicator is positioned at zero.
- Do not attach a weight that is either too heavy or too light to a spring scale. A weight that is too heavy could break the scale or exert too great a force for the scale to measure. A weight that is too light may not exert enough force to be measured accurately.

Graduated Cylinder

- Use a graduated cylinder to measure the volume of a liquid.
- Be sure that the graduated cylinder is on a flat surface so that your measurement will be accurate.
- When reading the scale on a graduated cylinder, be sure to have your eyes at the level of the surface of the liquid.
- The surface of the liquid will be curved in the graduated cylinder. Read the volume of the liquid at the bottom of the curve, or meniscus (muh-NIHS-kuhs).
- You can use a graduated cylinder to find the volume of a solid object by measuring the increase in a liquid's level after you add the object to the cylinder.

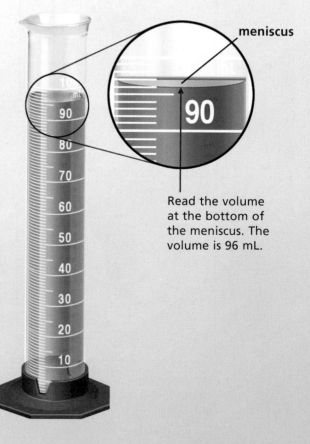

meniscus

Read the volume at the bottom of the meniscus. The volume is 96 mL.

Metric Rulers

- Use metric rulers or meter sticks to measure objects' lengths.

- Do not measure an object from the end of a metric ruler or meter stick, because the end is often imperfect. Instead, measure from the 1-centimeter mark, but remember to subtract a centimeter from the apparent measurement.

- Estimate any lengths that extend between marked units. For example, if a meter stick shows centimeters but not millimeters, you can estimate the length that an object extends between centimeter marks to measure it to the nearest millimeter.

- **Controlling Variables** If you are taking repeated measurements, always measure from the same point each time. For example, if you're measuring how high two different balls bounce when dropped from the same height, measure both bounces at the same point on the balls—either the top or the bottom. Do not measure at the top of one ball and the bottom of the other.

EXAMPLE

How to Measure a Leaf

1. Lay a ruler flat on top of the leaf so that the 1-centimeter mark lines up with one end. Make sure the ruler and the leaf do not move between the time you line them up and the time you take the measurement.

2. Look straight down on the ruler so that you can see exactly how the marks line up with the other end of the leaf.

3. Estimate the length by which the leaf extends beyond a marking. For example, the leaf below extends about halfway between the 4.2-centimeter and 4.3-centimeter marks, so the apparent measurement is about 4.25 centimeters.

4. Remember to subtract 1 centimeter from your apparent measurement, since you started at the 1-centimeter mark on the ruler and not at the end. The leaf is about 3.25 centimeters long (4.25 cm – 1 cm = 3.25 cm).

Triple-Beam Balance

This balance has a pan and three beams with sliding masses, called riders. At one end of the beams is a pointer that indicates whether the mass on the pan is equal to the masses shown on the beams.

1. Make sure the balance is zeroed before measuring the mass of an object. The balance is zeroed if the pointer is at zero when nothing is on the pan and the riders are at their zero points. Use the adjustment knob at the base of the balance to zero it.

2. Place the object to be measured on the pan.

3. Move the riders one notch at a time away from the pan. Begin with the largest rider. If moving the largest rider one notch brings the pointer below zero, begin measuring the mass of the object with the next smaller rider.

4. Change the positions of the riders until they balance the mass on the pan and the pointer is at zero. Then add the readings from the three beams to determine the mass of the object.

300 g	position of largest rider
90 g	position of middle rider
+ 3 g	position of smallest rider
393 g	mass of beaker

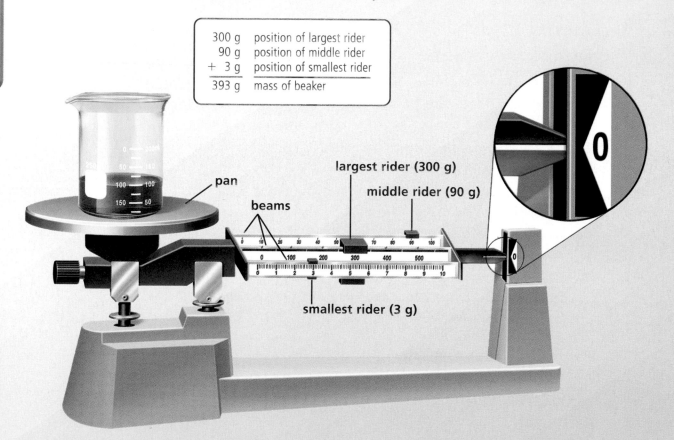

Double-Pan Balance

This type of balance has two pans. Between the pans is a pointer that indicates whether the masses on the pans are equal.

1. Make sure the balance is zeroed before measuring the mass of an object. The balance is zeroed if the pointer is at zero when there is nothing on either of the pans. Many double-pan balances have sliding knobs that can be used to zero them.

2. Place the object to be measured on one of the pans.

3. Begin adding standard masses to the other pan. Begin with the largest standard mass. If this adds too much mass to the balance, begin measuring the mass of the object with the next smaller standard mass.

4. Add standard masses until the masses on both pans are balanced and the pointer is at zero. Then add the standard masses together to determine the mass of the object being measured.

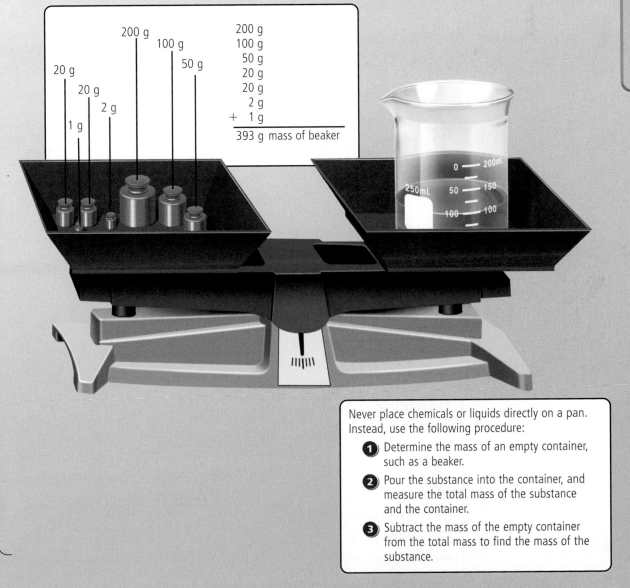

Never place chemicals or liquids directly on a pan. Instead, use the following procedure:

1. Determine the mass of an empty container, such as a beaker.

2. Pour the substance into the container, and measure the total mass of the substance and the container.

3. Subtract the mass of the empty container from the total mass to find the mass of the substance.

The Metric System and SI Units

Scientists use International System (SI) units for measurements of distance, volume, mass, and temperature. The International System is based on multiples of ten and the metric system of measurement.

Basic SI Units		
Property	**Name**	**Symbol**
length	meter	m
volume	liter	L
mass	kilogram	kg
temperature	kelvin	K

SI Prefixes		
Prefix	**Symbol**	**Multiple of 10**
kilo-	k	1000
hecto-	h	100
deca-	da	10
deci-	d	$0.1 \left(\frac{1}{10}\right)$
centi-	c	$0.01 \left(\frac{1}{100}\right)$
milli-	m	$0.001 \left(\frac{1}{1000}\right)$

Changing Metric Units

You can change from one unit to another in the metric system by multiplying or dividing by a power of 10.

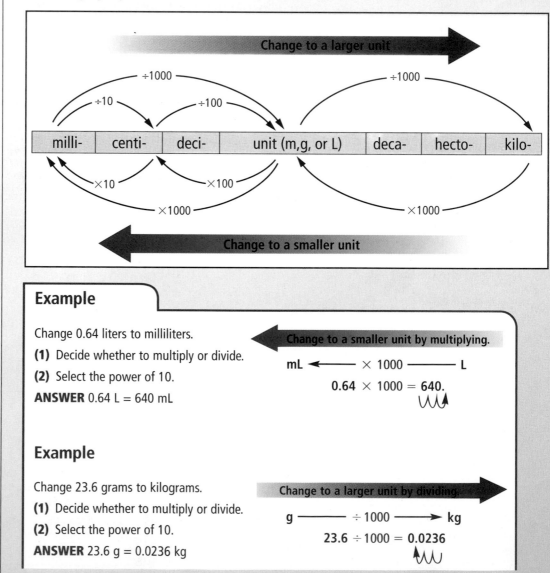

Example

Change 0.64 liters to milliliters.

(1) Decide whether to multiply or divide.

(2) Select the power of 10.

ANSWER 0.64 L = 640 mL

Change to a smaller unit by multiplying.

mL ⟵ × 1000 ⟶ L

0.64 × 1000 = **640.**

Example

Change 23.6 grams to kilograms.

(1) Decide whether to multiply or divide.

(2) Select the power of 10.

ANSWER 23.6 g = 0.0236 kg

Change to a larger unit by dividing.

g ⟶ ÷ 1000 ⟶ kg

23.6 ÷ 1000 = **0.0236**

LAB HANDBOOK

Temperature Conversions

Even though the kelvin is the SI base unit of temperature, the degree Celsius will be the unit you use most often in your science studies. The formulas below show the relationships between temperatures in degrees Fahrenheit (°F), degrees Celsius (°C), and kelvins (K).

$$°C = \frac{5}{9}(°F - 32)$$

$$°F = \frac{9}{5}°C + 32$$

$$K = °C + 273$$

See page R42 for help with using formulas.

Examples of Temperature Conversions		
Condition	Degrees Celsius	Degrees Fahrenheit
Freezing point of water	0	32
Cool day	10	50
Mild day	20	68
Warm day	30	86
Normal body temperature	37	98.6
Very hot day	40	104
Boiling point of water	100	212

LAB HANDBOOK

Converting Between SI and U.S. Customary Units

Use the chart below when you need to convert between SI units and U.S. customary units.

SI Unit	From SI to U.S. Customary			From U.S. Customary to SI		
Length	**When you know**	**multiply by**	**to find**	**When you know**	**multiply by**	**to find**
kilometer (km) = 1000 m	kilometers	0.62	miles	miles	1.61	kilometers
meter (m) = 100 cm	meters	3.28	feet	feet	0.3048	meters
centimeter (cm) = 10 mm	centimeters	0.39	inches	inches	2.54	centimeters
millimeter (mm) = 0.1 cm	millimeters	0.04	inches	inches	25.4	millimeters
Area	**When you know**	**multiply by**	**to find**	**When you know**	**multiply by**	**to find**
square kilometer (km^2)	square kilometers	0.39	square miles	square miles	2.59	square kilometers
square meter (m^2)	square meters	1.2	square yards	square yards	0.84	square meters
square centimeter (cm^2)	square centimeters	0.155	square inches	square inches	6.45	square centimeters
Volume	**When you know**	**multiply by**	**to find**	**When you know**	**multiply by**	**to find**
liter (L) = 1000 mL	liters	1.06	quarts	quarts	0.95	liters
	liters	0.26	gallons	gallons	3.79	liters
	liters	4.23	cups	cups	0.24	liters
	liters	2.12	pints	pints	0.47	liters
milliliter (mL) = 0.001 L	milliliters	0.20	teaspoons	teaspoons	4.93	milliliters
	milliliters	0.07	tablespoons	tablespoons	14.79	milliliters
	milliliters	0.03	fluid ounces	fluid ounces	29.57	milliliters
Mass	**When you know**	**multiply by**	**to find**	**When you know**	**multiply by**	**to find**
kilogram (kg) = 1000 g	kilograms	2.2	pounds	pounds	0.45	kilograms
gram (g) = 1000 mg	grams	0.035	ounces	ounces	28.35	grams

Precision and Accuracy

When you do an experiment, it is important that your methods, observations, and data be both precise and accurate.

low precision

precision, but not accuracy

precision and accuracy

Precision

In science, **precision** is the exactness and consistency of measurements. For example, measurements made with a ruler that has both centimeter and millimeter markings would be more precise than measurements made with a ruler that has only centimeter markings. Another indicator of precision is the care taken to make sure that methods and observations are as exact and consistent as possible. Every time a particular experiment is done, the same procedure should be used. Precision is necessary because experiments are repeated several times and if the procedure changes, the results will change.

EXAMPLE

Suppose you are measuring temperatures over a two-week period. Your precision will be greater if you measure each temperature at the same place, at the same time of day, and with the same thermometer than if you change any of these factors from one day to the next.

Accuracy

In science, it is possible to be precise but not accurate. **Accuracy** depends on the difference between a measurement and an actual value. The smaller the difference, the more accurate the measurement.

EXAMPLE

Suppose you look at a stream and estimate that it is about 1 meter wide at a particular place. You decide to check your estimate by measuring the stream with a meter stick, and you determine that the stream is 1.32 meters wide. However, because it is hard to measure the width of a stream with a meter stick, it turns out that you didn't do a very good job. The stream is actually 1.14 meters wide. Therefore, even though your estimate was less precise than your measurement, your estimate was actually more accurate.

Making Data Tables and Graphs

Data tables and graphs are useful tools for both recording and communicating scientific data.

Making Data Tables

You can use a **data table** to organize and record the measurements that you make. Some examples of information that might be recorded in data tables are frequencies, times, and amounts.

EXAMPLE

Suppose you are investigating photosynthesis in two elodea plants. One sits in direct sunlight, and the other sits in a dimly lit room. You measure the rate of photosynthesis by counting the number of bubbles in the jar every ten minutes.

1. Title and number your data table.
2. Decide how you will organize the table into columns and rows.
3. Any units, such as seconds or degrees, should be included in column headings, not in the individual cells.

Table 1. Number of Bubbles from Elodea

Time (min)	Sunlight	Dim Light
0	0	0
10	15	5
20	25	8
30	32	7
40	41	10
50	47	9
60	42	9

> Always number and title data tables.

The data in the table above could also be organized in a different way.

Table 1. Number of Bubbles from Elodea

Light Condition	Time (min)						
	0	10	20	30	40	50	60
Sunlight	0	15	25	32	41	47	42
Dim light	0	5	8	7	10	9	9

> Put units in column heading.

Making Line Graphs

You can use a **line graph** to show a relationship between variables. Line graphs are particularly useful for showing changes in variables over time.

EXAMPLE

Suppose you are interested in graphing temperature data that you collected over the course of a day.

Table 1. Outside Temperature During the Day on March 7

	Time of Day						
	7:00 A.M.	9:00 A.M.	11:00 A.M.	1:00 P.M.	3:00 P.M.	5:00 P.M.	7:00 P.M.
Temp (°C)	8	9	11	14	12	10	6

1. Use the vertical axis of your line graph for the variable that you are measuring—temperature.

2. Choose scales for both the horizontal axis and the vertical axis of the graph. You should have two points more than you need on the vertical axis, and the horizontal axis should be long enough for all of the data points to fit.

3. Draw and label each axis.

4. Graph each value. First find the appropriate point on the scale of the horizontal axis. Imagine a line that rises vertically from that place on the scale. Then find the corresponding value on the vertical axis, and imagine a line that moves horizontally from that value. The point where these two imaginary lines intersect is where the value should be plotted.

5. Connect the points with straight lines.

> Be sure to add a number and a title to your graph.

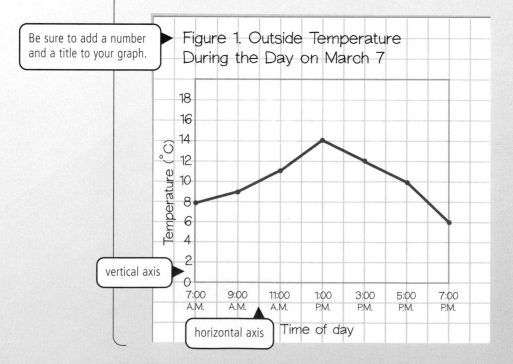

Figure 1. Outside Temperature During the Day on March 7

vertical axis

horizontal axis

LAB HANDBOOK

Making Circle Graphs

You can use a **circle graph,** sometimes called a pie chart, to represent data as parts of a circle. Circle graphs are used only when the data can be expressed as percentages of a whole. The entire circle shown in a circle graph is equal to 100 percent of the data.

EXAMPLE

Suppose you identified the species of each mature tree growing in a small wooded area. You organized your data in a table, but you also want to show the data in a circle graph.

1. To begin, find the total number of mature trees.

    $$56 + 34 + 22 + 10 + 28 = 150$$

2. To find the degree measure for each sector of the circle, write a fraction comparing the number of each tree species with the total number of trees. Then multiply the fraction by 360°.

    Oak: $\dfrac{56}{150} \times 360° = 134.4°$

3. Draw a circle. Use a protractor to draw the angle for each sector of the graph.

4. Color and label each sector of the graph.

5. Give the graph a number and title.

Table 1. Tree Species in Wooded Area

Species	Number of Specimens
Oak	56
Maple	34
Birch	22
Willow	10
Pine	28

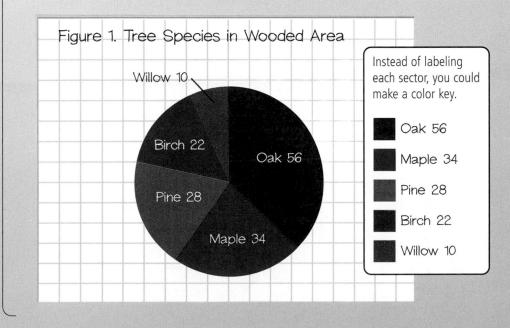

Figure 1. Tree Species in Wooded Area

Willow 10
Birch 22
Oak 56
Pine 28
Maple 34

Instead of labeling each sector, you could make a color key.

Oak 56
Maple 34
Pine 28
Birch 22
Willow 10

Bar Graph

A **bar graph** is a type of graph in which the lengths of the bars are used to represent and compare data. A numerical scale is used to determine the lengths of the bars.

EXAMPLE

To determine the effect of water on seed sprouting, three cups were filled with sand, and ten seeds were planted in each. Different amounts of water were added to each cup over a three-day period.

Table 1. Effect of Water on Seed Sprouting

Daily Amount of Water (mL)	Number of Seeds That Sprouted After 3 Days in Sand
0	1
10	4
20	8

1. Choose a numerical scale. The greatest value is 8, so the end of the scale should have a value greater than 8, such as 10. Use equal increments along the scale, such as increments of 2.

2. Draw and label the axes. Mark intervals on the vertical axis according to the scale you chose.

3. Draw a bar for each data value. Use the scale to decide how long to make each bar.

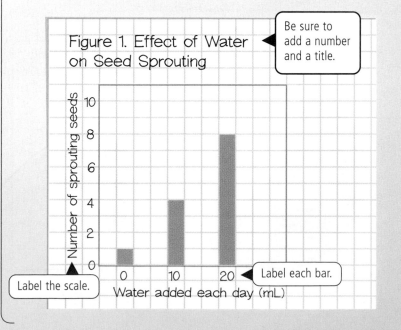

Figure 1. Effect of Water on Seed Sprouting

Be sure to add a number and a title.

Label the scale.

Label each bar.

Double Bar Graph

A **double bar graph** is a bar graph that shows two sets of data. The two bars for each measurement are drawn next to each other.

EXAMPLE

The seed-sprouting experiment was done using both sand and potting soil. The data for sand and potting soil can be plotted on one graph.

1. Draw one set of bars, using the data for sand, as shown below.

2. Draw bars for the potting-soil data next to the bars for the sand data. Shade them a different color. Add a key.

Table 2. Effect of Water and Soil on Seed Sprouting

Daily Amount of Water (mL)	Number of Seeds That Sprouted After 3 Days in Sand	Number of Seeds That Sprouted After 3 Days in Potting Soil
0	1	2
10	4	5
20	8	9

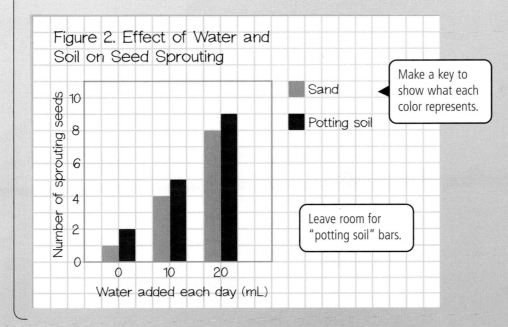

Figure 2. Effect of Water and Soil on Seed Sprouting

Make a key to show what each color represents.

Leave room for "potting soil" bars.

Designing an Experiment

Use this section when designing or conducting an experiment.

Determining a Purpose

You can find a purpose for an experiment by doing research, by examining the results of a previous experiment, or by observing the world around you. An **experiment** is an organized procedure to study something under controlled conditions.

Don't forget to learn as much as possible about your topic before you begin.

1. Write the purpose of your experiment as a question or problem that you want to investigate.

2. Write down research questions and begin searching for information that will help you design an experiment. Consult the library, the Internet, and other people as you conduct your research.

EXAMPLE

Middle school students observed an odor near the lake by their school. They also noticed that the water on the side of the lake near the school was greener than the water on the other side of the lake. The students did some research to learn more about their observations. They discovered that the odor and green color in the lake came from algae. They also discovered that a new fertilizer was being used on a field nearby. The students inferred that the use of the fertilizer might be related to the presence of the algae and designed a controlled experiment to find out whether they were right.

> ### Problem
> How does fertilizer affect the presence of algae in a lake?
>
> ### Research Questions
> - Have other experiments been done on this problem? If so, what did those experiments show?
> - What kind of fertilizer is used on the field? How much?
> - How do algae grow?
> - How do people measure algae?
> - Can fertilizer and algae be used safely in a lab? How?

Research
As you research, you may find a topic that is more interesting to you than your original topic, or learn that a procedure you wanted to use is not practical or safe. It is OK to change your purpose as you research.

Writing a Hypothesis

A **hypothesis** is a tentative explanation for an observation or scientific problem that can be tested by further investigation. You can write your hypothesis in the form of an "If . . . , then . . . , because . . ." statement.

> ### Hypothesis
>
> If the amount of fertilizer in lake water is increased, then the amount of algae will also increase, because fertilizers provide nutrients that algae need to grow.

Hypotheses
For help with hypotheses, refer to page R3.

Determining Materials

Make a list of all the materials you will need to do your experiment. Be specific, especially if someone else is helping you obtain the materials. Try to think of everything you will need.

> ### Materials
>
> - 1 large jar or container
> - 4 identical smaller containers
> - rubber gloves that also cover the arms
> - sample of fertilizer-and-water solution
> - eyedropper
> - clear plastic wrap
> - scissors
> - masking tape
> - marker
> - ruler

Determining Variables and Constants

EXPERIMENTAL GROUP AND CONTROL GROUP

An experiment to determine how two factors are related always has two groups—a control group and an experimental group.

1. Design an experimental group. Include as many trials as possible in the experimental group in order to obtain reliable results.

2. Design a control group that is the same as the experimental group in every way possible, except for the factor you wish to test.

> **Experimental Group:** two containers of lake water with one drop of fertilizer solution added to each
>
> **Control Group:** two containers of lake water with no fertilizer solution added

> Go back to your materials list and make sure you have enough items listed to cover both your experimental group and your control group.

VARIABLES AND CONSTANTS

Identify the variables and constants in your experiment. In a controlled experiment, a **variable** is any factor that can change. **Constants** are all of the factors that are the same in both the experimental group and the control group.

> **Hypothesis**
> If the amount of fertilizer in lake water is increased, then the amount of algae will also increase, because fertilizers provide nutrients that algae need to grow.

1. Read your hypothesis. The **independent variable** is the factor that you wish to test and that is manipulated or changed so that it can be tested. The independent variable is expressed in your hypothesis after the word *if*. Identify the independent variable in your laboratory report.

2. The **dependent variable** is the factor that you measure to gather results. It is expressed in your hypothesis after the word *then*. Identify the dependent variable in your laboratory report.

Table 1. Variables and Constants in Algae Experiment

Independent Variable	Dependent Variable	Constants
Amount of fertilizer in lake water	Amount of algae that grow	• Where the lake water is obtained • Type of container used • Light and temperature conditions where water will be stored

> Set up your experiment so that you will test only one variable.

MEASURING THE DEPENDENT VARIABLE

Before starting your experiment, you need to define how you will measure the dependent variable. An **operational definition** is a description of the one particular way in which you will measure the dependent variable.

Your operational definition is important for several reasons. First, in any experiment there are several ways in which a dependent variable can be measured. Second, the procedure of the experiment depends on how you decide to measure the dependent variable. Third, your operational definition makes it possible for other people to evaluate and build on your experiment.

EXAMPLE 1

An operational definition of a dependent variable can be qualitative. That is, your measurement of the dependent variable can simply be an observation of whether a change occurs as a result of a change in the independent variable. This type of operational definition can be thought of as a "yes or no" measurement.

Table 2. Qualitative Operational Definition of Algae Growth

Independent Variable	Dependent Variable	Operational Definition
Amount of fertilizer in lake water	Amount of algae that grow	Algae grow in lake water

A qualitative measurement of a dependent variable is often easy to make and record. However, this type of information does not provide a great deal of detail in your experimental results.

EXAMPLE 2

An operational definition of a dependent variable can be quantitative. That is, your measurement of the dependent variable can be a number that shows how much change occurs as a result of a change in the independent variable.

Table 3. Quantitative Operational Definition of Algae Growth

Independent Variable	Dependent Variable	Operational Definition
Amount of fertilizer in lake water	Amount of algae that grow	Diameter of largest algal growth (in mm)

A quantitative measurement of a dependent variable can be more difficult to make and analyze than a qualitative measurement. However, this type of data provides much more information about your experiment and is often more useful.

Writing a Procedure

Write each step of your procedure. Start each step with a verb, or action word, and keep the steps short. Your procedure should be clear enough for someone else to use as instructions for repeating your experiment.

If necessary, go back to your materials list and add any materials that you left out.

Controlling Variables
The same amount of fertilizer solution must be added to two of the four containers.

Controlling Variables
All four containers must receive the same amount of light.

Procedure

1. Put on your gloves. Use the large container to obtain a sample of lake water.

2. Divide the sample of lake water equally among the four smaller containers.

3. Use the eyedropper to add one drop of fertilizer solution to two of the containers.

4. Use the masking tape and the marker to label the containers with your initials, the date, and the identifiers "Jar 1 with Fertilizer," "Jar 2 with Fertilizer," "Jar 1 without Fertilizer," and "Jar 2 without Fertilizer."

5. Cover the containers with clear plastic wrap. Use the scissors to punch ten holes in each of the covers.

6. Place all four containers on a window ledge. Make sure that they all receive the same amount of light.

7. Observe the containers every day for one week.

8. Use the ruler to measure the diameter of the largest clump of algae in each container, and record your measurements daily.

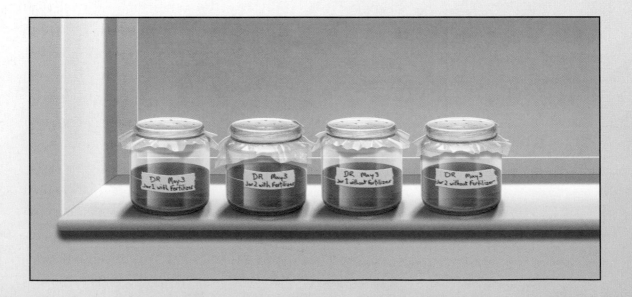

Recording Observations

Once you have obtained all of your materials and your procedure has been approved, you can begin making experimental observations. Gather both quantitative and qualitative data. If something goes wrong during your procedure, make sure you record that too.

> **Observations**
> For help with making qualitative and quantitative observations, refer to page R2.

> For more examples of data tables, see page R23.

Table 4. Fertilizer and Algae Growth

Date and Time	Experimental Group		Control Group		Observations
	Jar 1 with Fertilizer (diameter of algae in mm)	Jar 2 with Fertilizer (diameter of algae in mm)	Jar 1 without Fertilizer (diameter of algae in mm)	Jar 2 without Fertilizer (diameter of algae in mm)	
5/3 4:00 P.M.	0	0	0	0	condensation in all containers
5/4 4:00 P.M.	0	3	0	0	tiny green blobs in jar 2 with fertilizer
5/5 4:15 P.M.	4	5	0	3	green blobs in jars 1 and 2 with fertilizer and jar 2 without fertilizer
5/6 4:00 P.M.	5	6	0	4	water light green in jar 2 with fertilizer
5/7 4:00 P.M.	8	10	0	6	water light green in jars 1 and 2 with fertilizer and in jar 2 without fertilizer
5/8 3:30 P.M.	10	18	0	6	cover off jar 2 with fertilizer
5/9 3:30 P.M.	14	23	0	8	drew sketches of each container

> Notice that on the sixth day, the observer found that the cover was off one of the containers. It is important to record observations of unintended factors because they might affect the results of the experiment.

Drawings of Samples Viewed Under Microscope on 5/9 at 100x

> Use technology, such as a microscope, to help you make observations when possible.

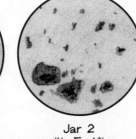

Jar 1 with Fertilizer

Jar 2 with Fertilizer

Jar 1 without Fertilizer

Jar 2 without Fertilizer

Summarizing Results

To summarize your data, look at all of your observations together. Look for meaningful ways to present your observations. For example, you might average your data or make a graph to look for patterns. When possible, use spreadsheet software to help you analyze and present your data. The two graphs below show the same data.

EXAMPLE 1

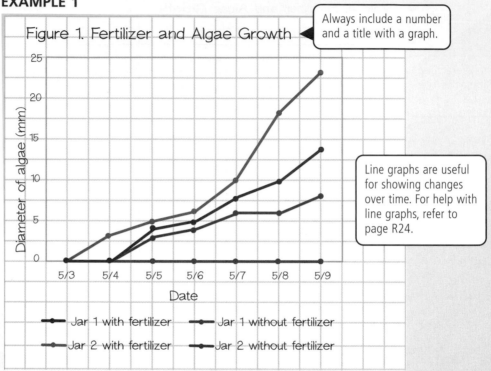

Always include a number and a title with a graph.

Line graphs are useful for showing changes over time. For help with line graphs, refer to page R24.

EXAMPLE 2

Bar graphs are useful for comparing different data sets. This bar graph has four bars for each day. Another way to present the data would be to calculate averages for the tests and the controls, and to show one test bar and one control bar for each day.

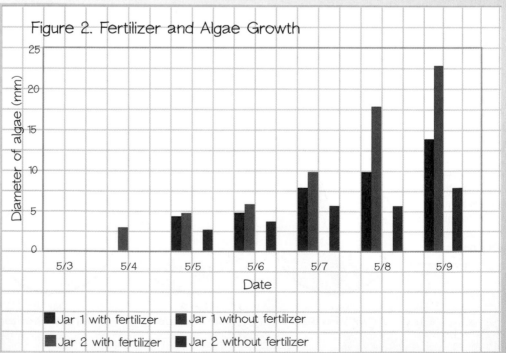

Drawing Conclusions

RESULTS AND INFERENCES

To draw conclusions from your experiment, first write your results. Then compare your results with your hypothesis. Do your results support your hypothesis? Be careful not to make inferences about factors that you did not test.

> For help with making inferences, see page R4.

Results and Inferences

The results of my experiment show that more algae grew in lake water to which fertilizer had been added than in lake water to which no fertilizer had been added. My hypothesis was supported. I infer that it is possible that the growth of algae in the lake was caused by the fertilizer used on the field.

> Notice that you cannot conclude from this experiment that the presence of algae in the lake was due only to the fertilizer.

QUESTIONS FOR FURTHER RESEARCH

Write a list of questions for further research and investigation. Your ideas may lead you to new experiments and discoveries.

Questions for Further Research

- What is the connection between the amount of fertilizer and algae growth?
- How do different brands of fertilizer affect algae growth?
- How would algae growth in the lake be affected if no fertilizer were used on the field?
- How do algae affect the lake and the other life in and around it?
- How does fertilizer affect the lake and the life in and around it?
- If fertilizer is getting into the lake, how is it getting there?

Math Handbook

Describing a Set of Data

Means, medians, modes, and ranges are important math tools for describing data sets such as the following widths of fossilized clamshells.

13 mm   25 mm   14 mm   21 mm   16 mm   23 mm   14 mm

Mean

The **mean** of a data set is the sum of the values divided by the number of values.

Example

To find the mean of the clamshell data, add the values and then divide the sum by the number of values.

$$\frac{13 \text{ mm} + 25 \text{ mm} + 14 \text{ mm} + 21 \text{ mm} + 16 \text{ mm} + 23 \text{ mm} + 14 \text{ mm}}{7} = \frac{126 \text{ mm}}{7} = 18 \text{ mm}$$

ANSWER The mean is 18 mm.

Median

The **median** of a data set is the middle value when the values are written in numerical order. If a data set has an even number of values, the median is the mean of the two middle values.

Example

To find the median of the clamshell data, arrange the values in order from least to greatest. The median is the middle value.

13 mm   14 mm   14 mm   **16 mm**   21 mm   23 mm   25 mm

ANSWER The median is 16 mm.

Mode

The **mode** of a data set is the value that occurs most often.

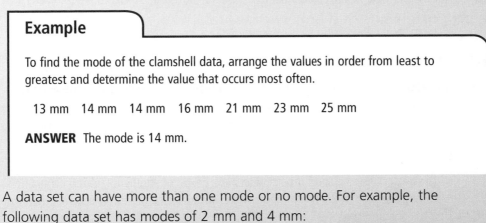

> ### Example
>
> To find the mode of the clamshell data, arrange the values in order from least to greatest and determine the value that occurs most often.
>
> 13 mm   14 mm   14 mm   16 mm   21 mm   23 mm   25 mm
>
> **ANSWER** The mode is 14 mm.

A data set can have more than one mode or no mode. For example, the following data set has modes of 2 mm and 4 mm:

2 mm   2 mm   3 mm   4 mm   4 mm

The data set below has no mode, because no value occurs more often than any other.

2 mm   3 mm   4 mm   5 mm

Range

The **range** of a data set is the difference between the greatest value and the least value.

> ### Example
>
> To find the range of the clamshell data, arrange the values in order from least to greatest.
>
> 13 mm   14 mm   14 mm   16 mm   21 mm   23 mm   25 mm
>
> Subtract the least value from the greatest value.
>
> 13 mm is the least value.
> 25 mm is the greatest value.
>
> 25 mm − 13 mm = 12 mm
>
> **ANSWER** The range is 12 mm.

Using Ratios, Rates, and Proportions

You can use ratios and rates to compare values in data sets. You can use proportions to find unknown values.

Ratios

A **ratio** uses division to compare two values. The ratio of a value a to a nonzero value b can be written as $\frac{a}{b}$.

Example

The height of one plant is 8 centimeters. The height of another plant is 6 centimeters. To find the ratio of the height of the first plant to the height of the second plant, write a fraction and simplify it.

$$\frac{8\text{ cm}}{6\text{ cm}} = \frac{4 \times \overset{1}{\cancel{2}}}{3 \times \underset{1}{\cancel{2}}} = \frac{4}{3}$$

ANSWER The ratio of the plant heights is $\frac{4}{3}$.

You can also write the ratio $\frac{a}{b}$ as "a to b" or as $a:b$. For example, you can write the ratio of the plant heights as "4 to 3" or as $4:3$.

Rates

A **rate** is a ratio of two values expressed in different units. A unit rate is a rate with a denominator of 1 unit.

Example

A plant grew 6 centimeters in 2 days. The plant's rate of growth was $\frac{6\text{ cm}}{2\text{ days}}$. To describe the plant's growth in centimeters per day, write a unit rate.

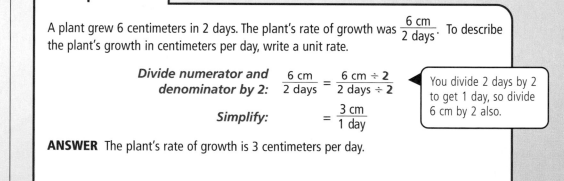

Divide numerator and denominator by 2: $\frac{6\text{ cm}}{2\text{ days}} = \frac{6\text{ cm} \div 2}{2\text{ days} \div 2}$

Simplify: $= \frac{3\text{ cm}}{1\text{ day}}$

You divide 2 days by 2 to get 1 day, so divide 6 cm by 2 also.

ANSWER The plant's rate of growth is 3 centimeters per day.

Proportions

A **proportion** is an equation stating that two ratios are equivalent. To solve for an unknown value in a proportion, you can use cross products.

Example

If a plant grew 6 centimeters in 2 days, how many centimeters would it grow in 3 days (if its rate of growth is constant)?

Write a proportion:	$\dfrac{6 \text{ cm}}{2 \text{ days}} = \dfrac{x}{3 \text{ days}}$
Set cross products:	$6 \text{ cm} \cdot 3 = 2x$
Multiply 6 and 3:	$18 \text{ cm} = 2x$
Divide each side by 2:	$\dfrac{18 \text{ cm}}{2} = \dfrac{2x}{2}$
Simplify:	$9 \text{ cm} = x$

ANSWER The plant would grow 9 centimeters in 3 days.

Using Decimals, Fractions, and Percents

Decimals, fractions, and percentages are all ways of recording and representing data.

Decimals

A **decimal** is a number that is written in the base-ten place value system, in which a decimal point separates the ones and tenths digits. The values of each place is ten times that of the place to its right.

Example

A caterpillar traveled from point *A* to point *C* along the path shown.

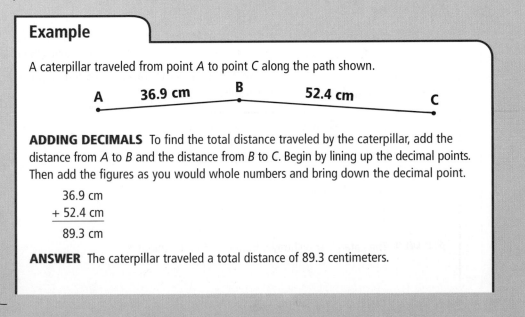

ADDING DECIMALS To find the total distance traveled by the caterpillar, add the distance from *A* to *B* and the distance from *B* to *C*. Begin by lining up the decimal points. Then add the figures as you would whole numbers and bring down the decimal point.

```
  36.9 cm
+ 52.4 cm
---------
  89.3 cm
```

ANSWER The caterpillar traveled a total distance of 89.3 centimeters.

Example continued

SUBTRACTING DECIMALS To find how much farther the caterpillar traveled on the second leg of the journey, subtract the distance from *A* to *B* from the distance from *B* to *C*.

$$\begin{array}{r} 52.4 \text{ cm} \\ -\ 36.9 \text{ cm} \\ \hline 15.5 \text{ cm} \end{array}$$

ANSWER The caterpillar traveled 15.5 centimeters farther on the second leg of the journey.

Example

A caterpillar is traveling from point *D* to point *F* along the path shown. The caterpillar travels at a speed of 9.6 centimeters per minute.

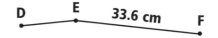

MULTIPLYING DECIMALS You can multiply decimals as you would whole numbers. The number of decimal places in the product is equal to the sum of the number of decimal places in the factors.

For instance, suppose it takes the caterpillar 1.5 minutes to go from *D* to *E*. To find the distance from *D* to *E*, multiply the caterpillar's speed by the time it took.

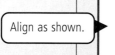
Align as shown.

$$\begin{array}{rl} 9.6 & \quad 1 \quad \text{decimal place} \\ \times\ 1.5 & \quad +\ 1 \quad \text{decimal place} \\ \hline 480 & \\ 96 & \\ \hline 14.40 & \quad 2 \quad \text{decimal places} \end{array}$$

ANSWER The distance from *D* to *E* is 14.4 centimeters.

DIVIDING DECIMALS When you divide by a decimal, move the decimal points the same number of places in the divisor and the dividend to make the divisor a whole number.

For instance, to find the time it will take the caterpillar to travel from *E* to *F*, divide the distance from *E* to *F* by the caterpillar's speed.

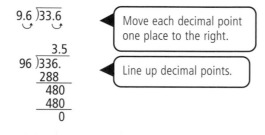

Move each decimal point one place to the right.

Line up decimal points.

ANSWER The caterpillar will travel from *E* to *F* in 3.5 minutes.

Fractions

A **fraction** is a number in the form $\frac{a}{b}$, where b is not equal to 0. A fraction is in **simplest form** if its numerator and denominator have a greatest common factor (GCF) of 1. To simplify a fraction, divide its numerator and denominator by their GCF.

Example

A caterpillar is 40 millimeters long. The head of the caterpillar is 6 millimeters long. To compare the length of the caterpillar's head with the caterpillar's total length, you can write and simplify a fraction that expresses the ratio of the two lengths.

Write the ratio of the two lengths: $\quad \dfrac{\text{Length of head}}{\text{Total length}} = \dfrac{6 \text{ mm}}{40 \text{ mm}}$

Write numerator and denominator as products of numbers and the GCF: $\quad = \dfrac{3 \times 2}{20 \times 2}$

Divide numerator and denominator by the GCF: $\quad = \dfrac{3 \times \overset{1}{\cancel{2}}}{20 \times \underset{1}{\cancel{2}}}$

Simplify: $\quad = \dfrac{3}{20}$

ANSWER In simplest form, the ratio of the lengths is $\frac{3}{20}$.

Percents

A **percent** is a ratio that compares a number to 100. The word *percent* means "per hundred" or "out of 100." The symbol for *percent* is %.

For instance, suppose 43 out of 100 caterpillars are female. You can represent this ratio as a percent, a decimal, or a fraction.

Percent	Decimal	Fraction
43%	0.43	$\frac{43}{100}$

Example

In the preceding example, the ratio of the length of the caterpillar's head to the caterpillar's total length is $\frac{3}{20}$. To write this ratio as a percent, write an equivalent fraction that has a denominator of 100.

Multiply numerator and denominator by 5: $\quad \dfrac{3}{20} = \dfrac{3 \times 5}{20 \times 5}$

$\quad = \dfrac{15}{100}$

Write as a percent: $\quad = 15\%$

ANSWER The caterpillar's head represents 15 percent of its total length.

Using Formulas

A **formula** is an equation that shows the general relationship between two or more quantities.

The term *variable* is also used in science to refer to a factor that can change during an experiment.

In science, a formula often has a word form and a symbolic form. The formula below expresses Ohm's law.

Word Form

$$\text{Current} = \frac{\text{voltage}}{\text{resistance}}$$

Symbolic Form

$$I = \frac{V}{R}$$

In this formula, *I*, *V*, and *R* are variables. A mathematical **variable** is a symbol or letter that is used to represent one or more numbers.

Example

Suppose that you measure a voltage of 1.5 volts and a resistance of 15 ohms. You can use the formula for Ohm's law to find the current in amperes.

Write the formula for Ohm's law: $I = \dfrac{V}{R}$

Substitute 1.5 volts for V and 15 ohms for R: $I = \dfrac{1.5 \text{ volts}}{15 \text{ ohms}}$

Simplify: $I = 0.1 \text{ amp}$

ANSWER The current is 0.1 ampere.

If you know the values of all variables but one in a formula, you can solve for the value of the unknown variable. For instance, Ohm's law can be used to find a voltage if you know the current and the resistance.

Example

Suppose that you know that a current is 0.2 amperes and the resistance is 18 ohms. Use the formula for Ohm's law to find the voltage in volts.

Write the formula for Ohm's law: $I = \dfrac{V}{R}$

Substitute 0.2 amp for I and 18 ohms for R: $0.2 \text{ amp} = \dfrac{V}{18 \text{ ohms}}$

Multiply both sides by 18 ohms: $0.2 \text{ amp} \cdot 18 \text{ ohms} = V$

Simplify: $3.6 \text{ volts} = V$

ANSWER The voltage is 3.6 volts.

Finding Areas

The area of a figure is the amount of surface the figure covers.

Area is measured in square units, such as square meters (m²) or square centimeters (cm²). Formulas for the areas of three common geometric figures are shown below.

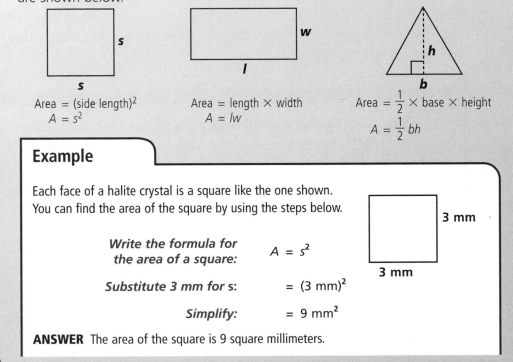

Area = (side length)²
$A = s^2$

Area = length × width
$A = lw$

Area = $\frac{1}{2}$ × base × height
$A = \frac{1}{2} bh$

Example

Each face of a halite crystal is a square like the one shown. You can find the area of the square by using the steps below.

Write the formula for the area of a square:	$A = s^2$
Substitute 3 mm for s:	$= (3 \text{ mm})^2$
Simplify:	$= 9 \text{ mm}^2$

ANSWER The area of the square is 9 square millimeters.

Finding Volumes

The volume of a solid is the amount of space contained by the solid.

Volume is measured in cubic units, such as cubic meters (m³) or cubic centimeters (cm³). The volume of a rectangular prism is given by the formula shown below.

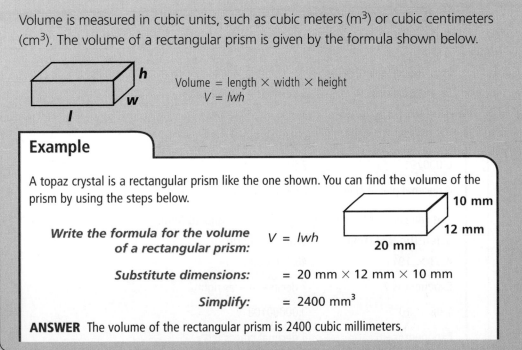

Volume = length × width × height
$V = lwh$

Example

A topaz crystal is a rectangular prism like the one shown. You can find the volume of the prism by using the steps below.

Write the formula for the volume of a rectangular prism:	$V = lwh$
Substitute dimensions:	$= 20 \text{ mm} \times 12 \text{ mm} \times 10 \text{ mm}$
Simplify:	$= 2400 \text{ mm}^3$

ANSWER The volume of the rectangular prism is 2400 cubic millimeters.

Using Significant Figures

The **significant figures** in a decimal are the digits that are warranted by the accuracy of a measuring device.

When you perform a calculation with measurements, the number of significant figures to include in the result depends in part on the number of significant figures in the measurements. When you multiply or divide measurements, your answer should have only as many significant figures as the measurement with the fewest significant figures.

Example

Using a balance and a graduated cylinder filled with water, you determined that a marble has a mass of 8.0 grams and a volume of 3.5 cubic centimeters. To calculate the density of the marble, divide the mass by the volume.

Write the formula for density: $\text{Density} = \dfrac{\text{mass}}{\text{Volume}}$

Substitute measurements: $= \dfrac{8.0 \text{ g}}{3.5 \text{ cm}^3}$

Use a calculator to divide: $\approx 2.285714286 \text{ g/cm}^3$

ANSWER Because the mass and the volume have two significant figures each, give the density to two significant figures. The marble has a density of 2.3 grams per cubic centimeter.

Using Scientific Notation

Scientific notation is a shorthand way to write very large or very small numbers. For example, 73,500,000,000,000,000,000,000 kg is the mass of the Moon. In scientific notation, it is 7.35×10^{22} kg.

Example

You can convert from standard form to scientific notation.

Standard Form	Scientific Notation
720,000 5 decimal places left	7.2×10^5 Exponent is 5.
0.000291 4 decimal places right	2.91×10^{-4} Exponent is −4.

You can convert from scientific notation to standard form.

Scientific Notation	Standard Form
4.63×10^7 Exponent is 7.	46,300,000 7 decimal places right
1.08×10^{-6} Exponent is −6.	0.00000108 6 decimal places left

Note-Taking Handbook

Note-Taking Strategies

Taking notes as you read helps you understand the information. The notes you take can also be used as a study guide for later review. This handbook presents several ways to organize your notes.

Content Frame

1. Make a chart in which each column represents a category.
2. Give each column a heading.
3. Write details under the headings.

NAME	GROUP	CHARACTERISTICS	DRAWING
snail	mollusks	mantle, shell	
ant	arthropods	six legs, exoskeleton	
earthworm	segmented worms	segmented body, circulatory and digestive systems	
heartworm	roundworms	digestive system	
sea star	echinoderms	spiny skin, tube feet	
jellyfish	cnidarians	stinging cells	

categories

details

Combination Notes

1. For each new idea or concept, write an informal outline of the information.
2. Make a sketch to illustrate the concept, and label it.

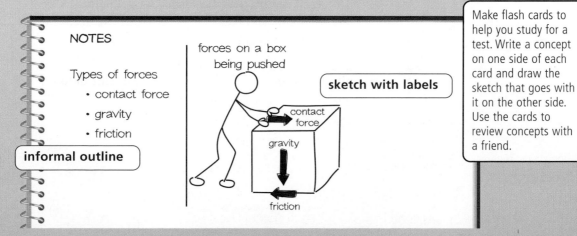

NOTES

Types of forces
- contact force
- gravity
- friction

informal outline

forces on a box being pushed

sketch with labels

contact force

gravity

friction

Make flash cards to help you study for a test. Write a concept on one side of each card and draw the sketch that goes with it on the other side. Use the cards to review concepts with a friend.

Main Idea and Detail Notes

1. In the left-hand column of a two-column chart, list main ideas. The blue headings express main ideas throughout this textbook.

2. In the right-hand column, write details that expand on each main idea.

You can shorten the headings in your chart. Be sure to use the most important words.

When studying for tests, cover up the detail notes column with a sheet of paper. Then use each main idea to form a question—such as "How does latitude affect climate?" Answer the question, and then uncover the detail notes column to check your answer.

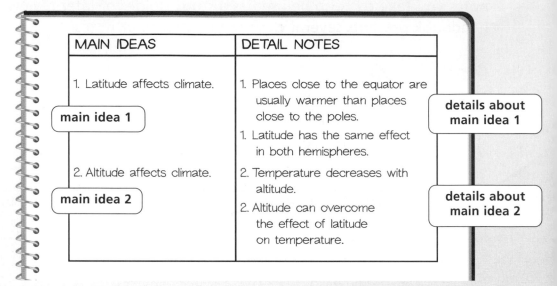

MAIN IDEAS	DETAIL NOTES
1. Latitude affects climate. *main idea 1*	1. Places close to the equator are usually warmer than places close to the poles. *details about main idea 1* 1. Latitude has the same effect in both hemispheres.
2. Altitude affects climate. *main idea 2*	2. Temperature decreases with altitude. *details about main idea 2* 2. Altitude can overcome the effect of latitude on temperature.

Main Idea Web

1. Write a main idea in a box.

2. Add boxes around it with related vocabulary terms and important details.

You can find definitions near highlighted terms.

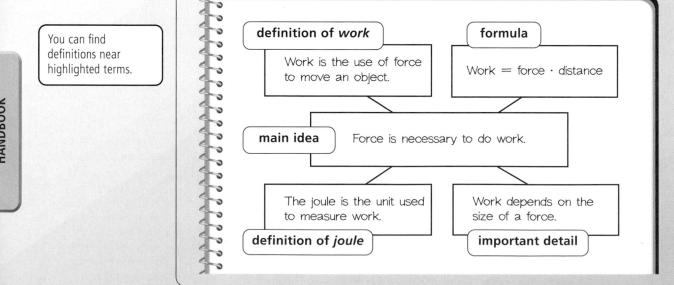

definition of *work*
Work is the use of force to move an object.

formula
Work = force · distance

main idea
Force is necessary to do work.

The joule is the unit used to measure work.
definition of *joule*

Work depends on the size of a force.
important detail

Mind Map

1. Write a main idea in the center.

2. Add details that relate to one another and to the main idea.

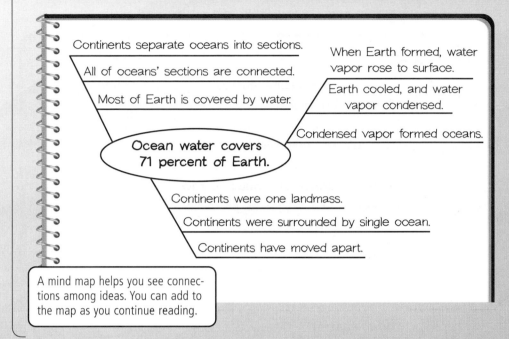

Continents separate oceans into sections.

All of oceans' sections are connected.

Most of Earth is covered by water.

When Earth formed, water vapor rose to surface.

Earth cooled, and water vapor condensed.

Condensed vapor formed oceans.

Ocean water covers 71 percent of Earth.

Continents were one landmass.

Continents were surrounded by single ocean.

Continents have moved apart.

A mind map helps you see connections among ideas. You can add to the map as you continue reading.

Supporting Main Ideas

1. Write a main idea in a box.

2. Add boxes underneath with information—such as reasons, explanations, and examples—that supports the main idea.

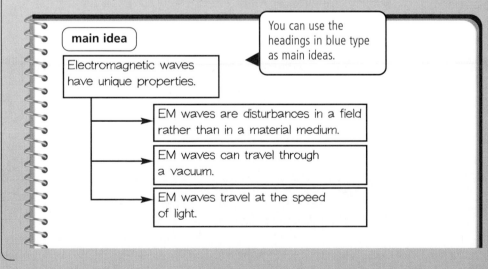

main idea

Electromagnetic waves have unique properties.

You can use the headings in blue type as main ideas.

EM waves are disturbances in a field rather than in a material medium.

EM waves can travel through a vacuum.

EM waves travel at the speed of light.

Outline

1. Copy the chapter title and headings from the book in the form of an outline.
2. Add notes that summarize in your own words what you read.

Cell Processes

1st key idea

I. Cells capture and release energy.

1st subpoint of I

A. All cells need energy.

2nd subpoint of I

B. Some cells capture light energy.

1st detail about B

   1. Process of photosynthesis

2nd detail about B

   2. Chloroplasts (site of photosynthesis)

   3. Carbon dioxide and water as raw materials

   4. Glucose and oxygen as products

C. All cells release energy.

   1. Process of cellular respiration

   2. Fermentation of sugar to carbon dioxide

   3. Bacteria that carry out fermentation

II. Cells transport materials through membranes.

A. Some materials move by diffusion.

   1. Particle movement from higher to lower concentrations

   2. Movement of water through membrane (osmosis)

B. Some transport requires energy.

   1. Active transport

   2. Examples of active transport

Correct Outline Form

Include a title.

Arrange key ideas, subpoints, and details as shown.

Indent the divisions of the outline as shown.

Use the same grammatical form for items of the same rank. For example, if A is a sentence, B must also be a sentence.

You must have at least two main ideas or subpoints. That is, every A must be followed by a B, and every 1 must be followed by a 2.

Concept Map

1. Write an important concept in a large oval.
2. Add details related to the concept in smaller ovals.
3. Write linking words on arrows that connect the ovals.

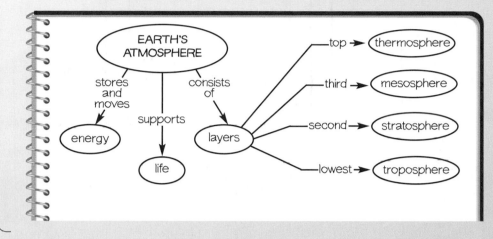

The main ideas or concepts can often be found in the blue headings. An example is "The atmosphere stores and moves energy." Use nouns from these concepts in the ovals, and use the verb or verbs on the lines.

Venn Diagram

1. Draw two overlapping circles, one for each item that you are comparing.
2. In the overlapping section, list the characteristics that are shared by both items.
3. In the outer sections, list the characteristics that are peculiar to each item.
4. Write a summary that describes the information in the Venn diagram.

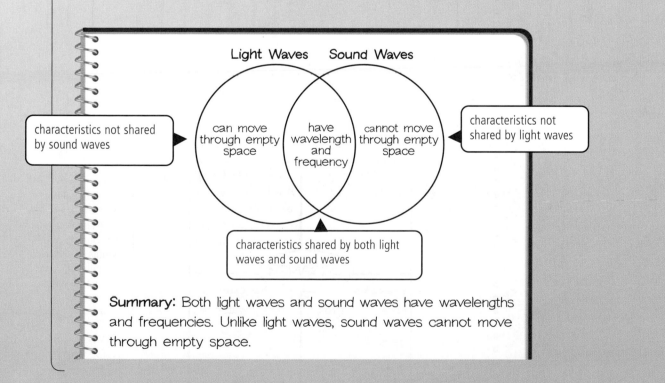

NOTE-TAKING HANDBOOK

Vocabulary Strategies

Important terms are highlighted in this book. A definition of each term can be found in the sentence or paragraph where the term appears. You can also find definitions in the Glossary. Taking notes about vocabulary terms helps you understand and remember what you read.

Description Wheel

1. Write a term inside a circle.
2. Write words that describe the term on "spokes" attached to the circle.

When studying for a test with a friend, read the phrases on the spokes one at a time until your friend identifies the correct term.

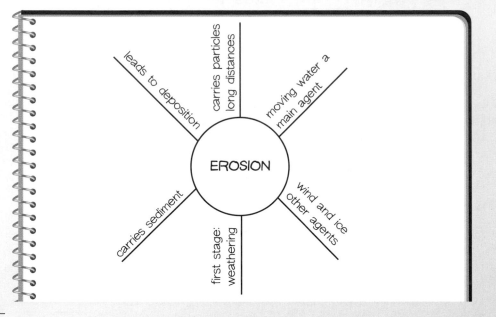

Four Square

1. Write a term in the center.
2. Write details in the four areas around the term.

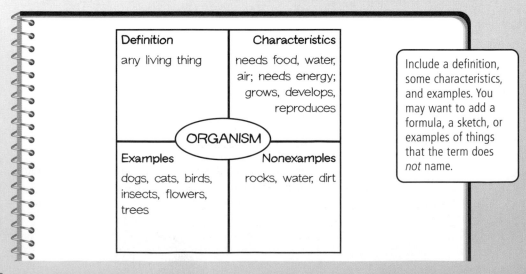

Include a definition, some characteristics, and examples. You may want to add a formula, a sketch, or examples of things that the term does *not* name.

Frame Game

1. Write a term in the center.
2. Frame the term with details.

Include examples, descriptions, sketches, or sentences that use the term in context. Change the frame to fit each new term.

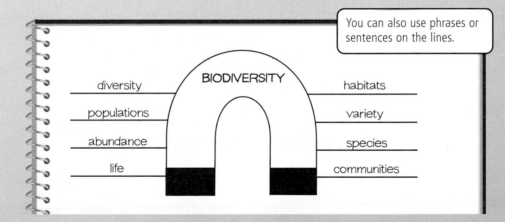

$ME = PE + KE$

MECHANICAL ENERGY

bouncing ball

energy of position and motion

Magnet Word

1. Write a term on the magnet.
2. On the lines, add details related to the term.

You can also use phrases or sentences on the lines.

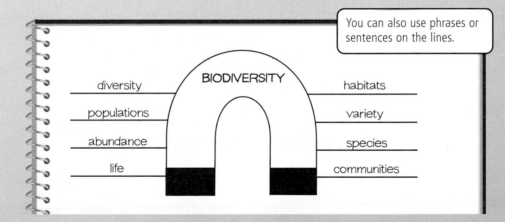

BIODIVERSITY

diversity

populations

abundance

life

habitats

variety

species

communities

Word Triangle

1. Write a term and its definition in the bottom section.
2. In the middle section, write a sentence in which the term is used correctly.
3. In the top section, draw a small picture to illustrate the term.

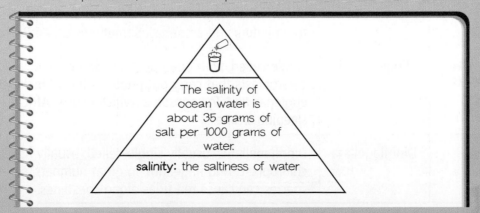

The salinity of ocean water is about 35 grams of salt per 1000 grams of water.

salinity: the saltiness of water

Appendix

Classification of Living Things

Living things are classified into three domains. These domains are further divided into kingdoms, and then phyla. Major phyla are described in the table below, along with important features that are used to distinguish each group.

Classification of Living Things

Domain	Kingdom	Phylum	Common Name and Description
Archaea	**Archaea**		Single-celled, with no nucleus. Live in some of Earth's most extreme environments, including salty, hot, and acid environments, and the deep ocean.
Bacteria	**Bacteria**		Single-celled, with no nucleus, but chemically different from Archaea. Live in all types of environments, including the human body; reproduce by dividing from one cell into two. Includes blue-green bacteria (cyanobacteria), *Streptococcus,* and *Bacillus.*
Eukarya			Cells are larger than archaea or bacteria and are eukaryotic (have a nucleus containing DNA). Single-celled or multicellular.
	Protista		Usually single-celled, but sometimes multicellular. DNA contained in a nucleus. Many phyla resemble plants, fungi, or animals but are usually smaller or simpler in structure.
	Animal-like protists	Ciliophora	Ciliates; have many short, hairlike extensions called cilia, which they use for feeding and movement. Includes paramecium.
		Zoomastigina	Zooflagellates; have usually one or two long, hairlike extensions called flagella.
		Sporozoa	Cause diseases in animals such as birds, fish, and humans. Includes *Plasmodium,* which causes malaria.
		Sarcodina	Use footlike extensions to move and feed. Includes foraminifers and amoebas. Sometimes called Rhizopoda.
	Plantlike protists	Euglenozoa	Single-celled, with one flagellum. Some have chloroplasts that carry out photosynthesis. Includes euglenas and *Trypanosoma,* which causes African sleeping sickness.
		Dinoflagellata	Dinoflagellates; usually single-celled; usually have chloroplasts and flagellum. In great numbers, some species can cause red tides along coastlines.

Classification of Living Things (cont.)

Domain	Kingdom	Phylum	Common Name and Description
		Chrysophyta	Yellow algae, golden-brown algae, and diatoms; single-celled; named for the yellow pigments in their chloroplasts (*chrysophyte*, in Greek, means "golden plant").
		Chlorophyceae	Green algae; have chloroplasts and are chemically similar to land plants. Unicellular or forms simple colonies of cells. Includes *Chlamydomonas, Ulva* (sea lettuce), and *Volvox*.
		Phaeophyta	Brown seaweed; contain a special brown pigment that gives these organisms their color. Multicellular, live mainly in salt water; includes kelp.
		Rhodophyta	Red algae; contain a red pigment that makes these organisms red, purple, or reddish-black. Multicellular, live in salt water.
	Funguslike protists	Acrasiomycota	Cellular slime molds; live partly as free-living single-celled organisms, then fuse together to form a many-celled mass. Live in damp, nutrient-rich environments; decomposers.
		Myxomycota	Acellular slime molds; form large, slimy masses made of many nuclei but technically a single cell.
		Oomycota	Water molds and downy mildews; produce thin, cottonlike extensions called hyphae. Feed off of dead or decaying material, often in water.
	Fungi		Usually multicellular; eukaryotic; cells have a thick cell wall. Obtain nutrients through absorption; often function as decomposers.
		Chytridiomycota	Oldest and simplest fungi; usually aquatic (fresh water or brackish water); single-celled or multicellular.
		Basidiomycota	Multicellular; reproduce with a club-shaped structure that is commonly seen on forest floors. Includes mushrooms, puffballs, rusts, and smuts.
		Zygomycota	Mostly disease-causing molds; often parasitic.
		Ascomycota	Includes single-celled yeasts and multicellular sac fungi. Includes *Penicillium*.

Classification of Living Things (cont.)

Domain	Kingdom	Phylum	Common Name and Description
	Plantae		Multicellular and eukaryotic; make sugars using energy from sunlight. Cells have a thick cell wall of cellulose.
		Bryophyta	Mosses; small, grasslike plants that live in moist, cool environments. Includes sphagnum (peat) moss. Seedless, nonvascular plants.
		Hepatophyta	Liverworts; named for the liver-shaped structure of one part of the plant's life cycle. Live in moist environments. Seedless, nonvascular plants.
		Anthoceratophyta	Hornworts; named for the visible hornlike structures with which they reproduce. Live on forest floors and other moist, cool environments. Seedless, nonvascular plants.
		Psilotophyta	Simple plant, just two types. Includes whisk ferns found in tropical areas, a common greenhouse weed. Seedless, vascular plants.
		Lycophyta	Club mosses and quillworts; look like miniature pine trees; live in moist, wooded environments. Includes *Lycopodium* (ground pine). Seedless vascular plants.
		Sphenophyta	Plants with simple leaves, stems, and roots. Grow about a meter tall, usually in moist areas. Includes *Equisetum* (scouring rush). Seedless, vascular plants.
		Pterophyta	Ferns; fringed-leaf plants that grow in cool, wooded environments. Includes many species. Seedless, vascular plants.
		Cycadophyta	Cycads; slow-growing palmlike plants that grow in tropical environments. Reproduce with seeds.
		Ginkgophyta	Includes only one species: *Ginkgo biloba*, a tree that is often planted in urban environments. Reproduce with seeds in cones.
		Gnetophyta	Small group includes desert-dwelling and tropical species. Includes *Ephedra* (Mormon tea) and *Welwitschia*, which grows in African deserts. Reproduce with seeds.
		Coniferophyta	Conifers, including pines, spruces, firs, sequoias. Usually evergreen trees; tend to grow in cold, dry environments; reproduce with seeds produced in cones.

Classification of Living Things (cont.)

Domain	Kingdom	Phylum	Common Name and Description
		Anthophyta	Flowering plants; includes grasses and flowering trees and shrubs. Reproduce with seeds produced in flowers, becoming fruit.
	Animalia		Multicellular and eukaryotic; obtain energy by consuming food. Usually able to move around.
		Porifera	Sponges; spend most of their lives fixed to the ocean floor. Feed by filtering water (containing nutrients and small organisms) through their body.
		Cnidaria	Aquatic animals with a radial (spokelike) body shape; named for their stinging cells (cnidocytes). Includes jellyfish, hydras, sea anemones, and corals.
		Ctenophora	Comb jellies; named for the comblike rows of cilia (hairlike extensions) that are used for movement.
		Platyhelminthes	Flatworms; thin, flattened worms with simple tissues and sensory organs. Includes planaria and tapeworms, which cause diseases in humans and other hosts.
		Nematoda	Roundworms; small, round worms; many species are parasites, causing diseases in humans, such as trichinosis and elephantiasis.
		Annelida	Segmented worms; body is made of many similar segments. Includes earthworms, leeches, and many marine worms.
		Mollusca	Soft-bodied, aquatic animals that usually have an outer shell. Includes snails, mussels, clams, octopus, and squid.
		Arthropoda	Animals with an outer skeleton (exoskeleton) and jointed appendages (for example, legs or wings). Very large group that includes insects, spiders and ticks, centipedes, millipedes, and crustaceans.
		Echinodermata	Marine animals with a radial (spokelike) body shape. Includes feather stars, sea stars (starfish), sea urchins, sand dollars, and sea cucumbers.
		Chordata	Mostly vertebrates (animals with backbones) that share important stages of early development. Includes tunicates (sea squirts), fish, sharks, amphibians, reptiles, birds, and mammals.

The Periodic Table of the Elements

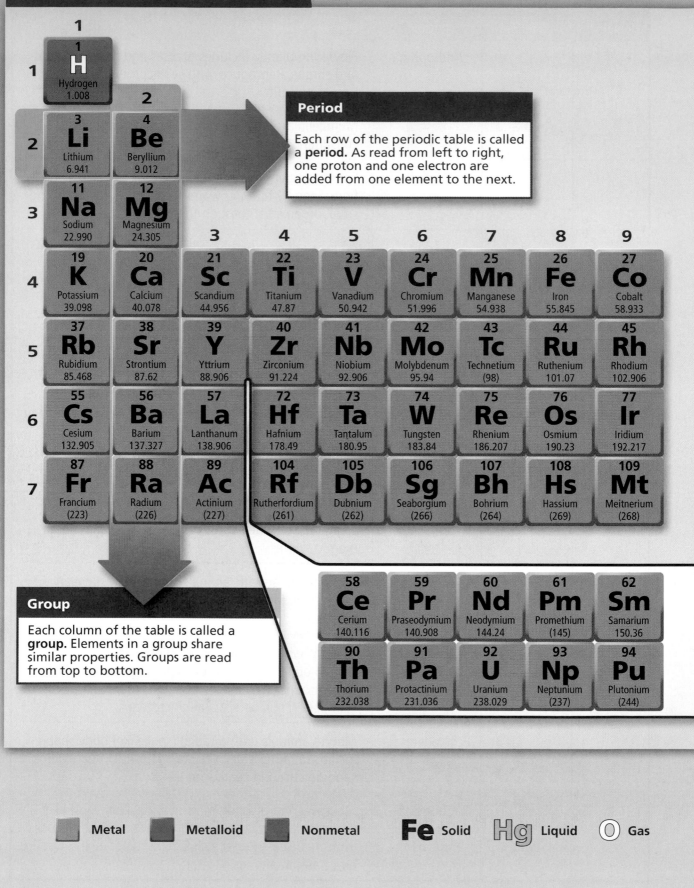

Period

Each row of the periodic table is called a **period**. As read from left to right, one proton and one electron are added from one element to the next.

Group

Each column of the table is called a **group**. Elements in a group share similar properties. Groups are read from top to bottom.

Metal	**Metalloid**	**Nonmetal**

Fe Solid   **Hg** Liquid   **O** Gas

APPENDIX

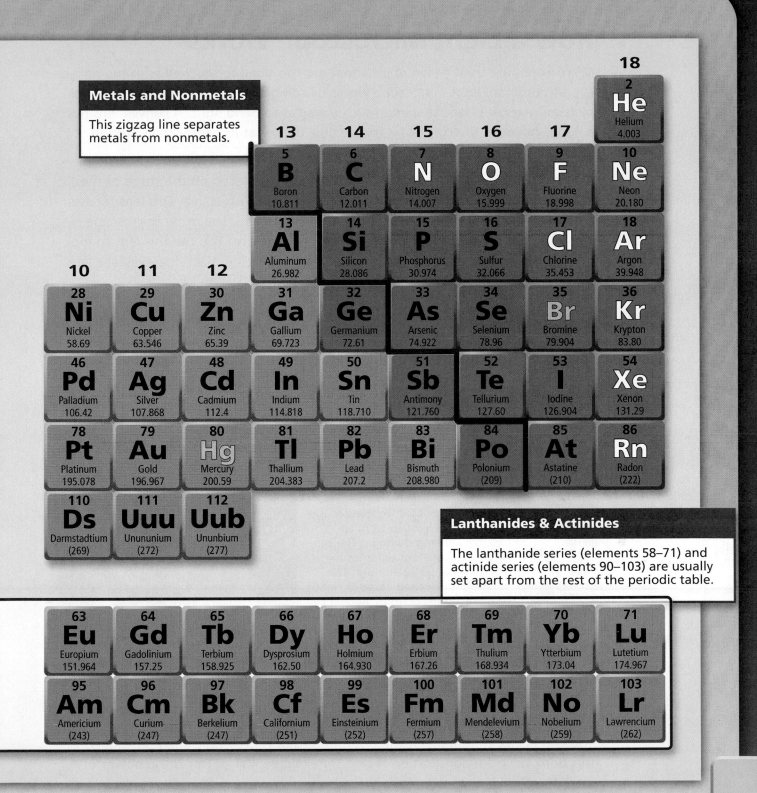

Metals and Nonmetals

This zigzag line separates metals from nonmetals.

18

| 2 He Helium 4.003 |

13 | **14** | **15** | **16** | **17**

5 B Boron 10.811 | 6 C Carbon 12.011 | 7 N Nitrogen 14.007 | 8 O Oxygen 15.999 | 9 F Fluorine 18.998 | 10 Ne Neon 20.180

13 Al Aluminum 26.982 | 14 Si Silicon 28.086 | 15 P Phosphorus 30.974 | 16 S Sulfur 32.066 | 17 Cl Chlorine 35.453 | 18 Ar Argon 39.948

10 | **11** | **12**

28 Ni Nickel 58.69 | 29 Cu Copper 63.546 | 30 Zn Zinc 65.39 | 31 Ga Gallium 69.723 | 32 Ge Germanium 72.61 | 33 As Arsenic 74.922 | 34 Se Selenium 78.96 | 35 Br Bromine 79.904 | 36 Kr Krypton 83.80

46 Pd Palladium 106.42 | 47 Ag Silver 107.868 | 48 Cd Cadmium 112.4 | 49 In Indium 114.818 | 50 Sn Tin 118.710 | 51 Sb Antimony 121.760 | 52 Te Tellurium 127.60 | 53 I Iodine 126.904 | 54 Xe Xenon 131.29

78 Pt Platinum 195.078 | 79 Au Gold 196.967 | 80 Hg Mercury 200.59 | 81 Tl Thallium 204.383 | 82 Pb Lead 207.2 | 83 Bi Bismuth 208.980 | 84 Po Polonium (209) | 85 At Astatine (210) | 86 Rn Radon (222)

110 Ds Darmstadtium (269) | 111 Uuu Unununium (272) | 112 Uub Ununbium (277)

Lanthanides & Actinides

The lanthanide series (elements 58–71) and actinide series (elements 90–103) are usually set apart from the rest of the periodic table.

63 Eu Europium 151.964 | 64 Gd Gadolinium 157.25 | 65 Tb Terbium 158.925 | 66 Dy Dysprosium 162.50 | 67 Ho Holmium 164.930 | 68 Er Erbium 167.26 | 69 Tm Thulium 168.934 | 70 Yb Ytterbium 173.04 | 71 Lu Lutetium 174.967

95 Am Americium (243) | 96 Cm Curium (247) | 97 Bk Berkelium (247) | 98 Cf Californium (251) | 99 Es Einsteinium (252) | 100 Fm Fermium (257) | 101 Md Mendelevium (258) | 102 No Nobelium (259) | 103 Lr Lawrencium (262)

Atomic Number number of protons in the nucleus of the element

Symbol Each element has a symbol. The symbol's color represents the element's state at room temperature.

1 H Hydrogen 1.008

Name

Atomic Mass average mass of isotopes of this element

How a Light Microscope Works

Microscopes are used to see objects that are too small to see well with the naked eye. An ordinary light microscope works by combining convex lenses. A lens is a piece of glass or plastic shaped in such a way as to bend light. A convex lens has a bend similar to the curve of a sphere. It is thicker at its center than around the edges.

The object being viewed is mounted on a slide and placed on the stage of the microscope. The lens closer to the object is called the objective. This lens focuses an enlarged image of the object inside the microscope. The other microscope lens—the one you look through—is called the eyepiece. You use this lens to look at the image formed by the objective. Like a magnifying glass, the eyepiece lens forms an enlarged image of the first image.

Very small objects do not reflect much light. Most microscopes use a lamp or a mirror to shine more light on the object.

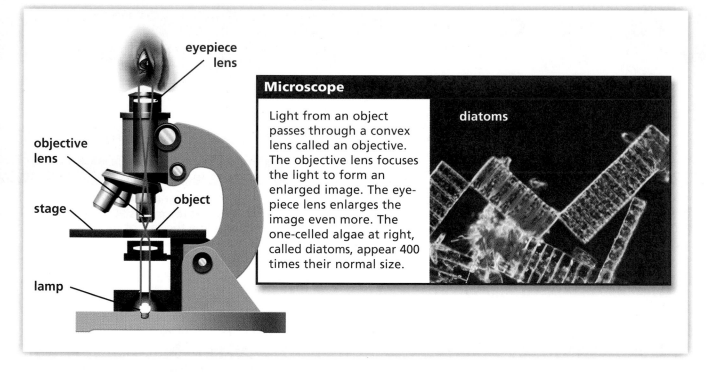

eyepiece lens

objective lens

stage

lamp

object

Microscope

Light from an object passes through a convex lens called an objective. The objective lens focuses the light to form an enlarged image. The eyepiece lens enlarges the image even more. The one-celled algae at right, called diatoms, appear 400 times their normal size.

diatoms

You will notice that many of the photographs of microscopic images included in this book have a magnification factor, for example 400×. This is the power of magnification of the microscope.

Glossary

A

active transport
The process of using energy to move materials through a membrane. (p. 60)

transporte activo El proceso de usar energía para mover sustancias a través de una membrana.

adaptation
A characteristic, a behavior, or any inherited trait that makes a species able to survive and reproduce in a particular environment. (p. xxi)

adaptación Una característica, un comportamiento o cualquier rasgo heredado que permite a una especie sobrevivir o reproducirse en un medio ambiente determinado.

allele (uh-LEEL)
An alternate form of a gene for a specific trait or gene product. (p. 103)

alelo Una forma alterna de un gen para un rasgo específico o un producto del gen.

asexual reproduction
The process by which a single organism produces offspring that have the same genetic material. (p. 88)

reproducción asexual El proceso mediante el cual un solo organismo produce crías que tienen el mismo material genético.

atom
The smallest particle of an element that has the chemical properties of that element.

átomo La partícula más pequeña de un elemento que tiene las propiedades químicas de ese elemento.

B

bacteria (bak-TEER-ee-uh)
A large group of one-celled organisms that sometimes cause disease. *Bacteria* is a plural word; the singular is *bacterium*. (p. 14)

bacterias Un grupo grande de organismos unicelulares que algunas veces causan enfermedades.

binary fission
A form of asexual reproduction by which some single-celled organisms reproduce. The genetic material is copied, and one cell divides into two independent cells that are each a copy of the original cell. Prokaryotes such as bacteria reproduce by binary fission. (p. 89)

fisión binaria Una forma asexual de reproducción mediante la cual algunos organismos unicelulares se reproducen. El material genético se copia y una célula se divide en dos células independientes las cuales son copias de la célula original. Los organismos procariotas, tales como las bacterias, se reproducen mediante fisión binaria.

biodiversity
The number and variety of living things found on Earth or within an ecosystem. (p. xxi)

biodiversidad La cantidad y variedad de organismos vivos que se encuentran en la Tierra o dentro de un ecosistema.

budding
A process of asexual reproduction in which an organism develops as an outgrowth of the parent. Each bud can grow into a new organism, breaking free and becoming separate and independent. (p. 89)

gemación Un proceso de reproducción asexual en el cual un organismo se desarrolla a partir de una porción del progenitor. Cada yema puede convertirse en un nuevo organismo, separándose del progenitor y volviéndose independiente.

C

carbohydrate (KAHR-boh-HY-drayt)
A type of molecule made up of subunits of sugars and used for energy and structure. (p. 42)

carbohidrato Un tipo de molécula compuesta de unidades de azúcares y usada como fuente de energía y como material estructural.

cell
The smallest unit that is able to perform the basic functions of life. (p. xv)

célula La unidad más pequeña capaz de realizar las funciones básicas de la vida.

cell cycle
The normal sequence of growth, maintenance, and division in a cell. (p. 80)

ciclo celular La secuencia normal de crecimiento, mantenimiento y división en una célula.

cell membrane
The outer boundary of the cytoplasm, a layer that controls what enters or leaves the cell; a protective covering enclosing an entire cell. (p. 20)

membrana celular El límite exterior del citoplasma, una capa que controla lo que entra y sale de la célula, una cubierta protectora que encierra una célula entera.

cell wall
A protective outer covering that lies just outside the cell membrane of plant cells. (p. 21)

pared celular Una cubierta exterior protectora que se encuentra justo fuera de la membrana celular de las células vegetales.

cellular respiration
A process in which cells use oxygen to release energy stored in sugars. (p. 50)

respiración celular Un proceso en el cual las células usan oxígeno para liberar energía almacenada en las azúcares.

chemical energy
Energy that is stored in the chemical composition of matter. The amount of chemical energy in a substance depends on the types and arrangement of its atoms. When wood or gasoline burns, chemical energy produces heat. The energy used by the cells in your body comes from chemical energy in the foods you eat. (p. 47)

energía química Energía almacenada en la composición química de la materia. La cantidad de energía química en una sustancia depende de los tipos y la disposición de sus átomos. Cuando se quema madera o gasolina, la energía química produce calor. La energía usada por las células en tu cuerpo proviene de la energía química en los alimentos que comes.

chemical reaction
The process by which chemical changes occur. In a chemical reaction, atoms are rearranged, and chemical bonds are broken and formed. (p. 42)

reacción química El proceso mediante el cual ocurren cambios químicos. En una reacción química, se reacomodan átomos y se rompen y se forman enlaces químicos.

chlorophyll (KLAWR-uh-fihl)
A light-absorbing chemical, a pigment, that traps the energy in sunlight and converts it to chemical energy. Found in chloroplasts of plant cells and the cells of other photosynthetic organisms. (p. 48)

clorofila Una sustancia química que absorbe luz, un pigmento, que atrapa la energía de la luz solar y la convierte a energía química. Se encuentra en los cloroplastos de células vegetales y en las células de otros organismos fotosintéticos.

chloroplast (KLAWR-uh-PLAST)
An organelle in a plant cell that contains chlorophyll, a chemical that uses the energy from sunlight to make sugar. (p. 23)

cloroplasto Un organelo en una célula vegetal que contiene clorofila, una sustancia química que usa la energía de la luz solar para producir azúcar.

chromosome
The physical structure in a cell that contains the cell's genetic material. (p. 75)

cromosoma Una estructura corporal en la célula que contiene el material genético de la célula.

classification
The systematic grouping of different types of organisms by their shared characteristics.

clasificación La agrupación sistemática de diferentes tipos de organismos en base a las características que comparten.

cloning
The process of using DNA technology to produce an offspring that is genetically identical to its one parent. (p. 154)

clonación El proceso de usar tecnología de ADN para producir una cría que es genéticamente idéntica a su único progenitor.

compound
A substance made up of two or more different types of atoms.

compuesto Una sustancia formada por dos o más diferentes tipos de átomos enlazados.

cycle

n. A series of events or actions that repeat themselves regularly; a physical and/or chemical process in which one material continually changes locations and/or forms. Examples include the water cycle, the carbon cycle, and the rock cycle.

v. To move through a repeating series of events or actions.

> **ciclo** Una serie de eventos o acciones que se repiten regularmente; un proceso físico y/o químico en el cual un material cambia continuamente de lugar y/o forma. Ejemplos: el ciclo del agua, el ciclo del carbono y el ciclo de las rocas.

cytokinesis (SY-toh-kuh-NEE-sihs)

The division of a parent cell's cytoplasm following mitosis. (p. 81)

> **citocinesis** La división del citoplasma de la célula madre después de la mitosis.

cytoplasm (SY-tuh-PLAZ-uhm)

A thick, gelatin-like material contained within the cell membrane. Most of the work of the cell is carried out in the cytoplasm. (p. 20)

> **citoplasma** Un material espeso, parecido a la gelatina, contenido dentro de la membrana celular. La mayor parte del trabajo de la célula se realiza en el citoplasma.

D

data

Information gathered by observation or experimentation that can be used in calculating or reasoning. *Data* is a plural word; the singular is *datum.*

> **datos** Información reunida mediante observación o experimentación y que se puede usar para calcular o para razonar.

density

A property of matter representing the mass per unit volume.

> **densidad** Una propiedad de la materia que representa la masa por unidad de volumen.

diffusion (dih-FYOO-zhuhn)

The tendency of a substance to move from an area of higher concentration to an area of lower concentration. (p. 56)

> **difusión** La tendencia de una sustancia a moverse de un área de mayor concentración a un área de menor concentración.

DNA

The genetic material found in all living cells that contains the information needed for an organism to grow, maintain itself, and reproduce. Deoxyribonucleic acid (dee-AHK-see-RY-boh-noo-KLEE-ihk). (p. 74)

> **ADN** El material genético que se encuentra en todas las céulas vivas y que contiene la información necesaria para que un organismo crezca, se mantenga a sí mismo y se reproduzca. Ácido desoxiribunucleico.

dominant

A term that describes the allele that determines the phenotype of an individual organism when two different copies are present in the genotype. (p. 107)

> **dominante** Un término que describe al alelo que determina el fenotipo de un organismo cuando están presentes dos copias diferentes en el genotipo.

E

egg

A female reproductive cell (gamete) that forms in the reproductive organs of a female and has just a single copy of the genetic material of the parent. (p. 118)

> **óvulo** Una célula reproductiva femenina (gameto) que se forma en los órganos reproductivos de una hembra y tiene una sola copia del material genético de la madre.

element

A substance that cannot be broken down into a simpler substance by ordinary chemical changes. An element consists of atoms of only one type.

> **elemento** Una sustancia que no puede descomponerse en otra sustancia más simple por medio de cambios químicos normales. Un elemento consta de átomos de un solo tipo.

energy

The ability to do work or to cause a change. For example, the energy of a moving bowling ball knocks over pins; energy from food allows animals to move and to grow; and energy from the Sun heats Earth's surface and atmosphere, which causes air to move.

> **energía** La capacidad para trabajar o causar un cambio. Por ejemplo, la energía de una bola de boliche en movimiento tumba los pinos; la energía proveniente de su alimento permite a los animales moverse y crecer; la energía del Sol calienta la superficie y la atmósfera de la Tierra, lo que ocasiona que el aire se mueva.

environment
Everything that surrounds a living thing. An environment is made up of both living and nonliving factors. (p. xix)

medio ambiente Todo lo que rodea a un organismo vivo. Un medio ambiente está compuesto de factores vivos y factores sin vida.

eukaryotic cell (yoo-KAR-ee-AHT-ihk)
A cell in which the genetic material is enclosed within a nucleus, surrounded by its own membrane. (p. 20)

célula eucariota Una célula en la cual el material genético esta dentro de un núcleo, rodeado por su propia membrana.

experiment
An organized procedure to study something under controlled conditions. (p. xxiv)

experimento Un procedimiento organizado para estudiar algo bajo condiciones controladas.

extinction
The permanent disappearance of a species. (p. xxi)

extinción La desaparición permanente de una especie.

F

fermentation
A chemical process by which cells release energy from sugar when no oxygen is present. (p. 52)

fermentación Un proceso químico mediante el cual las células liberan energía del azúcar cuando no hay oxígeno presente.

fertilization
Part of the process of sexual reproduction in which a male reproductive cell and a female reproductive cell combine to make a new cell that can develop into a new organism. (p. 118)

fertilización El proceso mediante el cual una célula reproductiva masculina y una célula reproductiva femenina se combinan para formar una nueva célula que puede convertirse en un organismo nuevo.

G

gamete
A sperm or egg cell, containing half the usual number of chromosomes of an organism (one chromosome from each pair), which is found only in the reproductive organs of a plant or animal. (p. 118)

gameto Un óvulo o un espermatozoide, que contiene la mitad del número usual de cromosomas de un organismo (un cromosoma de cada par), que se encuentra sólo en los órganos reproductivos de una planta o de un animal.

gene
The basic unit of heredity that consists of a segment of DNA on a chromosome. (p. 102)

gen La unidad básica de herencia que consiste en un segmento de ADN en un cromosoma.

genetic engineering
The scientific process in which DNA is separated from an organism, changed, and then reinserted into the same or a different organism. (p. 151)

ingeniería genética El proceso científico en el cual se extrae el ADN de un organismo, se modifica y luego se reinserta en el mismo organismo o en uno diferente.

genetic material
The nucleic acid DNA that is present in all living cells and contains the information needed for a cell's growth, maintenance, and reproduction.

material genético El ácido nucleico ADN, ue esta presente en todas las células vivas y que contiene la información necesaria para el crecimiento, el mantenimiento y la reproducción celular.

genome (JEE-nohm)
All the DNA of an organism, including its genes; the genetic material of an organism. (p. 154)

genoma Todo el ADN de un organismo, incluyendo sus genes; el material genético de un organismo.

genotype (JEHN-uh-typ)
The genetic makeup of an organism; all the genes that an organism has. (p. 106)

genotipo La estructura genética de un organismo; todos los genes que tiene un organismo.

glucose
A sugar molecule that is a major energy source for most cells, produced by the process of photosynthesis. (p. 47)

glucosa Una molécula de azúcar que es la principal fuente de energía para la mayoría de las células, producida mediante el proceso de fotosíntesis.

H

heredity
The passing of genes from parents to offspring; the genes are expressed in the traits of the offspring. (p. 102)

herencia La transferencia de genes de los progenitores a la crías; los genes se expresan en los rasgos de las crías.

homeostasis (HOH-mee-oh-STAY-sihs)
A condition needed for health and functioning in which an organism or cell maintains a relatively stable internal environment.

homeostasis Una condición necesaria para la salud y el funcionamiento en la cual un organismo o una célula mantiene un medio ambiente estable e interna.

hypothesis
A tentative explanation for an observation or phenomenon. A hypothesis is used to make tentative predictions. (p. xxiv)

hipótesis Una explicación provisional de una observación o de un fenómeno. Una hipótesis se usa para hacer predicciones que se pueden probar.

I, J, K

interaction
The condition of acting or having an influence upon something. Living things in an ecosystem interact with both the living and nonliving parts of their environment. (p. xix)

interacción La condición de actuar o influir sobre algo. Los organismos vivos en un ecosistema interactúan con las partes vivas y las partes sin vida de su medio ambiente.

interphase
The period in the cell cycle in which a cell grows, maintains itself, and prepares for division. (p. 81)

interfase El período en el ciclo celular en el cual una célula crece, se mantiene y se prepara para la división.

L

law
In science, a rule or principle describing a physical relationship that always works in the same way under the same conditions. The law of conservation of energy is an example.

ley En las ciencias, una regla o un principio que describe una relación física que siempre funciona de la misma manera bajo las mismas condiciones. La ley de la conservación de la energía es un ejemplo.

lipid
A type of molecule made up of subunits of fatty acids. Lipids are found in the fats, oils, and waxes used for structure and to store energy. (p. 43)

lípido Un tipo de molécula compuesta de unidades de ácidos grasos. Los lípidos se encuentran en las grasas, los aceites y las ceras usadas como materiales estructurales y para almacenar energía.

M

mass
A measure of how much matter an object is made of.

masa Una medida de la cantidad de materia de la que está compuesto un objeto.

matter
Anything that has mass and volume. Matter exists ordinarily as a solid, a liquid, or a gas.

materia Todo lo que tiene masa y volumen. Generalmente la materia existe como sólido, líquido o gas.

meiosis (my-OH-sihs)
A part of sexual reproduction in which cells divide to form sperm cells in a male and egg cells in a female. Meiosis occurs only in reproductive cells. (p. 119)

meiosis Una parte de la reproducción sexual en la cual las células se dividen para formar espermatozoides en los machos y óvulos en las hembras. La meiosis sólo ocurre en las células reproductivas.

microscope
An instrument that uses glass lenses to magnify an object. (p. 12)

microscopio Un instrumento que usa lentes de vidrio para magnificar un objeto.

mitochondria (MY-tuh-KAWN-dree-uh)
Organelles that release energy by using oxygen to break down sugars. (p. 23)

> **mitocondrias** Organelos que liberan energía usando oxígeno para romper los azúcares.

mitosis
The phase in the cell cycle during which the nucleus divides. (p. 81)

> **mitosis** La fase en el ciclo celular durante la cual se divide el núcleo.

molecule
A group of atoms that are held together by covalent bonds so that they move as a single unit.

> **molécula** Un grupo de átomos que están unidos mediante enlaces covalentes de tal manera que se mueven como una sola unidad.

multicellular
A term used to describe an organism that is made up of many cells. (p. 11)

> **multicelular** Un término usado para describir a un organismo que esta formado por muchas células.

mutation
Any change made to DNA. (p. 145)

> **mutación** Cualquier cambio hecho al ADN.

N

nucleic acid (noo-KLEE-ihk)
A type of molecule, made up of subunits of nucleotides, that is part of the genetic material of a cell and is needed to make proteins. DNA and RNA are nucleic acids. (p. 43)

> **ácido nucleico** Un tipo de molécula, compuesto de unidades de nucleótidos, que es parte del material genético de una célula y se necesita para producir proteínas. El ADN y el ARN son ácidos nucleicos.

nucleus (NOO-klee-uhs)
The structure in a eukaryotic cell that contains the genetic material a cell needs to reproduce and function. (p. 20)

> **núcleo** La estructura en una célula eucariota que contiene el material genético que la célula necesita para reproducirse y funcionar.

O

offspring
The new organisms produced by one or two parent organisms.

> **crías** Los nuevos organismos producidos por uno o dos organismos progenitores.

organ
A structure in a plant or an animal that is made up of different tissues working together to perform a particular function. (p. 30)

> **órgano**
>
> Una estructura en una planta o en un animal compuesta de diferentes tejidos que trabajan juntos para realizar una función determinada.

organelle (AWR-guh-NEHL)
A structure in a cell that is enclosed by a membrane and that performs a particular function. (p. 20)

> **organelo** Una estructura en una célula, envuelta en una membrana, que realiza una función determinada.

organism
An individual living thing, made up of one or many cells, that is capable of growing and reproducing. (p. xv)

> **organismo** Un individuo vivo, compuesto de una o muchas células, que es capaz de crecer y reproducirse.

osmosis (ahz-MOH-sihs)
The movement of water through a membrane from an area of higher concentration to an area of lower concentration. (p. 59)

> **osmosis** El movimiento de agua a través de una membrana desde un área de mayor concentración hacia un área de menor concentración.

P, Q

parent
An organism that produces a new organism or organisms similar to or related to itself. (p. 93)

> **progenitor** Un organismo que produce un nuevo organismo u organismos parecidos a o relacionados a él.

passive transport
The movement of materials through a membrane without any input of energy. (p. 58)

> **transporte pasivo** El movimiento de sustancias a través de una membrana sin aporte de energía.

pedigree
A chart that shows family relationships, including two or more generations. (p. 147)

pedigrí Un diagrama de las relaciones de dos o más generaciones de una familia.

percentage
A ratio that states the number of times an outcome is likely to occur out of a possible 100 times. (p. 112)

porcentaje Una razón que establece el número de veces que es probable que ocurra un resultado en 100 veces.

phenotype
The observable characteristics or traits of an organism. (p. 106)

fenotipo Las características o rasgos visibles de un organismo.

photosynthesis (FOH-toh-SIHN-thih-sihs)
The process by which green plants and other producers use simple compounds and energy from light to make sugar, an energy-rich compound. (p. 48)

fotosíntesis El proceso mediante el cual las plantas verdes y otros productores usan compuestos simples y energía de la luz para producir azúcares, compuestos ricos en energía.

probability
The likelihood or chance that a specific outcome will occur out of a total number of outcomes. (p. 112)

probabilidad La posibilidad de que ocurra un resultado específico en un número total de resultados.

prokaryotic cell (proh-KAR-ee-AWT-ihk)
A cell that lacks a nucleus and other organelles, with DNA that is not organized into chromosomes. (p. 20)

célula procariota Una célula que carece de núcleo y otros organelos, con ADN que no esta organizado en cromosomas.

protein
One of many types of molecules made up of chains of amino acid subunits. Proteins control the chemical activity of a cell and support growth and repair. (p. 43)

proteína Uno de muchos tipos de moléculas formadas por cadenas de aminoácidos. Las proteínas controlan la actividad química de una célula y sustentan el crecimiento y la reparación.

Punnett square
A chart used to show all the ways genes from two parents can combine and be passed to offspring; used to predict all genotypes that are possible. (p. 110)

cuadro de Punnett Una tabla que se usa para mostrar todas las formas en que los genes de dos progenitores pueden combinarse y pasarse a la crías; se usa para predecir todos los genotipos que son posibles.

R

ratio
A comparison between two quantities, often written with a colon, as 3 : 4. (p. 112)

razón Una comparación entre dos cantidades, a menudo se escribe con dos puntos, como 3 : 4.

recessive
A term that describes an allele that is not expressed when combined with a dominant form of the gene. (p. 107)

recesivo Un término que describe un alelo que no se expresa cuando se combina con una forma dominante del gen.

regeneration
In some organisms, the process by which certain cells produce new tissue growth at the site of a wound or lost limb; also a form of asexual reproduction. (p. 90)

regeneración En algunos organismos, el proceso mediante el cual ciertas células producen crecimiento de tejido nuevo en el sitio de una herida o de una extremidad perdida; también un tipo de reproducción asexual.

replication
The process by which DNA is copied before it condenses into chromosomes. Replication takes place before a cell divides. (p. 137)

replicación El proceso mediante el cual el ADN se copia antes de condensarse en los cromosomas. La replicación se realiza antes de que una célula se divida.

RNA
A molecule that carries genetic information from DNA to a ribosome, where the genetic information is used to bring together amino acids to form a protein. Ribonucleic acid (RY-boh-noo-KLEE-ihk). (p. 138)

ARN Una molécula que lleva información genética del ADN al ribosoma, donde la información genética se usa para unir aminoácidos para formar una proteína. Ácido ribonucleico.

S

selective breeding
The process of breeding plants and animals with specific traits to produce offspring that have these traits. (p. 151)

reproducción selectiva El proceso de reproducir plantas y animales con rasgos específicos para producir crías que tengan estos rasgos.

sexual reproduction
A type of reproduction in which male and female reproductive cells combine to form offspring with genetic material from both cells. (p. 102)

reproducción sexual Un tipo de reproducción en el cual se combinan las células reproductivas femeninas y masculinas para formar una cría con material genético de ambas células.

specialization
The specific organization of a cell and its structure that allows it to perform a specific function. (p. 28)

especialización La organización específica de una célula y de su estructura que le permite realizar una función específica.

species
A group of organisms so closely related that they can breed with one another and produce offspring that are able to breed. (p. xxi)

especie Un grupo de organismos que están tan estrechamente relacionados que pueden aparearse entre sí y producir crías que también pueden aparearse.

sperm
A male reproductive cell (gamete) that forms in the reproductive organs of a male and has just a single copy of the genetic material of the parent. (p. 118)

espermatozoide Una célula reproductiva masculina (gameto) que se forma en los órganos reproductivos de un macho y tiene una sola copia del material genético del progenitor.

system
A group of objects or phenomena that interact. A system can be as simple as a rope, a pulley, and a mass. It also can be as complex as the interaction of energy and matter in the four parts of the Earth system.

sistema Un grupo de objetos o fenómenos que interactúan. Un sistema puede ser algo tan sencillo como una cuerda, una polea y una masa. También puede ser algo tan complejo como la interacción de la energía y la materia en las cuatro partes del sistema de la Tierra.

T

technology
The use of scientific knowledge to solve problems or engineer new products, tools, or processes.

tecnología El uso de conocimientos científicos para resolver problemas o para diseñar nuevos productos, herramientas o procesos.

theory
In science, a set of widely accepted explanations of observations and phenomena. A theory is a well-tested explanation that is consistent with all available evidence.

teoría En las ciencias, un conjunto de explicaciones de observaciones y fenómenos que es ampliamente aceptado. Una teoría es una explicación bien probada que es consecuente con la evidencia disponible.

tissue
A group of similar cells that are organized to do a specific job. (p. 29)

tejido Un grupo de células parecidas que juntas realizan una función específica en un organismo.

U

unicellular
A term used to describe an organism that is made up of a single cell. (p. 11)

unicelular Un término usado para describir a un organismo que está compuesto de una sola célula.

V, W, X, Y, Z

variable
Any factor that can change in a controlled experiment, observation, or model. (p. R30)

variable Cualquier factor que puede cambiar en un experimento controlado, en una observación o en un modelo.

volume
An amount of three-dimensional space, often used to describe the space that an object takes up.

volumen Una cantidad de espacio tridimensional; a menudo se usa este término para describir el espacio que ocupa un objeto.

Index

Page numbers for definitions are printed in **boldface** type.
Page numbers for illustrations, maps, and charts are printed in *italics*.

environment
of archaea, 27, *27*
of organisms, 10
enzymes, 43
Eukarya, 28, *R52–R55*
eukaryotes, 28. *See also* cell division
compared with prokaryotes, 81, 89
eukaryotic cells, **20**, *20*, 20–24
organelles in, 23–24
plant and animal, 21, *21*, *22*
and protein, 138
evaluating, **R8**
media claims, R8
evidence, collection of, xxiv
exercise, 54
exocytosis, 61, *61*
experiment, **xxiv**. *See also* labs
conclusions, drawing, R35
constants, determining, R30
controlled, **R28**, R30
designing, R28–R35
hypothesis, writing, R29
materials, determining, R29
observations, recording, R33
procedure, writing, R32
purpose, determining, R28
results, summarizing, R34
variables, R30–R31, R32
experimental group, R30

F

fact, **R9**
different from opinion, R9
fatty acids, **43**, *43*
faulty reasoning, **R7**
fermentation, **52**, 52–54
and exercise, 54
fertilization, **118**, *118*. *See also* heredity
fibers, 46
fingerprints, DNA, 130, 131, *131*, 153
first generation, 104–105, *105*
formulas, **R42**
fractions, **R41**
Franklin, Rosalind, 32, 130
fruit flies, 3, 123
fungi, 28

G

gametes, **118**, *118*. *See also* meiosis
genes, **102**, *102*, 102–103. *See also* DNA; heredity
discovery of, 129
and disease, *146*, 146–148, *147*, *148*
Hox, *3*, 3–5, *4*, *5*
mapping, 123
variations and mutations of, 145
genetic disorders, *146*, 146–148, *147*, *148*
genetic engineering, 130, **151**, 151–153
genetic material. *See also* DNA; heredity
and cell division, *74*, 74–75, *75*
and cell structure, 20
genetics, 132–159. *See also* cells; DNA; heredity
development of, 128–131
and disease, *146*, 146–148, *147*, *148*
and DNA identification, 130, 131, *131*, 153
and genetic code, 135–137
and genetic engineering, 130, 151–153
and genomes, 131, **154**
Internet Activity on, 133
and replication, *137*, 137–138
and species history, 155
and transcription, 138–139, *139*
and translation, 139–141, *140*
and variation and mutation, 144–148
genomes, 131, **154**
Internet Activity on, 133
genotypes, **106**
and Punnett squares, 111, 112, *113*
germs, 14. *See also* bacteria
glucose, **47**. *See also* sugar
and cellular respiration, 50, *51*, *52*
and diffusion, 58, *58*
and energy, 50
and photosynthesis, 48, *49*, *52*
glycerol, **43**, *43*
Golgi apparatus, *22*, 24
graphs
bar, R26, R31
circle, R25
double bar, R27
line, R24, R34
growth
and cell division, 73, 76–77, *77*
of organisms, 10
guanine (G), 136, 138–139

microorganisms. *See* bacteria; organisms; unicellular organisms
microscope, **12**, *12*, *R14*, R14–R15, R58, *R58*
discovery of, 128–130
electron, 19, *19*, 130
making a slide or wet mount, R15, *R15*
viewing an object, R15
mitochondria, 22, **23**, *23*
and cellular respiration, 50, *51*, *52*
mitosis, **81**, *81*, 81–82, *83*
and meiosis, 122
mode, **R37**
models, scientific, 32, *32*
and mapping genes, 123
molecules, 42
types of, 42–44
mordants, 46
multicellular organisms, **11**, *11*. *See also* cell division; cells
cell structure of, 20
organization of, 11, 28–31
muscle cells, and exercise, 54
mutation, **145**
and disease, *146*, 146–148, *147*, *148*

N

nerve cells, 79
note-taking strategies, R45–R49
combination notes, R45, *R45*
concept map, R49, *R49*
content frame, R45, *R45*
main idea and detail notes, R46, *R46*
main idea web, R46, *R46*
mind map, R47, *R47*
outline, R48, *R48*
supporting main ideas, R47, *R47*
Venn diagram, R49, *R49*
nucleic acids, **43**, *43*, 43–44
nucleotides, *43*, 43–44, *136*, 136–140
and replication, 137, *137*
and transcription, 138–140, *139*
and translation, 139–141, *140*
nucleus, **20**, *20*, 20–23, *21*, *22*
discovery of, 129
and DNA, 75, *75*, 82, *83*

O

observations, **xxiv**, **R2**, R5, R33
qualitative, R2
quantitative, R2
offspring, 88
operational definition, **R31**
opinion, **R9**
different from fact, R9
organelles, **20**, 23–25
chloroplasts, 22, **23**, *23*
Golgi apparatus, 22, 24
lysosomes, 22, 24
mitochondria, *22*, **23**, *23*
vacuoles, *22*, 24, *24*
organisms, 9
archaea, 27
bacteria, 14–15, 27
characteristics of, 10
and endoplasmic reticulum, *22*, 23–24
Eukarya, 28
genetically modified, 151
multicellular, **11**, 20, 28–31
needs of, 10
organization of, 29–31, *30*
unicellular, **11**, 20, 26–27, 88–89
organization
of cells, 20–24
of humans, 31
of multicellular organisms, 29, 29–31, *30*
of organisms, 10, 11
of paramecium, 28, *28*
of prokaryotes, 27
organs, **30**, *30*, 30–31
organ systems, *30*, 31
osmosis, **59**, *59*
oxygen
and cellular respiration, 50, *51*, *52*
and diffusion, 57–58, *58*
and photosynthesis, 48, *49*, *52*

P, Q

paramecium, 28, *28*, 89
parent cells, 82
passive transport, **58**, *58*. *See also* diffusion
Pasteur, Louis, 14–15
pasteurization, 14
pedigree, **147**
percentage, **112**
percents, **R41**
periodic table, *R56–R57*

R

S

Acknowledgments

Photography

Cover © Dr. Gopal Murti/Photo Researchers, Inc.; **iii** Photograph of James Trefil by Evan Cantwell; Photograph of Rita Ann Calvo by Joseph Calvo; Photograph of Kenneth Cutler by Kenneth A. Cutler; Photograph of Douglas Carnine by McDougal Littell; Photograph of Linda Carnine by Amilcar Cifuentes; Photograph of Donald Steely by Marni Stamm; Photograph of Sam Miller by Samuel Miller; Photograph of Vicky Vachon by Redfern Photographics; **vi** *bottom* © Kent Foster Photographs/Bruce Coleman, Inc.; **ix** *top* © Photodisc/Getty Images; *bottom left* Photograph by Ken O'Donoghue; *bottom right* Photograph by Frank Siteman; **xiv, xv** © Mark Hamblin/Age Fotostock; **xvi, xvii** © Georgette Duowma/Taxi/Getty Images; **xviii, xix** © Ron Sanford/Corbis; **xx, xxi** © Nick Vedros & Assoc./Stone/Getty Images; **xxii** *left* © Michael Gadomski/Animals Animals; *right* © Shin Yoshino/Minden Pictures; **xxiii** © Laif Elleringmann/Aurora Photos; **xxiv** © Pascal Goetgheluck/Science Photo Library/Photo Researchers, Inc.; **xxv** *top left* © David Parker/Science Photo Library/Photo Researchers, Inc.; *top right* © James King-Holmes/Science Photo Library/Photo Researchers, Inc.; *bottom* Sinsheimer Labs/University of California, Santa Cruz; **xxvi, xxvii** *background* © Maximillian Stock/Photo Researchers, Inc.; **xxvi** Courtesy, John Lair, Jewish Hospital, University of Louisville; **xxvii** *top* © Brand X Pictures/Alamy; *center* Courtesy, AbioMed; **xxxii** © Chedd-Angier Production Company; **2, 3** © Mark Smith/Photo Researchers, Inc.; **4** *top left to right* © Dr. Richard Kessel and Dr. Gene Shih/Visuals Unlimited; *bottom* © Chedd-Angier Production Company; **5** *left* © Carolina Biological/Visuals Unlimited; *right* © Inga Spence/Visuals Unlimited; **6, 7** © Biophoto Associates/Photo Researchers, Inc.; **7** *top right* Photograph by Ken O'Donoghue; *center right* Photograph by Frank Siteman; **9** Photograph by Ken O'Donoghue; **10** © Heintges/Premium Stock/PictureQuest ; **11** *bottom* © David Stone/Rainbow/PictureQuest; *inset* © Science VU/Visuals Unlimited; **12** *left* © American Registry of Photography; *right* Library of Congress, Prints and Photographs Division, #LC-USZ62-95187; **13** *bottom* © Tom Walker/Visuals Unlimited; *inset* © Greg Theiman; **14** © Will & Demi McIntyre/Corbis; **16** *top* © Science VU/Visuals Unlimited; *center* Photograph by Frank Siteman; *bottom left, bottom right* Photographs by Ken O'Donoghue; **18** *left* Photograph by Ken O'Donoghue; *right* © Dr. Gary Gaugler/Visuals Unlimited **19** © Eye of Science/Photo Researchers, Inc.; **20** *left* © Eric Grave/Photo Reseachers, Inc.; *right* © CNRI/Photo Reseachers, Inc.; **21** *bottom left* © Biophoto Associates/Science Source/Photo Researchers, Inc.; *bottom right* © Dennis Kunkel/Phototake; **22** *background* © John Edwards/Getty Images; *inset* © Gary Braasch/Getty Images; **23** © Dr. Martha Powell/Visuals Unlimited; **24** *top* © Dr. Henry Aldrich/Visuals Unlimited; *bottom* © Biophoto Associates/Photo Researchers, Inc.; **25** *top* © Dr. Gary Gaugler/Visuals Unlimited; *bottom* © Dr. Tony Brain and David Parker/Photo Reseachers, Inc.; **26** Photograph by Ken O'Donoghue; **27** *center* © Ralph White/Corbis; *inset* © Alfred Pasieka/Photo Researchers, Inc.; **28** © Stan Flegler/Visuals Unlimited; **29** *left to right* © Ted Whittenkraus/Visuals Unlimited; © Gustav Verderber/Visuals Unlimited; © Dwight R. Kuhn; **30** *left* © Eric and David Hosking/Corbis; *right* © Frans Lanting/Minden Pictures; **31** Photograph by Ken O'Donoghue; **32** *top* © Ken Eward/BioGrafx/Photo Researchers, Inc.; *inset* © A. Barrington Brown/Photo Researchers, Inc.; **33** *left* © Photo Researchers, Inc.; *inset* © Dr. Linda Stannard, UCT/Photo Researchers, Inc.; **34** *top left* David Stone/Rainbow/PictureQuest; *top right* © Science VU/Visuals Unlimited; *center left* © CNRI/Photo Reseachers, Inc.; © *bottom* Frans Lanting/Minden Pictures; **35** © Dr. Martha Powell/Visuals Unlimited; **36** *top* © Tom Walker/Visuals Unlimited; *inset* © Greg Theiman; **38, 39** © Kent Foster Photographs/Bruce Coleman, Inc.; **39** *top, center* Photographs by Ken O'Donoghue; **41** Photograph by Ken O'Donoghue; **42** © Corbis-Royalty Free; **44** *top* © Alfred Pasieka/Photo Researhers, Inc.; *bottom* Photograph by Ken O'Donoghue; **46** *background* © Andrew Syred/Photo Researchers, Inc.; *bottom left* © Anna Clopet/Corbis; *center right* Photograph by Tim Nihoff; *montage top to bottom* © Dr. Jeremy Burgess/Photo Researchers, Inc.; © Andrew Syred/Photo Researchers, Inc.; **47** *top right* © David Young-Wolff/PhotoEdit; *top inset* John Durham/Photo Researchers, Inc.; *bottom inset* © Innerspace Imaging/Photo Researchers, Inc.; **48** © Dr. Jeremy Burgess/Photo Researchers, Inc.; **49** *top center* © Biophoto Associates/Science Source/Photo Researchers, Inc.; **51** *top left* © Dr. Gopal Murti/Photo Researchers, Inc.; *top right* © Biophoto Associates/Science Source/Photo Researchers, Inc.; **53** Photograph by Ken O'Donoghue; **54** © Bob Daemmrich Photo, Inc.; **55** © Roger Ressmeyer/Corbis; **56** Photograph by Ken O'Donoghue; **59** © Marilyn Schaller/Photo Researchers, Inc.; **60** © Fred Bavendam/Peter Arnold, Inc.; **62** Photograph by Frank Siteman; **64** *top* Corbis/Royalty Free; *all others* Photograph by Frank Siteman; **66** *bottom left* Photograph by Frank Siteman; *bottom right* © Fred Bavendam/Peter Arnold, Inc.; **70, 71** © CNRI/Photo Researchers, Inc.; **71** *top right* Photograph by Ken O'Donoghue; *center right* Photograph by Frank Siteman; **73** Photograph by Ken

O'Donoghue; **74** © Will & Deni McIntyre/Photo Researchers, Inc.; **76** Photograph by Frank Siteman; **77** *background* © Rudiger Lehnen/Photo Researchers, Inc.; *left inset* © Alexis Rosenfeld/Photo Researchers, Inc.; *right inset* © David Hughes/Bruce Coleman, Inc.; **79** *left* © Nancy Kedersha/UCLA/Photo Researchers, Inc.; *top right* Photograph of Elizabeth Gould by Denise Applewhite; **80** © IFA/eStock Photo/PictureQuest; **83** © Ed Reschke; **84** Photograph by Ken O'Donoghue; **85** *left* © Dr. Gopal Murti/Photo Researchers, Inc.; *right* © Carolina Biological/Visuals Unlimited; **86** *top* © Michael Newman/PhotoEdit, Inc.; *top right, bottom left, bottom right* Photographs by Ken O'Donoghue; *center right* © Science VU/Visuals Unlimited; *center* © Custom Medical Stock Photo; **88** © M.I. Walker/Photo Researchers, Inc.; **89** *top* © CNRI/Photo Researchers, Inc.; *bottom* © Biophoto Associates/Photo Researchers, Inc.; **90** © David B. Fleetham/Visuals Unlimited; **91** *top* © Cytographics/Visuals Unlimited; *bottom* Photograph by Ken O'Donoghue; **93** © CNRI/Phototake; **94** © Will & Deni McIntyre/Photo Researchers, Inc.; **98, 99** © Norbert Rosing/National Geographic Image Collection; **99** *top right* © Photodisc/Getty Images; *center right* Photograph by Ken O'Donoghue; **101** © Florence Delva/Getty Images; **103** *left* © CNRI/Photo Researchers, Inc.; *right* © Biophoto Associates/Photo Researchers, Inc.; **106** © Mary Kate Denny/PhotoEdit; **107** © Ken Weingart/Corbis; **108** *top* © Johnny Johnson/Animals Animals; *bottom* Photograph by Ken O'Donoghue; **109, 110** Photographs by Ken O'Donoghue; **113** *background* © Ludovic Maisant/Corbis; *bottom right* © Jane Burton/Bruce Coleman, Inc.; **114** Photograph by Frank Siteman; **116** © Robert Dowling/Corbis; **117** Photograph by Ken O'Donoghue; **118** © Pascal Goetgheluck/Photo Researchers, Inc.; **119** Photograph by Ken O'Donoghue; **123** © David M. Phillips/Photo Researchers, Inc.; **128** *center* Library of Congress, Prints and Photographs Division, #LC-USZ62-95187; *center right* Courtesy of The Royal Society of London; *bottom* Courtesy of Professor John Doebley, Genetics Department, University of Wisconsin; **129** *top left* Library and Archives of the Royal Botanical Gardens, Kew; *center* Drawing by Edward Strasburger; *center left* © Margaret Stones; *center right* © Oliver Meckes/Photo Researchers, Inc.; *bottom* © Vic Small; **130** *top left* Reproduced from *The Journal of Experimental Medicine*, 1944, vol. 79, 158-159, by copyright permission of the Rockefeller University Press; *top right* © Dr. Gopal Murti/Photo Researchers, Inc.; *center* © Omikron/Photo Researchers, Inc.; *bottom left* © Lennart Nilsson/Albert Bonniers Forlag AB; **131** *top* © David Parker/Photo Researchers, Inc.; *center* Courtesy of The Whitehead Institute/MIT Center for Genome Research and reprinted by permission of Nature, 409:745-964 (2001), Macmillan Publishers Ltd.; *bottom* Courtesy of the USC-Keck School of Medicine and Ashanti DeSilva; **132, 133** © Ted Horowitz/Corbis; **133** *top right* Photograph by Ken O'Donoghue; *bottom right* © Corbis-Royalty Free; **135** Photography by Ken O'Donoghue; **139** Photograph by Ken O'Donoghue; **142** *top* © Ken Eward/Photo Researchers, Inc.; *center* Photograph by Frank Siteman; *bottom* Photography by Ken O'Donoghue; **143** Photograph by Frank Siteman; **144** Photograph by Ken O'Donoghue; **145** © David Pollack/Corbis; **146** Photograph by Frank Siteman; **147** © Meckes/Ottawa/Photo Researchers, Inc.; **148** © Gladden Willis/Visuals Unlimited, Inc; **149** © Dennis Kunkel Microscopy, Inc.; **150** © Geoff Tompkinson/Photo Researchers, Inc.; **151** © Doug Loneman/AP Wide World Photos; **152** © Richard T. Nowitz/Corbis; **153** © Mark C. Burnett/Stock Boston, Inc./PictureQuest ; **154** © Getty Images; **155** *left* © ImageState- Pictor/PictureQuest; *right* © PJ Green/Ardea London Limited; **156** © Getty Images; **160** Photograph by Ken O'Donoghue; **168** *bottom right* Photograph by Ken O'Donoghue; **R28** © PhotoDisc/Getty Images; **R58** © Andrew Syred/Photo Reseachers, Inc.

Illustration and Maps

Peter Bull/Wildlife Art Ltd. **32**
Patrick Gnan/Deborah Wolfe Ltd. **61**
Keith Kasnot **49, 51, 52, 66**
George Kelvin **15, 17**
George Kelvin and Richard McMahon **19** *(montage)*
Myriam Kirkman-Oh/KO Studios **43** *(center)*, **140**
Debbie Maizels **3** *(right)*, **22, 30, 34, 42, 43** *(top, bottom)*, **45, 58, 60, 61, 75** *(center right)*, **136** *(bottom)*
Steve Oh/KO Studios **75** *(left)*, **83, 96** *(right)*, **121, 122, 124, 136, 137, 139**
Mick Posen/Wildlife Art Ltd. **78, 105, 111, 113, 116**
Dan Stuckenschneider/Uhl Studios **R58**
Bart Vallecoccia and Richard McMahon **3** *(montage)*